D1001155

BEHIND THE HEDGES

BEHIND THE HEDGES

*Big Money and Power Politics
at the University of Georgia*

RICH WHITT

NEWSOUTH BOOKS
Montgomery | Louisville

A Note from the Publisher

Richard Whitt, the author of this book, died from a heart attack at his home in Marietta, Georgia, the very day the book's final edits were completed. He was 64. A native of eastern Kentucky, he had been a journalist for more than thirty-five years. He worked first at several small newspapers, then for more than a decade at the Louisville *Courier-Journal,* where he won the Pulitzer Prize for local reporting for his investigation of the causes of a 1977 fire that claimed 165 lives at a northern Kentucky supper club. He finished his newspaper career at the *Atlanta Journal-Constitution* where he retired in 2006. He was a well-respected investigative reporter on state and local government in Georgia and had a legion of admiring friends and colleagues. He attended the University of Kentucky and was inducted into the school's Journalism Hall of Fame in 1995. The UK Journalism School has established the Richard Whitt Memorial Fund for Rural Journalists in his honor.

NewSouth Books
105 South Court Street
Montgomery, AL 36104

Library of Congress Cataloging-in-Publication Data
Whitt, Rich.
Behind the hedges : big money and power politics at the University of Georgia / Rich Whitt.
p. cm.
ISBN-13: 978-1-58838-206-1
ISBN-10: 1-58838-206-0
1. University of Georgia—History—21st century. 2. University of Georgia—Finance. 3. Adams,
Michael F., 1948– 4. Higher education and state—Georgia. I. Title.
LD1983.W54 2008
378.758'18—dc22
2008052462

Design by Randall Williams
Printed in the United States of America by the Maple-Vail Book Manufacturing Group.

*For my wife Terri,
without whose support and encouragement
this book would not have been possible.*

For Hayes, Emily, and Christen, who are the lights of my life.

*Finally, I dedicate this book to truth,
as our creator has given us the wisdom to discern it,
and to the men and women who soldier for truth
in the face of scorn and ridicule and persecution.*

CONTENTS

INTRODUCTION

Little noticed outside the realm of higher education, a sea change has occurred over the past few decades in how America supports its great public institutions of higher learning. As enrollments and programs have steadily increased, so too have budgets, endowments, tuition, and fees. These shifting tides have buffeted the major universities and created stress fractures in the financial underpinnings of some traditional bases of support for higher education. Nowhere are these cracks more apparent than in Athens, Georgia, home of the state's flagship university.

This book examines the circumstances and aftermath of a highly public family squabble that erupted in 2003 within the usually collegial University of Georgia community. The clash involved a controversial new president, a powerful and eccentric wealthy businessman, a revered and iconic football coach, spineless politicians, other wealthy businessmen, backroom deals, hanky-panky, and a compliant media that proved itself a toothless watchdog over the public interest.

There was also Big Money, Big Football, adultery, and more than a whiff of Big Daddy's "odor of mendacity."

What went on at Georgia—and is still unresolved—was unique and highly personal to many of its participants, but the conditions leading up to the events were symptomatic of the pressures facing most big public universities across the country.

Historically, private colleges and universities have depended heavily on student tuition and private support as their major source of revenue, while public institutions have been funded from a combination of state appropriations and student tuition. But in recent years, enrollment pressures and infrastructure costs have skyrocketed, while state funding has remained static or declined. "Even within the public sector with its government funding, revenues from tuition and fees increased 318 percent from 1980 to 1996 while revenues from government appropriations during that time only increased 125 percent. Little evidence exists that this trend will change between now and 2010," the National Center for Education Statistics presciently observed in a summary on higher education accounting for the online Education Encyclopedia at StateUniversity.com. In fact, by 2008, most major public universities seemed to be receiving less than half of their annual budgets from their respective states' taxes. The implications for the nation's public universities are profound.

The University of Georgia, for example, now gets less than a third of its budget from state tax dollars, down from 45 percent just a decade ago. Other states have seen even more dramatic change. The Colorado legislature cut state support for its higher education institutions to less than 10 percent of their annual revenues and began issuing "vouchers" to students who attend both public and private universities. South Carolina's governor suggested privatizing some of his state's public universities. The University of Virginia, among others, has bargained decreased state funding in return for greater autonomy in dealing with private financial sources.

This dramatic shift in funding has given rise not only to huge tuition increases but also to increased reliance on private gifts to supplement public university budgets. In 2007, colleges and universities collected $29.75 billion in charitable contributions, according to the Council for Aid to Education. Many universities, both private and public, have built up huge endowments through capital campaigns tapping alumni, corporations, and charitable foundations for gifts. As of 2007, endowments to higher education institutions nationwide totaled a staggering $411 billion. Even the richest public school endowment is peanuts compared to Harvard's $34.6 billion and Yale's $22.5 billion, but the public institutions are working hard. However, the 2008 stock market crash has hammered all college endowments. Nearly every public university in America seems to have a major fundraising campaign underway or in the planning stage. Like their private sisters, public universities now rely on private donations to attract top academics, pay for construction projects, and often to keep the lights burning. Without private dollars and the volunteers who raise the money for them, America's great public universities would cease to function or at least would be forced to operate on a greatly reduced scale.

Not surprisingly, this shift has enormously increased the prestige and power of the affiliated private foundations that have emerged to raise money for public schools. As we shall see, a large pot of privately controlled money earmarked for a public institution was at the heart of the trouble between the University of Georgia Foundation and the University System of Georgia Board of Regents from 2000 to 2003.

IN GEORGIA—THE SOUTHEAST'S FASTEST growing state—demand for higher education has soared. The University System of thirty-five public colleges and universities expects to expand student capacity by 40 percent by 2020, with enrollment increasing from the current 260,000 to more than 360,000. The system is adding about 10,000 students every year. Ironically, an innovative step by state government to make college education more affordable to average students had the unintended consequence of exacerbating the conflict between the UGA Foundation and UGA President Michael Adams and his supporters among the Regents.

The University of Georgia is not just any school. Chartered in 1785 as the nation's first state-supported university, it has grown from a place "where young men, primarily sons of the privileged, came to receive a classical education that included Greek and Latin" and a place that "turned out the future political leaders of the state—a tradition that continues to this day" into a major public research institution. It is an NCAA Division 1 athletic powerhouse, the home of generations of the nation's most famous bulldog, an incubator for both science and rock music, a place known for partying *and* studying, and, not incidentally, was the employer of an institution named Vince Dooley.

For many years, generations of Georgia families had followed one another to Athens, creating not only a legacy of loyalty but a sense of entitlement. That began changing after the Georgia General Assembly passed the HOPE Scholarship program in 1993 and the voters approved a lottery to fund it. The HOPE Scholarship offers free college tuition to in-state students who maintain a "B" average in high school and college. Many of these high-achieving Georgia students decided they wanted to get their free educations at the University of Georgia. Applications increased, SAT averages rose correspondingly, and soon a school known more for tailgating parties and football was beginning to gain national attention for academics.

Meanwhile, some children and grandchildren of UGA graduates whose families had attended the school for generations found themselves turned away because of the rising standards. Their resentment naturally found its symbolic target in the UGA president's office, which by 1997 was occupied by one Michael Adams, whose rather interesting personality, leadership style, and behavior we will explore further in this book.

PRESIDENT ADAMS WAS ONE flash point of the 2003 explosion. The University of Georgia Foundation was another.

Publicly funded institutions like the University of Georgia and Georgia Tech are relative Johnnies-come-lately in the business of private educational fundraising. Nevertheless, the Georgia Tech Foundation has amassed more than $1 billion in endowments and the UGA Foundation has just more than $500 million.

A private arm of the university, the UGA Foundation had for years acted as a club whose mission was simply to raise money for the university. The Foundation members—mainly wealthy, conservative business leaders who are passionately committed to the university—met annually at Sea Island to choose officers, play golf, and talk about the glory that was "Old Georgia." But the growing reliance on private fundraising meant that the Foundation was increasingly important and powerful. The UGA Foundation had not been a big player in fundraising efforts, but now it was embarking on the largest capital campaign in the university's history. And in addition to its fundraising role, the Foundation had begun paying nearly half of Adams's annual salary as well as a stipend to his wife. Many on the Foundation had opposed and deeply resented putting Mrs. Adams on the payroll. There was a sense among Foundation members that it ought to have some say in who was spending their money.

University foundations are private corporations and are registered by the

IRS as public charities. They receive tax-deductible gifts and pledges, manage investments of assets, and distribute endowment gifts for scholarships and other purposes. They exist to support their schools and have no role in the hiring and firing of university personnel. Yet because of the importance of private financial support, foundations hold enormous sway with university governing bodies. Sometimes that leads to conflict and at Georgia, the stage was set for a clash.

Tremendous growth coupled with cutbacks in state funding had put the university on shaky financial footing. Programs were being cut back, tuition increased, and professors' wages frozen while Adams's own income was increasing substantially. Meanwhile, UGA had fallen well behind comparable institutions in raising private cash to supplement dwindling state support. School officials had identified $1 billion of critical needs but were jittery about a fundraising effort that large. The Foundation ultimately undertook a more modest $500 million campaign, with plans to launch a second fundraising campaign once they met the first goal. Foundation leaders were predictably anxious that spending construed as unnecessary could turn off potential contributors. Reports that Adams was spending lavishly on various pet projects did not endear him to the Foundation officers.

Nothing is more harmful to private fundraising efforts than the appearance of abuse by a college president. In his handbook on university foundations, Joseph F. Phelan, founding president of the University of New Hampshire Foundation, warns against presidents using foundation discretionary accounts for questionable purposes. Specifically, Phelan cautioned against using foundation funding to augment a president's salary or to underwrite exclusive club memberships or social or political activities.

As we shall see, Adams was violating most of these cardinal sins. He got Foundation money to pay for expensive meals, trips, and a salary supplement. No other UGA president had ever tried to get his wife onto the Foundation payroll. Tensions escalated when some members of the Foundation's governing board repeatedly called his hand on questionable spending.

However, in the aftermath of 2003, many observers felt that the Foundation had overstepped its bounds in the clashes with Adams. The Phelan handbook also cautioned that foundations sometimes take their independence too seriously and attempt to exert undue influence on their university, *"including the president's length of service."*

IN THE END, OF course, the UGA Foundation failed in its effort to get Adams fired. The conflict over the Adams affair split the Bulldog nation into warring camps, but by the time the story disappeared from the front pages of the newspapers it was still not clear exactly what had been contested, why, or who won. This book, based on a thorough review of documents and on interviews with as many of the principals as were willing to speak, explores those questions.

At the time, Adams's decision to retire the popular athletic director and former football coach Vince Dooley was widely proffered by the media as the cause of the conflagration. But the seeds of strife were sown years earlier. Dramatic political and institutional shifts within the state of Georgia and its flagship university had created new fault lines that set the stage for upheaval.

Adams had been an unpopular choice with the UGA faculty when he was named president in 1997 because of what the academics saw as his lightweight credentials. He did little after his arrival to win over the hearts and minds of the faculty, which saw him as arrogant, aloof, and dismissive of their concerns. And even though he wanted its money, Adams's relationship with the University of Georgia Foundation was no better.

As it would turn out, Adams had support where it counted.

In Atlanta, the once dormant Republican Party had captured both the governor's office and the state senate. In January 2003 George Ervin "Sonny" Perdue III was sworn in as Georgia's first Republican governor since Reconstruction. Perdue's surprising victory over Democrat Roy Barnes set in motion a realignment of alliances that played out dramatically behind the scenes as Georgia's elite wrestled for power and control. Traditional power centers were shifting and long-time political alliances fell apart. Several conservative Democrats in the legislature switched parties.

By 2003, Adams had been in Athens for five years. He had survived a major scandal in the men's basketball program and questions about his spending habits and had engineered himself a hefty salary increase. But he had made some powerful enemies on and off the UGA Foundation. Some prominent Atlanta alumni had already begun discussions about whether Adams was up to the task of running a major research university. When the Dooley story broke, Adams's critics figured the time was ripe to go after him. Thousands of Dooley supporters came out of the shadows to make their opinions known. What they could not know was that Adams had won the Dooley battle before it began. In conversations with Dooley and others, Adams had subtly let him know that he had the backing of "some people" who felt it was time for a change in athletic directors.

That brings us to Donald Leebern, the colorful and wealthy liquor distributor who is a University System Regent and one of the most interesting pieces in this complex story. Adams never identified to Dooley those "some people" but it now seems obvious that Adams had the backing of Governor Perdue and Leebern. Adams also told reporters that he had consulted with people "at every level" before making the Dooley decision.

The public uproar over the Dooley dispute was contrasted by the UGA faculty's reaction to it. Not a single faculty member stepped forward to defend the beleaguered president. Fourteen academic deans issued a statement saying only that the university's interests would be served by moving past the controversy. Adams simply shrugged it all off, perhaps knowing that his job was secure. As the weeks wore on, the UGA Foundation commissioned the auditing firm of Deloitte & Touche to conduct an investigation of Adams's salary and expenses and other issues they felt Adams had mishandled. The report, released in October 2003, confirmed Adams's misuse of Foundation funds but stopped short of accusing him of criminal acts.

Nevertheless, it was a broad indictment of Adams's performance and Foundation members thought they had a smoking gun. Several members pushed for a vote of no confidence. But Griffin Bell, the Atlanta lawyer and former U.S. attorney general who was advising the Foundation at the time, and has since died, urged restraint. Bell felt the audit was damning enough but he understood that the Board of Regents, as Adams's employer, might see it as meddling in their affairs. So Bell advised the Foundation to pass the audit on to the Regents for further action, hoping the Regents would ask Georgia Attorney General Thurbert Baker for an investigation.

That never happened, and instead the Regents and Governor Perdue quickly gave public statements of support to Adams. To the utter consternation of Foundation members, the *Atlanta Journal-Constitution* (where I worked at the time) picked up on a few paragraphs of the audit mildly criticizing the Foundation for inadequate oversight over Adams's spending and ran this headline: "Audit targets UGA Foundation oversight, spending by Adams."

The audit report thus had the opposite effect of that intended by the concerned Foundation members.

Attorney General Baker, meanwhile, took the matter under advisement. For almost three years a spokesman for the attorney general claimed the office was investigating the case. The "investigation" turned out to be merely a review of the audit and of letters written to the attorney general. After his reelection in November 2006, Baker wrote the Board of Regents, strongly condemning some of Adams's transactions, calling some of them possibly unconstitutional. But the attorney general took no further action.

The Regents' reaction to the Foundation's audit report drove a wedge deeper between the two UGA powers centers. The Foundation threatened to quit paying Adams's salary stipend. The Regents responded by ordering Adams to terminate the university's association with its foundation. There followed a period of negotiations that lasted almost two years. At various times both sides indicated they had worked out an agreement, but in April, 2005, the Regents pulled the plug on the Foundation a second time and began organizing a new fundraising body. This ended a seventy-year relationship between the two entities.

MOST GEORGIANS HAVE NOW moved past the extraordinary public squabble and few of the key players are eager to revisit the issues. But five years after the blowup, the fallout still haunts the university and hinders fundraising efforts. Although UGA met its $500 million capital campaign goal, it did so only by counting donations required for priority purchase of football tickets. Those monies were never supposed to be part of the capital campaign, according to Billy Espy, a leader of the campaign.

And the Foundation members who witnessed close up what they saw as Adams's perfidy can't forget.

"The issue to me is trust. And Dr. Adams violated our trust," one trustee said shortly after the audit report was released. The critics feel the same way today.

The late Griffin Bell didn't believe the controversy would die until Adams is gone from the university. "At some point," he said, "we are going to have to deal with the problem."

This book examines in some detail the "problem" Bell referred to. It reviews the history of the relationship between the university and the Foundation, profiles Michael Adams and looks at how he was selected as UGA president, examines his actions as president that caused conflict with Foundation officials, and puts in perspective the crisis which unfolded in 2003 and its implications for the university and the state today. Along the way we learn more about Michael Adams, Vince Dooley, and Donald Leebern, as well as a number of other people who are not as well known but who were and are involved in this controversy.

Like most big stories, this one involves money, power, and personalities. And to keep it moving, it also has football, sex, and fistfights.

I

LEGACY

Chartered two years before the founding fathers gathered in Philadelphia to adopt the U.S. Constitution, the University of Georgia was the first college in America to be created by a state government. The concepts underpinning its charter—which established the school as the head of the state's educational system—laid the foundation for public higher education in America. In 1784, at the urging of Governor Lyman Hall, the state set aside forty thousand acres to endow a university. The following year, Abraham Baldwin introduced legislation that passed in the General Assembly creating the university's charter. Baldwin then served as the first president of the University of Georgia, during its planning phase from 1786 until it opened to students in 1801. (By then, North Carolina had followed Georgia's lead and moved to a faster track in establishing a state-supported institution of higher learning, the University of North Carolina, which opened in 1795.)

Governor Hall and President Baldwin were both Yale-educated Connecticut Yankees; the architecture of their new campus in Athens was modeled on that of Yale, and the bulldog is the mascot for both schools. Baldwin and Hall shared a vision of the importance of education to a developing state and nation. Baldwin once said that Georgia must place its youth "under the forming hand of Society, that by instruction they may be moulded to the love of Virtue and good Order." Two centuries later, it would be hard to overstate the importance of the University of Georgia to the people of the Peach State. The school motto, "To teach, to serve and to inquire into the nature of things," spells out its broad mission. The oldest, largest, and most comprehensive educational institution in the state, the university's first mission is to educate Georgia's people. But it is also charged with improving the quality of life of all Georgians and discovering new knowledge through research. Though it has neither medical nor engineering schools, it has in most respects fulfilled that mission admirably.

The university has also carved its legacy deeply into Georgia's political landscape. Alliances formed in its law and business schools have often been tempered and honed in the arenas of state government. Since 1851, UGA has educated twenty-five governors and countless state and local politicians. Luminaries of every political persuasion have advanced through the famous arches at Athens. Georgia's current Republican governor, Sonny Perdue, and both of Georgia's U.S. senators, Saxby Chambliss of Moultrie and Johnny Isakson of Marietta, are UGA graduates. Perdue, who hails from the town of Bonaire in central Georgia, is the fifth consecutive governor and seventh of the last nine to hold a degree from the University of Georgia. Other prominent graduates include Dan Amos, CEO of AFLAC; Robert Benham, the first African American chief justice of the Georgia Supreme Court; Robert D. McTeer, former CEO of the Federal Reserve Bank in Dallas; Charles S. Sanford Jr., former chairman/CEO of Banker's Trust Company; Pete Correll Jr., retired CEO of Georgia-Pacific Corporation; retired Synovus CEO James Blanchard; Billy Payne, chairman of the Augusta National Golf Club; and the late humorist Lewis Grizzard, to name just a handful.

YET GEORGIA WAS NEVER an institution for the elite only. In its first two centuries—with one big exception—the university's doors were open to just about anyone who could afford the modest tuition and board. Generations of Georgians from small towns and large cities alike followed one another to Athens, creating an interwoven tribe of alumni whose devotion to their alma mater almost needed to be experienced to be fully understood. It's not uncommon today to hear a Georgian boast of being the third- or fourth-generation Georgia Bulldog in his or her family. This loyalty was partly by design: until 2002, so-called "legacy" admissions gave preferential treatment to applicants whose immediate family members had attended UGA. This policy no doubt contributed to the historical discrimination against blacks—the exception to the open admission philosophy noted above—and ended only after the school's affirmative action program for African American students was struck down by the courts in 2001.

Like most Southern institutions, the University of Georgia struggled with the race issue. Although the original charter pledged that no citizen could be denied enrollment at the university because of religious affiliation, sex, or race, slaves were never considered citizens, even after the Emancipation Proclamation in 1863. And even after the end of the Civil War, African Americans were barred from the University of Georgia for another hundred years.

Race, of course, has been at the heart of some of Georgia's greatest trials and triumphs. It boiled to the surface in 1941 when a University of Georgia secretary gave a sworn statement that the dean of the School of Education favored racial integration. Governor Eugene Talmadge, an avowed segregationist, demanded that the Board of Regents fire Dean Walter Cocking. To appease the governor, the Regents voted 8–4 to dismiss Cocking. However, the Regents reconsidered after President Harmon Caldwell threatened to resign in protest. At a special executive session two weeks later, the Regents reversed themselves and voted 8–7 to retain Cocking. The Regents' action infuriated Talmadge, who snapped his galluses and demanded the resignations of three of his own appointees so he could pack the board with more subservient members. The three Regents refused to resign but two other members did quit and the Board was reconstituted more to the governor's liking. The Regents then voted 10–5 to fire Cocking and also dismissed Marvin Pittman, the president of Georgia State Teachers College (now Georgia Southern University).

Both the Georgia university system and Talmadge would pay dearly. The Southern Association of Colleges and Universities met later that year and voted unanimously to strip most of Georgia's public colleges of their accreditation. That stern action helped turn Georgia voters against the race-baiting Talmadge and his meddling in higher education. In 1942, voters instead elected as governor a progressive young legislator, Ellis Arnall, who promised to remove the university system from political interference.

Arnall—a Georgia law graduate—kept his promise. One of Governor Arnall's first acts was to sign legislation creating a constitutionally independent Board of Regents, thus ending overt political interference in Georgia's higher education system (although Georgia governors still appoint Regents and have retained considerable influence over the board).

The struggle to desegregate the University of Georgia began in earnest in 1950 when LaGrange native Horace Ward applied to attend law school. Ward had earned an undergraduate degree from Morehouse College and a master's degree in political science from Atlanta University.

The Regents weren't as supportive of a young black man as they had been of Dean Cocking. Responding to Ward's application, the University System Board of Regents established new criteria for admission, including personal recommendations from UGA alumni. Ward sued, but (in one of the many ironies of the segregated South) before the case could be heard, he was called on to serve the country that considered him a second-class citizen. When Ward returned from military service, he renewed his lawsuit and the case was finally set for trial in December 1956. The judge then dismissed the case as moot because Ward had meanwhile enrolled at Northwestern University's law school.

Ward was not finished with the University of Georgia, though. After graduating from Northwestern, he returned to Atlanta and soon joined famed civil rights attorney Donald Hollowell in representing Charlayne Hunter and Hamilton Holmes, who had applied for admission to UGA in 1959 after graduating from the segregated Turner High School in Atlanta. Both were honor students, but university officials threw up roadblocks, claiming, among other excuses, that the dorms were full.

On January 6, 1961, U.S. District Judge William A. Bootle ruled that the pair were fully qualified to enter the university and "would already have been admitted had it not been for their race and color." Three days later, on January 9, Hunter and Holmes were escorted to class as a crowd of white students chanted, "Two-four-six-eight. We don't want to integrate." There were no further demonstrations until January 11, when a student mob descended on Hunter's dormitory after a basketball game between Georgia and Georgia Tech (Georgia lost in overtime, 89–80). Sports reporter Jim Minter, later to become editor of the *Atlanta Journal-Constitution*, was on campus covering the game. Years later he wrote about the evening in a newspaper column: "I walked out of the gymnasium into rioting. Rocks were thrown, torches burned, threats shouted. The dean of students was hit in the head by a brick." Minter recalled that eighteen students left the university following the incident; some were expelled, others just refused to attend school with blacks.

Holmes and Hunter were escorted back to Atlanta by state troopers. Dean of Students J. A. Williams told them he was suspending them "in the interest of your personal safety and the welfare of more than seven thousand other students at the University of Georgia." More than four hundred faculty members signed a petition protesting the removal of Hunter and Holmes and calling for their return. A few days later, the pair did return, under the protection of a court order. Still, there was talk of closing the university. In 1956, the Georgia legislature had passed a resolution that forbade integration of schools and threatened the funding of any schools that did desegregate. However, Governor Ernest Vandiver, himself a Georgia graduate, kept the university from closing.

Hunter and Holmes graduated in 1963 (both had already gained some college credits elsewhere while their lawsuit was pending). Holmes had earned cum laude distinction and was elected to Phi Beta Kappa. He went on to receive a medical degree from Emory University and became an orthopedic surgeon in Atlanta. Hunter-Gault became a distinguished journalist, first in newspapers and later with PBS and CNN, winning two Emmys and two Peabodys. In 1988, she returned to the University of Georgia as the school's first black commencement speaker. Horace Ward was later appointed a U.S. district judge and presided over the 1986 Jan Kemp lawsuit (see Chapter 6). The University gave Donald Hollowell an honorary degree in 2002 in recognition of his legal battles on behalf of Hamilton and Hunter-Gault.

THE GENERATIONS OF WHITE Georgia alumni may have gotten over their resentment of integration more easily than they have accepted the loss of legacy admission entitlement for their children and grandchildren. The roots of this particular change can be traced to the 1990 gubernatorial campaign. Long-time Lieutenant Governor Zell Miller was seeking the Democratic Party's nomination for governor against four other candidates. Lottery fever was sweeping the nation but few Southern states had taken the plunge into state-sanctioned gambling. Many state politicians felt Georgia voters were too conservative and too "Baptist" to approve a lottery. But Miller was watching the caravans of Georgians streaming into Florida every week to play the numbers. Where other candidates saw danger, Miller saw opportunity.

An astute observer of all human condition except his own, Miller had been Georgia's lieutenant governor for sixteen years. His habit of taking multiple positions on every major issue had earned him the nickname "Zig-Zag Zell." Miller was not the favorite in a primary field that included Andrew Young and State Senator Roy Barnes. Young was popular and a civil rights legend, former aide to Martin Luther King, Jr., former congressman, former ambassador, and two-term former mayor of Atlanta. Barnes, considered a rising star in the Democratic Party, had the strong backing of the politically powerful Georgia House Speaker Tom Murphy, an arch-enemy of the lottery and Zell Miller.

Miller had cut his teeth in the executive branch as the chief of staff for segregationist Governor Lester Maddox, he of ax-handle and backwards-bicycle-riding fame. After the Georgia House of Representatives bottled up legislation to put the lottery issue on the ballot in 1990, Miller vowed to make it the central issue of his campaign. Miller had seen politically unknown Kentucky businessman Wallace Wilkinson ride the lottery issue into the governor's office in that state three years earlier. Wilkinson's campaign manager, James Carville, the "Ragin' Cajun" who would head Bill Clinton's 1992 presidential campaign, signed on as Miller's campaign manager.

Miller won 41 percent of the vote in the five-man primary and defeated Young in the runoff. Young had also supported a lottery but Miller had established himself as *the* lottery candidate. Miller then defeated the Republican nominee, State Senator Johnny Isakson, by 100,000 votes in the November general election.

Miller's election was seen as a mandate to create a state lottery for education and he quickly drove a proposed constitutional amendment through the General Assembly. Georgia voters approved it in 1992. The lottery proceeds were earmarked for pre-kindergarten, technology, and, most importantly, the HOPE Scholarship Program which pays the full tuition for any Georgia high school student who graduates with at least a "B" average in a core curriculum. Since its inception in 1993, the HOPE scholarships have paid more than $4 billion to students in tuition, books, and fees.

Many of Georgia's best and brightest students who once routinely left the state to attend other acclaimed universities are now staying home to take advantage of free tuition. Nearly 80 percent of the freshmen who enrolled at the University of Georgia in the fall of 2007 were from Georgia and 99 percent had received HOPE scholarships; they also had an average SAT score of 1233.

This rising tide of high-scoring students had unintended consequences for some of Georgia's most loyal alumni. Many among the generations of Georgians who have followed one another to Athens over recent decades have done so using so-called "legacy" points awarded to the sons and daughters of Georgia alumni. In some cases, those points meant the difference between admission and rejection.

Former Governor Roy Barnes, himself a UGA graduate, acknowledged that many Georgians view attending the state's flagship university as a birthright. And when their sons and daughters began being turned away, it ruffled feathers. "Some of these folks on the [University of Georgia] Foundation have been big givers," Barnes said. "Now a lot of their children can't get in the university and they blame [school officials]. I hear that all the time: 'I've been giving to the university and four generations have gone there and now my kid can't get in.'"

THE UNIVERSITY OF GEORGIA is a top-tier state university. Its sixteen schools and colleges offer twenty-two baccalaureate degrees in 140 fields, thirty master's degrees in 124 fields, and four doctoral degrees in 87 fields. And Georgia is a financial bargain. *U.S. News and World Report* has ranked UGA as high as seventh among public universities on its "Great Schools, Great Prices" list, which relates a school's academic quality to the cost of attending. *Kiplinger's* magazine has ranked UGA tenth on its list of best values among public colleges and universities based on academic quality, cost, and financial aid. The *Princeton Review's* "Best Academic Bang for Your Buck" has ranked UGA ninth among 345 public and private colleges. And because nearly all in-state first-year students come to Georgia on the HOPE scholarship, the university has been ranked by *Money* magazine as one of nine "unbeatable deals" nationwide where students can attend college tuition-free.

Princeton Review, by the way, has also ranked the university twelfth among the nation's best party schools, but if parties and academics aren't enough, Georgia has one of the most storied athletic programs in the country. The university fields competitive NCAA teams in basketball, track, swimming, gymnastics, baseball, and other sports, though football dominates. On a typical Saturday afternoon each fall more than ninety thousand crazed red-and-black-clad loyalists pour into Sanford Stadium to watch their Dawgs do battle, as they say, "between the hedges." Thousands more tailgate outside the stadium or tune into the radio broadcasts where for decades they listened to the legendary voice of the Bulldogs, Larry Munson. Georgia played its first football game in 1892, beating Mercer University 50–0. A month later UGA and Alabama Polytechnic Institute, better known today as Auburn University, met for the first time in what has become the Deep South's oldest football rivalry. UGA won that game 10–0. In 115 seasons, the Bulldogs have an overall record of 713–381 with 34 ties. The football team has won five national championships, and 1982 Heisman Trophy winner Hershel Walker no doubt could have gotten even the votes of geriatric woolhat segregationists if he had announced for governor after leading the Bulldogs to a 32-3 record in his three varsity years.

And Georgia has continued to move forward even in the midst of the controversy of the past few years which is the focus of this book. A new $42.2 million Student Learning Center opened in the heart of campus in 2003. It is considered one of the largest and most technologically advanced such facilities at an American university. The 206,000-square-foot building contains twenty-six classrooms and ninety-six small study rooms. An electronic library allows users to access materials in other university libraries. The building has five hundred public-access computers, and many classrooms and study rooms have wireless internet access. There is also a coffee shop and reading room.

A new medical school, to be jointly operated by and staffed with professors from UGA and the Medical College of Georgia in Augusta, is scheduled to open in 2009. The 200,000-square-foot Paul D. Coverdell Center for Biomedical and Health Sciences opened in 2006, providing space for faculty research in biomedicine, ecology and environmental sciences.

The University of Georgia today is big in every respect. Big in academics, with 32,000-plus students who boast rising test scores. Big in sports, with high-achieving athletes in almost every category and with distinguished alumni at all levels of professional and international competition. Big in business, with graduates in the executive suites of major corporations. Big in the professions, with its law graduates heading top firms and filling key judgeships. Big in politics, as previously noted. Big in philanthropy, with supporters giving the university about $100 million a year and with its endowment now approximately half a billion dollars. And big as a business itself, with an annual budget of $1.3 million.

When an institution is that big, and when it has a reputation built up over two centuries and carries with it the hopes and aspirations of an entire state, the person who heads up that institution becomes both its symbol and its lightning rod. The "forming hand of Society" and "the love of Virtue and good Order" come into play, as Lyman Hall and Abraham Baldwin might have put it.

Hall and Baldwin might have had quite a lot more to say if they could have been around in 1997 to see how Dr. Michael Adams was selected to be the next president of the University of Georgia, and to watch what unfolded over the next few years.

2

A Presidential Search

Charles B. Knapp, the twentieth president of the University of Georgia, announced in early 1997 that he would be leaving in the summer to head the Aspen Institute, a nonprofit specializing in leadership development. An economist, Knapp earned his PhD at the University of Wisconsin and then taught at the University of Texas before joining Jimmy Carter in Washington in 1976. Only four years out of graduate school, Knapp served in the Carter administration with his UT colleague Ray Marshall, who was Carter's Secretary of Labor; Knapp was Marshall's special assistant for two years, then Deputy Assistant Secretary for two more years, before exiting with Marshall at the beginning of the Ronald Reagan administration in 1981. Knapp then taught public policy at George Washington University for a year before transferring to Tulane University in 1982. At Tulane, he taught economics and gradually moved into administration, as senior and executive vice president. Then in 1987, he was named president at Georgia.

At the time of his appointment, Knapp was said to be the youngest president of a major U.S. research university. Despite his youth, he had solid academic credentials and experience in public policy, politics, and major-college administration. He was a popular choice for the UGA presidency, and if there were any anomalies or behind-the-scenes maneuvering around his selection, no one has said so.

Aside from a winning football team, what the power brokers who selected Knapp wanted from his tenure was more respect: they wanted Georgia's standing in academia moved up several notches. They wanted Georgia positioned for a "leadership role in national and global research, service, and higher education." They wanted higher test scores. They wanted more prestigious faculty. They wanted more of the state's best and brightest high school graduates to choose Georgia instead of the Vanderbilts, Dukes, Yales, and Penns. They wanted an upgraded and expanded campus and a larger endowment. They wanted an academic reputation to match the ones the university already had for athletics and partying.

Knapp himself said his goal was that the nation's oldest chartered public university should also be one of the nation's best public universities. Over the next decade, he arguably delivered.

His good-bye resolution in the Georgia state senate noted that he had "emphasized the importance of teaching . . . encouraged senior faculty to teach core undergraduate courses, and . . . supported the recognition of teaching excellence" by establishing honors such as "the Meigs Teaching Award and the Russell Undergraduate Teaching Award" and through an office of instructional development to provide more resources to faculty. The senate resolution praised Knapp for sharply increasing competition for admission, higher test and grade point averages for both undergraduate and graduate students, and significantly increased research activity. "Total research expenditures rose to more than $200 million in fiscal year 1995 . . . According to the latest data, the University now ranks thirty-second in the nation in total research expenditures and first in the nation among universities that have neither medical nor engineering colleges. The University is recognized as a Research Institution I by the Carnegie Foundation," the senate said. Knapp also helped design Governor Zell Miller's HOPE scholarship program and was a founding member of the Georgia Research Alliance, "a highly successful partnership among private corporations and the state's six major research universities that was created to foster technological innovation and economic growth in the state."

In fundraising, Knapp and an alumni steering committee led the Third Century Campaign—at that time the largest capital campaign in UGA history—to raise $150 million for scholarships, academics, and new buildings. The campaign reached its goal a year ahead of schedule, and even after the end of the campaign private gifts were running more than $30 million a year. The increased financial strength allowed Knapp to preside over the opening of a a new East Campus in the run-up to the 1996 Olympics, with UGA hosting competition in gymnastics, soccer, and volleyball. New construction during the Knapp decade included the Biological Sciences Complex (1992); Ramsey Center (1995); Music Department (1996); Hodgson Hall (1996); Georgia Museum of Art (1996); Rusk Center for Legal Research (1996); and the UGA Welcome Center (1996).

Knapp was praised by those he worked with in Athens and Atlanta for building coalitions between alumni, business and corporate leaders and benefactors, private donors, and state politicians. These good working relationships included, significantly, those with the UGA Foundation. Meanwhile, Knapp also held a faculty position as a professor of economics, chaired the board of directors of the National Association of State Universities and Land Grant Colleges, and served on the National School-to-Work Advisory Council and the NCAA President's Commission.

As he departed for the Aspen Institute in the summer of 1997, Knapp was leaving behind a land-grant university that on his watch had grown to more than 30,000 students, with 8,500 employees and an annual operating budget of more than $600 million. It was an institution said to be "poised on the edge of greatness as it moves with confidence into a new century and a new millenium."

AFTER KNAPP LET IT be known that he planned to move on, the powers that be at Georgia began talking amongst themselves about finding his successor. An outside observer would assume such a search would be for someone similar to Knapp—a solid academic with broad experience who had been steadily climbing the leadership ladder at major universities.

There was no shortage of such potential candidates spread across the American higher education landscape, although Savannah lawyer Frank W. "Sonny" Seiler said the search committee was ultimately disappointed that no sitting president of a large research university applied for the job. "Maybe we're too proud but we thought the job was attractive enough to get someone of that stature," he said. Nevertheless, some 130 hopefuls did seek the position. Seiler described the search as excruciatingly thorough. Some candidates sent the committee multiple boxes of supporting documents. "It was awful," he recalled. "I almost got hemorrhoids."

Seiler served on the search committee by virtue of his role as president of the alumni association. UGA business professor Betty Whitten was the chairwoman. Others on the committee included Columbus liquor dealer Donald Leebern; AFLAC insurance CEO Dan Amos; federal judge Julie Carnes; Athens businessman Howard "Ed" Benson; and Albany businesswoman Henrietta McArthur Singletary. The sixteen-member search committee also included six members of the UGA faculty and staff, and the student government association president.

The committee was reasonably diverse, if skewed toward influence, power, and wealth. One thing all the members had in common was that they bled red and black. Seiler himself is a good example of the lifelong loyalty many Georgians hold for their flagship university. He is also well-known in legal circles for his successful defense of a prominent Savannah antiques and art dealer in the shooting death of a local hustler, a murder made famous by the best-selling book, *Midnight in the Garden of Good and Evil*. Seiler was a prominent character in the book and even had a role in the movie, directed by Clint Eastwood. Seiler, seventy-five, a friendly and outgoing man, has also had roles in *Gingerbread Man* (1998) and *The Legend of Bagger Vance* (2000). But Seiler's favorite role is as the breeder and owner of UGA's English bulldog mascot. As a second-year law student in 1956 the newly married Seiler bought a white English bulldog puppy as a gift for his new bride. An avid UGA football fan, he took the puppy, which he named Uga, to the opening game at Sanford Stadium against Florida State. The Bulldogs won 3–0 and athletics department officials were so taken by the puppy they asked Seiler to bring the mutt to subsequent games, and a tradition was born. Uga became the official Georgia mascot and a succession of Ugas have followed (the current one is Uga VI), making Seiler's bulldogs among the most recognizable of college mascots. Uga V's mug made the cover of the April 28, 1997, *Sports Illustrated*, which named him the country's very best college mascot.

Seiler said he thought the presidential search committee was well-balanced. He recalls lively debates over the candidates, with members of the faculty generally on one side and businessmen on the other.

"The faculty wanted an agenda that would promote multi-cultural classes," Seiler said. "That was the first time I heard that term . . . Then tenure was a big issue. They didn't want anything to affect tenure. And when I tell you the faculty was 100 percent this way, it's true. We kind of felt like we were shopping for an energetic president and they were shopping for someone who would agree with their philosophy. It never got violent but it was sure as hell opinionated."

One person who was not on the committee was UGA Foundation chair Shell Hardman Knox of Augusta. Like many prominent Georgians, Shell Knox's family has long-established ties to UGA. She graduated in 1966 with a bachelor's degree in special education, is a founding member of the UGA Presidents Club, a former chairman of the UGA Foundation, was vice chairman of UGA's Board of Visitors, and was director of the university's Studies Abroad Program in Cortona, Italy. The granddaughter of former Governor Lamartine G. Hardman (1927–31), she is married to prominent attorney Wycliffe "Wyck" Knox, a former UGA Foundation treasurer. The couple are both avid Bulldog fans and significant donors.

Shell Knox had worked closely with Charles Knapp and was vitally interested in who would succeed him. She had wanted to be on the search committee but heard through others that Leebern didn't want her.

Over a period of five months and under a veil of secrecy, the search committee reduced the list of candidates to fourteen. The list included eleven men and three women; in accordance with state law, their names were not publicly released. Shell Knox, meanwhile, was following the process closely from the sidelines. Early in the search she was encouraged, she said. A friend on the search committee would call and say it's unbelievable how many people are interested in the job. But as the process wore on, the friend reported a "shift in focus." Adams was "in the mix," Knox was told, and she was warned that Adams probably wouldn't be her personal choice to succeed Knapp.

A round of interviews with the finalists was scheduled for May 1997 at the Hilton Hotel near the Atlanta airport. By then it seemed clear that Adams was a controversial front-runner. On paper, Adams may have been the unlikeliest of the candidates. As president of a small private college in Kentucky, he had no experience at a research university, let alone a flagship school like UGA. His record as president of tiny Centre College for nine years was solid but unspectacular. Before that he had been vice president for university affairs and professor of political communication at Pepperdine University, a Church of Christ school in Malibu, California. His academic resume was thin, but his credentials in fundraising and national politics had evidently earned him an inside track in the UGA search with some influential Regents, notably Leebern. Countering that was an equal lack of support from the UGA faculty representatives. Committee chairwoman and business professor Betty Whitten was reportedly unimpressed with Adams's background and warned the other committee members that he would "never be accepted" by the UGA faculty.

Whitten, who has since retired from Georgia, has steadfastly declined requests for interviews about Adams. Others familiar with the process say she believed he was the weakest candidate and thus scheduled his interview first. But when she arrived at the Hilton for the start of the interviews, she was told that Adams had a personal conflict and couldn't arrive in Atlanta until later. His interview was rescheduled for last.

Meanwhile, the committee had prepared a standard list of questions so the candidates' answers could be compared and assessed later. When Adams finally arrived and his interview began, it was apparent that someone had fed him the questions or at least had discussed with him the other candidates' answers. His response to the very first question was, "I understand there's been a lot of discussion about that in the last few days." Whitten has also told people that when Adams submitted his expense report for the trip to Atlanta, which she had to sign as chair of the search committee, it showed he had been in Georgia for the entire time of the interviews.

Adams's academic credentials were of little concern to others on the search committee. They were looking for a CEO-type who knew how to wield his authority and preferred to apologize rather than seek permission. They stressed Adams's intellect, his vision, and especially his political acumen and ability to connect with ordinary Georgians. Seiler said Adams was an impressive candidate. He had spent a day driving around the Athens campus before his interview, which impressed the committee. Although a native of Alabama, Adams grew up mostly in Georgia, which also helped his standing. Parties to the interview process say Adams was a great salesman of himself. He had a way of answering questions that made the questioner feel that he agreed with them, even when he didn't give the answer they wanted.

The necessity for academic standing apparently had been replaced by something more important—political skill and fundraising ability. The old days of the bookish college president, it seemed, were over.

AT THE CLOSE OF the Hilton interviews, the search committee narrowed the finalists to five "officially unranked" and still publicly anonymous candidates. These five names were submitted to a special Regents subcommittee chaired by Leebern, which cut two more from the list and submitted a shortlist of three finalists to the full Board of Regents. In June 1997, the Regents released the names of the three finalists. They were James Machen, vice president for academic affairs at the University of Michigan (now president of the University of Florida); Debra W. Stewart, vice provost and dean of the graduate school at North Carolina State University (now president of the Council of Graduate Schools); and Michael Adams, president of Centre College in Danville, Kentucky.

The final result was a foregone conclusion, according to insiders. Many of those interviewed for this book believe that Leebern had hand-picked Adams from the beginning. Leebern was by all accounts the most influential person on the search committee and he has remained one of Adams's staunchest backers throughout the subsequent controversies. Seiler acknowledged that Leebern played a pivotal role in Adams's hiring. "He's Leebern's kind of guy," Seiler said. "I don't think anybody would have been hired without Don's blessing."

Others quickly fell into line. Chancellor Stephen Portch, nearing retirement, gushed that Adams was a "perfect fit" for UGA. Portch praised the members of the Board of Regents, all appointed by Democrat governors, for choosing a partisan Republican to head the University of Georgia. Portch had insisted throughout the search that he wanted a president who would be as much at home in the onion fields of Vidalia as in the classrooms in Athens. He evidently felt that Adams was the complete package—intelligent yet down-to-earth and practical.

Governor Zell Miller praised Adams's "real world" political experience. Lieutenant Governor Pierre Howard drew on undisclosed information to proclaim that the Regents' choice of Adams demonstrated their dedication to classroom excellence.

The *Atlanta Journal-Constitution* observed that faculty and students were "taken aback" by the appointment due to reservations that a candidate from a school more similar to Georgia in size and stature had not been chosen. But the newspaper opined that the size doesn't matter when picking a university president. Adams brought unique qualities to the job, the newspaper said, noting his fundraising abilities and Centre College's traditional high ranking among small teaching colleges.

Even Betty Whitten seemed to have overcome her misgivings. When rumors of Adams's impending appointment began circulating several days before the official University System Board of Regents announcement on June 11, 1997, she stated that he would "do a great job."

3

MEET MICHAEL ADAMS

The twenty-first president of the University of Georgia made his first official appearance in Athens on June 26, 1997. Regent Donald Leebern, who some said had personally steered Adams through the selection process, sent his private airplane to Danville, Kentucky, on June 25 to fetch Adams's wife, Mary, and sons David and Taylor to join Dr. Adams in Atlanta. The boys were delivered to their grandparents' home in Stone Mountain, and Dr. and Mrs. Adams were driven to the home of Chancellor and Mrs. Stephen Portch to spend the night. Early the next morning, Dr. and Mrs. Adams, Chancellor Portch, and Leebern rode together to Athens. At precisely 9:45 A.M., holding hands like newlyweds, Mike and Mary Adams walked under the University Arch on the old North Campus while the Red Coat band played "Glory, Glory to Old Georgia."

"How're you doin'? I'm Mike Adams," the newly minted president said to a group of students. He was, according to news accounts, an instant hit with faculty and students. It is safe to say at that point the curious onlookers knew virtually nothing about him.

BORN MARCH 25, 1948, in Montgomery, Alabama, Michael F. Adams is the older of two children born to Hubert and Jean Adams. Hubert was a broker and sales manager with Kraft Foods, a job that required frequent family moves. By the time Adams finished elementary school he had lived in Albany, Macon, and Atlanta. The family moved to Chattanooga, Tennessee, after Adams's sophomore year in high school and Adams graduated there from City High School (living temporarily in a teacher's home after Hubert Adams was transferred to Raleigh, North Carolina, during his son's senior year).

Adams showed early ambition and leadership. He was class president during his sophomore and junior years of high school and student body president his senior year. He graduated in 1966. Although he hasn't lived there for many years, Adams has said he still considers Chattanooga as his home. After high school, he entered David Lipscomb College, a Nashville-based school associated with the Churches of Christ. The first in his family to attend college, Adams was a stellar student. He graduated magna cum laude with a degree in speech and history in 1970 and immediately began graduate studies at Ohio State University. He earned two graduate degrees in political communications.

Adams took an early interest in politics, particularly as practiced by the Republican party. His 1971 master's thesis at Ohio State University was on the "Role of the Ethos" of Spiro T. Agnew in the 1970 U.S. senate elections. That was followed two years later by his doctoral dissertation: "A Critical Analysis of the Rhetorical Strategies of Sen. Howard Baker Jr. in His 1972 Campaign for Re-election."

After earning his doctorate at Ohio State, Adams taught there for two years before taking a job in 1974 with Senator Baker, then U.S. Senate minority leader; he served as Baker's chief of staff from 1976–79. In 1980 Adams tested the political waters himself, running as the Republican candidate for a U.S. House seat in a solidly Democratic Tennessee district and was soundly defeated. It was his first and last political campaign. From 1980–82, Adams was a senior advisor to Tennessee Governor Lamar Alexander. His first job as a college administrator came the next year when he took a job as vice-president for university affairs and professor of political communication at Pepperdine University. He became president of Centre College in December 1988.

Adams's tenure at Centre is instructive for those who would seek to understand his behavior and performance at Georgia. As he was preparing to take the post at Centre, an Adams acquaintance at Pepperdine accurately predicted that he would be a forceful, dynamic, and at times controversial college president.

Centre College is a small but mighty private liberal arts school in Danville, Kentucky, about sixty miles southeast of Louisville and forty miles southwest of Lexington. Founded in 1819 by Presbyterians, it has become the top school in Kentucky in terms of academic rank and prestige. Whatever the *U.S. News and World Report* annual college rankings really mean, Centre was forty-fourth nationally in 2008, and *Consumer's Digest* declared Centre the nation's number one value among private, liberal arts schools in 2007. The campus sits on 150 immaculate acres and has sixty-four buildings, of which thirteen are on the National Register of Historic Places. However, the school is tiny, with only twelve hundred students. If anything, Centre's alumni are more fanatical and more loyal than Georgia's. Over the past quarter-century, Centre ranks first among U.S. colleges and universities for the percentage of alumni giving money to the school. And its alumni have excelled on the national stage disproportionately to their numbers, including two U.S. vice presidents, one chief justice of the United States, one associate justice of the Supreme Court, thirteen U.S. senators, forty-three U.S. representatives, ten moderators of the General Assemblies of the Presbyterian Church, and eleven governors. Centre even has a football team, the Colonels (formerly the Praying Colonels), who compete in the NCAA Division III Southern Collegiate Athletic Conference, with a 509-374-37 record compiled over the past 128 years. Centre's 6–0 defeat of top-ranked Harvard in 1921 is considered by the College Football Hall of Fame as one of the two greatest upsets ever in college football.

Against that backdrop of history and academic distinction, it is a fair question to ask how Adams ended up as Centre's president. The answer seems to be similar to the situation a decade later at UGA: he had a powerful patron.

Journalist Richard Wilson, former director of the University of Kentucky's School of Journalism and Telecommunications and retired education writer for the *Louisville Courier-Journal*, interviewed Adams when he was appointed at Centre. The interview began at Adams's Pepperdine office located high on a bluff overlooking Malibu beach and the blue Pacific Ocean. It ended at a beachfront bar over cocktails.

Wilson recalled that Adams's academic credentials were considered slim even for Centre, a school with just over eight hundred students at the time. "On the surface," Wilson wrote, "Adams may seem a strange choice for the presidency of what may be Kentucky's most elite private college. He didn't come up through the faculty ranks and was not groomed through a variety of bureaucratic posts within academe."

Wilson said Adams was the choice of J. David Grissom, a Louisville banker and entrepreneur and the long-time chair of Centre's trustees. Grissom liked Adams's down-to-earth style and the fact that he wasn't an academic. "We thought all of his experiences, when put together, made him a much more interesting and qualified candidate. He had not been in academe all of his life and we thought that would help him in dealing with the problems of a liberal arts college like ours," Grissom said at the time.

Adams replaced the popular Richard L. Morrill, who left Centre to become president of the University of Richmond. Educated at Brown, Yale and Duke, Morrill was the author of three books and numerous scholarly papers. Adams's body of research basically consisted of his master's thesis and doctoral dissertation, both unpublished. As his resume was being read for the first time to the assembled faculty at Centre in 1988, an administrator remembers that one professor turned to him and whispered: "Dr. Morrill had no peers on this campus . . . and neither does this guy."

ADAMS DID HAVE ENERGY, fundraising skill, and a network of political contacts. He put all to work at Centre, as he has throughout his career, following a consistent path as a builder of structures if not consensus. He established residential foreign studies programs in London, England, and Strasbourg, France. He also began the most ambitious fundraising program in the school's history, eventually more than tripling the school's endowment to $120 million and helping establish that previously mentioned enviable record of alumni giving. By the end of his tenure, private gifts and grants to Centre were approaching $9 million a year, up from $1.4 million when he arrived. As the money flowed in, Adams spent lavishly to improve Centre's physical facilities, according to faculty members. (After Adams left Centre, the school's financial officer was forced to resign, ostensibly for moving money from one fund to another to mask Adams's spending.)

One knock on Adams has been that he is hot-tempered and imperious. Predictably, these qualities did not universally endear him to Centre's faculty any more than they have at Georgia. In fact, some of Adams's most enthusiastic support for his being hired at UGA seems to have come from a faction within the Centre faculty.

Many had tired of nine years of what some described as bulldozer tactics. A quiet revolt was being plotted by eighteen senior professors at Centre after unilateral changes to the faculty handbook, in violation of the college's own policies. Adams blamed a dean for making the change without his permission; faculty members said they knew better. "It was done at Adams's instruction," said a senior faculty member who was at the meeting. "He stood right there and lied to sixteen senior faculty members. When you lie to sixteen faculty members you don't build capital." Three other faculty members confirmed the professor's recollection.

Trustee chairman David Grissom reportedly soured on Adams over the years; he did not respond to inquiries about his relationship with the former Centre president. Journalist Richard Wilson, who had written the 1988 Adams preview in the *Louisville Courier-Journal*, recalled getting a telephone call from Adams about a year later. Adams wanted to have lunch and chat. They met at the posh Lafayette Club atop Lexington's tallest bank building. "I sat and listened to him for an hour and a half and all he talked about was the rich and influential people he had met," Wilson said. "As if I cared. I thought it was not very savvy of him in dealing with media people."

Charles Vahlkamp, a retired Centre faculty member who attended the meeting with Adams, recalled that "there was a big sigh of relief" when Adams got the UGA job. "Tensions were building and so it really meant we didn't have to continue along that path," said Vahlkamp, meaning the path toward a showdown with Adams before the Centre board of trustees. Georgia saved them the trouble. A decade after Adams left the school, Centre professors still speak of Adams with a tinge of resentment and conflicted feelings.

"You'd like to say he's gone and forgotten but that's not the case," said Vahlkamp. "It's surprising he went to a school like [Georgia]. He's good at some aspects but he is a divisive character. Not a consensus builder. Still, I don't think anyone would say his presidency was detrimental to [Centre] in any way."

IF ADAMS HAD ANY misgivings about his ability to make the leap from Centre to UGA it certainly didn't show. Following his carefully scripted initial appearance at the University Arch, he toured the various UGA institutions, armed with talking points that had been prepared for him by the chancellor's office. Making note of the considerable concern about Adams's lack of experience, Chancellor Portch advised him to reach out to the existing administration and faculty at Georgia:

> You likely have read some of the press clipping since the announcement of your appointment and already have noted the questions about your past experience as an educator and administrator as it relates to large, land-grant, research institutions. In general, I suggest you appeal for help from those present, for time to learn, and give assurances that you are prepared to provide strong, decisive leadership within the context of close collaboration with the faculty and others who have the expertise to meet the needs of the University of Georgia. It would also be wise to state that you are aware of the positive role that the Staff Council has played in providing input and advice to the president.

4

THE ADAMS YEARS BEGIN

On his first work day in June 1997, the University of Georgia's new president met with community leaders, faculty and staff, sticking close to the guidelines Portch had scripted. Adams spoke of lofty goals for the university—of establishing international educational programs, of increasing research, of creating a system to reward teaching, and of becoming a part of the greater Athens community. He promised a team effort in "moving this great university to the next level." Students, he said, would be his primary focus.

In his first State of the University speech in January 1998, Adams elaborated on his plans to increase the school's foreign studies program, as he had done at Centre College. He emphasized that he wanted to take UGA to national prominence. The speech was well-received on and off campus, and at this point faculty and community response to Adams's vision for UGA seemed generally positive.

However, there were warning tremors. Shortly after settling into Charles Knapp's old office, Adams announced plans to restructure the school's upper management team, reducing the number of senior vice presidents from seven to three. Adams also created the Office of Provost and hired Karen Holbrook, Vice President for Research at the University of Florida, to the new position, a move explained as a way to free himself from some of the day-to-day management tasks, thus allowing him to be away from campus more often to raise funds. But it had the effect of isolating Adams from the faculty, some of whom were already grumbling about his corporate CEO management style. His early words about a "team effort" were beginning to ring hollow to senior faculty and staff who felt their input was ignored as Adams dismantled the existing hierarchy of university governance and replaced key administrators with his own loyal supporters.

In January 1999, Adams announced plans to add four schools and colleges to the Athens campus. A part of the expansion would have dismantled the prestigious Grady College of Journalism, creating in its place a new College of Communications that would include rhetorical studies, speech, and technology. Faculty and prominent alumni revolted. What stuck in the journalism faculty's craw was that Adams had not bothered to consult with them. "I am sickened and saddened by this," said journalism professor Conrad Fink. Grady College Dean Tom Russell knew nothing about the proposed changes until the evening before Adams was to announce them during his second State of the University speech.

Russell made no attempt to hide his disappointment. "As you can imagine, mass communication and speech therapy are not areas in the past that have had any [curriculum] relationship. I really think the reaction is somewhat surprised, simply because for all of us this really had not been something that had been considered." A month later, the well-regarded Russell, who had been at the school for thirty-four years, announced he was resigning as dean so he could to return to the classroom—not at UGA but seventy miles away at tiny Piedmont College. "It was too good of an opportunity to pass up," Russell wryly explained. Adams said he was surprised by the reaction of the journalism professors. The proposed change was an expansion of an existing program, which he said, is usually viewed favorably. But most journalism professors felt the change would adulterate what had been a clear focus.

The hostile reaction to the Grady College changes was severe enough that Adams was forced to abandon the proposal, but his top-down management continued to rankle faculty feathers. Criticism of Adams was widespread among the faculty. As botany professor Barry Palevitz observed, "Universities succeed best when the programs come from bottom up and this is from the top down."

The dawning of the twenty-first century also saw Adams publicly humiliated when one of his biggest administrative blunders was revealed after the firing of head football coach Jim Donnan. And the perception that Adams had little appreciation for the university's research mission persisted as twenty-six research faculty members sent a letter to Adams and Provost Holbrook expressing concern about the lack of administrative support. Adams met with them and pledged more support. Holbrook backed up Adams's promise by committing $4.1 million to recruit faculty to fill existing vacancies.

SOME OF ADAMS'S TROUBLES with the faculty and staff over administrative and academic issues were out in the open. But an even bigger storm was brewing in the background over issues of spending, compensation, and accountability. Criticism of Adams over spending began almost as soon as he arrived at Georgia. Eyebrows were raised when it became known that the university had spent $90,000 on his inauguration, followed by another $220,000 to renovate the president's sky box at Sanford Stadium. In response, Adams claimed that he and his wife used the sky box to entertain alumni, legislators, and potential donors at home football games.

Then there was the matter of his personal office. Adams first occupied the same office that his predecessors had used, a modest space in the uninspiring Lustrat House, a small two-story brick dwelling built in 1847 as a professor's home. The building was relocated to its present location on the old North Campus in 1903. That move so angered Professor Charles Morris that he vacated the premises, and the eponymous Professor Joseph Lustrat's family occupied the dwelling from 1904 until 1927. It was then converted into a museum, and later into the president's office.

When Adams took over at Georgia, a $2.1 million renovation was already planned for the 21,000-square-foot building that had housed the Georgia Museum of Art until 1996, when the museum moved into a new structure that was part of expansion of the campus during Knapp's tenure and in the run-up to the 1996 Olympics. Meanwhile the former museum, erected in 1907 as a library, was to be remade into offices for campus planning and legal affairs. Adams quickly decided the location, near the oldest building on campus, would make perfect digs for him and his senior staff. Two months later the Board of Regents approved Adams's request, with a price tag that had grown to $2.5 million. The spending occurred at a time of belt-tightening at UGA and drew criticism from among the faculty and students. Critics dubbed the opulent new office space "the winter palace," adding to a growing perception that Adams had too much appreciation for his personal concerns and too little for academics and research.

Still, Adams seemed to have solidified his support with the chancellor and the governor's office. In August 2000, Portch gave Adams a sparkling performance review and a $100,000 a year pay raise, bringing his annual compensation to $558,557. The pay hike was financed by the UGA Foundation, as was another $51,000 a year being paid to Mary Adams to accompany her husband and represent the university at various factions. All this spending was beginning not to sit well with some trustees of the UGA Foundation who felt Adams was too free with the private contributions that came in to the university's primary fundraising operation. In other words, with their money.

Coincidentally, Gerald McCarley, an auditor, had retired in 1999 from Deloitte & Touche, a Big Four professional services firm. He volunteered to set up auditing procedures for Foundation spending. Two inside auditors were assigned to audit cash disbursements on a quarterly basis, with McCarley supervising, and with reports issued to the Foundation board, which also meets quarterly. It wasn't long before McCarley's group began questioning Adams's expenditures. First, it was his use of a Foundation credit card to pay for personal expenses, dinners, and golf outings that seemed unrelated to his job. Sometimes Adams used the credit card for personal travel and would reimburse the Foundation, but even then the Foundation paid additional interest due to his late filings of expense reports. This might not have been a big deal to some, but to McCarley it was money that could have gone to a deserving student. The Foundation eventually revoked the credit card after auditors discovered Adams was using it to pay for expensive dinners for himself, his top assistants, and their wives.

In 2001, the internal auditors questioned a $13,490 charge for a charter airplane to take Adams and two university executives and their wives to Washington for George W. Bush's inauguration. Although Adams was listed as a passenger on the flight, Foundation officials later learned that he was not on either leg of the flight. He flew commercial to Washington and returned on January 19 and returned January 23 on a different charter at an additional cost of $2,422.50, according to records of that trip. Foundation Chief Financial Officer Cindy Coyle had already flagged the expense, forwarding a copy of the reimbursement request to UGA Vice President for External Affairs Kathryn Costello, who reported directly to Adams but was also executive director of the Foundation.

The auditors' recommendation on the matter was to "remind executives of the University that they are spending donor contributions and the travel policy of the foundation." The request was ultimately approved for payment but it resulted in policy changes that increased restrictions and provided for regular review of expenditures of funds that support the president's office.

For his part, Adams maintained the inauguration trip provided him and other senior university officials with a good opportunity to visit the Georgia congressional delegation. He also bristled at the auditing of presidential expenses, a practice he considered duplicative and unnecessary, and that was abandoned at his direction.

With his cherubic face and shock of white hair, Adams can sometimes seem reserved, almost shy. A devout church-goer, his undergraduate degree is from a school affiliated with the restorationist and generally fundamentalist Churches of Christ. But Adams also has an earthy side and can cuss a streak when riled. And he is quick to anger.

IN HINDSIGHT, NONE OF this behavior should have surprised Foundation member Wyck Knox, an Atlanta lawyer who gradually became one of Adams's most vocal critics. As mentioned earlier, he and his wife, Shell Hardman Knox, had been forewarned about Adams's hiring in 1997. Shell Knox had been unable to get a seat on the search committee, but she had followed the process through a friend, who had told the Knoxes they probably wouldn't be happy with Adams. The Knoxes learned of Adams's selection in an early morning phone call. "[The caller] was apologetic," said Wyck Knox. "He told us [Adams's] background and the reputation he had at Centre. The reputation was, watch the numbers. Watch the expenses. That's his reputation everywhere. He will fib on the numbers just like he's done with Georgia fundraising."

It's likely that Adams was told or intuited how Shell and Wyck Knox felt, but he nevertheless was friendly and solicitous toward them when he first arrived on campus. As time passed and Wyck Knox probed into more and more of Adams's expenditures and actions, the relationship grew tense.

Knox said he began to question the president's spending of Foundation money after he learned of the charter flight to the Bush inaugural. Following the airplane incident, Knox said he discovered that there were no written guidelines for reimbursement. He also learned about the Foundation credit card that Adams was using.

"In middle of that process Mike asked me to go to dinner with him at Bones [a restaurant in Atlanta's tony Buckhead neighborhood]," Knox said. "He wanted to talk me into not having any rules. And I remember looking him straight in the eye. I said, 'Mike, this is not about $5,000 or $10,000. This is about the success of a fundraising campaign. And your job is to raise money for the University of Georgia. Let me put it to you in Georgia vernacular. If somebody in rural Georgia is going to give $10,000 to the University of Georgia, they probably think that's the biggest gift they've ever given in their life. If they see you squandering money on a $500 dinner that ought to be $100, they're going to give their money to the First Baptist Church. They're not going to give it to the University of Georgia. That's what I'm talking about. You can't ruin your reputation with the image you're wasting money.'

"He did not like that one bit," Knox said. "I knew after that dinner we had trouble on our hands. So we wrote the rules and there was always friction. He was always hedging. If he and Mary went out to dinner we got the bill for it. He would co-opt the system."

AND THEN COMES THE firing of Vince Dooley, which opened a Pandora's box of Georgia tradition, university governance, the breaking of long-term friendships, high-profile hanky-panky, and, as always, intramural contests between the moneyed and the powerful. Through it all, it turns out that Adams held an ace hole card named Donald Leebern.

5

DON LEEBERN AND VINCE DOOLEY

To many in the Bulldog family, the name Vince Dooley is synonymous with the University of Georgia. During his forty-one-year career at Georgia, Dooley became one of the most respected figures in college athletics, serving twenty-five years as head football coach and nine years in the dual roles of coach and athletic director before giving up coaching in 1988 to serve exclusively as AD until 2004. A member of the College Football Hall of Fame, he was successful in one of the country's elite football conferences, bringing excitement and a sense of pride to his adopted state. His teams won six SEC championships, won eight bowl games and tied two in twenty appearances, and won a national championship. Rather studious for a football coach, Dooley has a master's degree in history and devours literature about the Civil War. His Athens home and office is filled not only with football memorabilia but with books on a wide range of subjects.

Georgia fans adore Dooley not only because he was successful, but also because they see him as a decent human being. He exhibits patience and good humor, has made thousands of speeches to Bulldog Clubs in even the smallest villages, and remains close to his former players, many of whom—like Billy Payne, who brought the 1996 Olympic Games to Atlanta—have become leaders in their communities. Others, like the Heisman-winning Herschel Walker, have become icons. All of them love their coach. And high school coaches love Dooley because he made it a policy to recruit Georgia kids first.

During Dooley's forty-one years with the school's athletic program, the University of Georgia got its swagger back. Meanwhile, the state of Georgia was dramatically changing. It has grown and prospered and progressed in many areas, race relations being one of the most significant and most visible. Dooley had a low-key hand in that. He had quietly signed five African American football players to scholarships a decade before Herschel Walker burst onto the scene and carried Georgia to a national championship. Horace King, Larry West, Chuck Kinnebrew, Richard Appleby, and Clarence Pope entered UGA in 1971. Forty years later, Dooley can still tick off their names without having to think. He dismisses the notion that their signings were controversial or even courageous acts. The South was rapidly integrating. Integrated high school teams were already competing. Georgia had signed Ronnie Hogue to a basketball scholarship in 1970. By the time Walker arrived, just twenty years after Georgia politicians threatened to close the university rather than admit blacks, bumper stickers proclaiming "Herschel Walker Is My Cousin" began appearing on whites' pickup trucks across the state. "I think sports did as much or more than any particular activity in the South to encourage acceptance of integration," Dooley said. "People accepted it. They want to win."

Although Dooley downplays his part in helping smooth the transition from all-white to integrated athletic teams, his role did not go unnoticed. In 2008, Dooley became only the second recipient of the Selig Mentoring Award given by a committee made up of fifteen Division I-A minority athletic directors. Established in 2007 and named in honor of Major League Baseball Commissioner Allan H. (Bud) Selig, the award is presented annually to a person in athletics administration who has been at the forefront in creating equal opportunities for minorities.

VINCENT JOSEPH DOOLEY was born September 4, 1932, in Mobile, Alabama. He attended McGill High, a Catholic boys' school run by the Brothers of the Sacred Heart. A gifted athlete, Dooley won a scholarship to Auburn University (then Alabama Polytechnic Institute) where he played quarterback for Coach Ralph "Shug" Jordan and basketball for Coach Joel Eaves. After graduating in 1954, Dooley spent two years in the Marine Corps and then took a job as an Auburn assistant football coach.

In 1963, a scandal erupted at Georgia after the *Saturday Evening Post* published a story alleging that Georgia's Athletic Director Wallace Butts and Alabama's Coach Bear Bryant had fixed a football game the previous year. Butts sued for libel and won $3 million in punitive damages, then the largest libel award in U.S. court history (later reduced to $500,000). However, Butts had retired as head football coach in 1960 (succeeded by Johnny Griffith), and he resigned as athletic director before the *Post* story broke. Georgia then hired Joel Eaves from Auburn to fill the AD job and Eaves tabbed Dooley, then coaching the Auburn freshmen, to take over as head football coach at Georgia, replacing Griffith.

Dooley's first game was an inauspicious beginning, as Bear Bryant's Crimson Tide gave the Bulldogs a 31–3 "whupping," but he rebounded quickly and went 7-3-1 and beat Texas Tech in the Sun Bowl in 1964.

Dooley was only thirty-one when he came to Athens, and he had to overcome the lack of previous head coach experience and the stigma of being "an Auburn man." Not only had he played and coached on the Plains, but he had married an Auburn girl. Auburn and Georgia have the oldest and perhaps most intense gridiron rivalry in the Deep South. After his best season at Georgia in 1980, Dooley received an offer from his alma mater to become head coach and athletic director. It was an overture Dooley felt he had to consider. But by this time he had been at Georgia for seventeen years and the Dooley children had grown up as Bulldogs. He recalls his son Derek, then ten years old, coming to him with tears in his eyes and saying, "Daddy, I hate Auburn." That pretty much sums up the feelings of both schools' fans.

Dooley refused Auburn's offer and went on to beat Notre Dame in the Sugar Bowl that year, finish 12-0, and win the national championship. By this time he was also the athletic director, having succeeded the retiring Joel Eaves in 1979. Dooley held both the AD and head football coach jobs until 1988, when he retired from active coaching and Dooley protege Ray Goff was chosen to replace him.

The *New Georgia Encyclopedia* notes that in his years as head coach:

> Dooley would usher the Bulldogs into the era of big-time, big-business college football, winning 201 games . . . and suffering through only one losing season (1977) . . . Dooley was also celebrated for his good fortune against two of Georgia's worst enemies: He had a 19-6 record against the Georgia Institute of Technology and a 17-7-1 record against the University of Florida. He was unable to go above .500 against his alma mater, however, posting a twenty-five-year record against Auburn of 11-13-1.

Nevertheless five of Georgia's SEC championships were clinched on the plains of Auburn.

. . . He was named National Collegiate Athletic Association (NCAA) National Coach of the Year in 1980 and 1982, and was honored as Southeastern Conference Coach of the Year seven times. He has been inducted into the College Football Hall of Fame, the Alabama Sports Hall of Fame, the Georgia Sports Hall of Fame, and the Sun Bowl Hall of Fame.

As impressive as that record is as head football coach, Dooley's accomplishments as AD were probably even more significant to the university as a whole. The *New Georgia Encyclopedia*, again:

> During his tenure as athletic director, UGA sports teams won [twenty-two] national championships and seventy-five Southeastern Conference championships, and the program broadened (thanks to federal Title IX regulations, which require female teams to equal male teams) to twenty-one sports. Georgia's prominence across the board in athletics is amply displayed in the annual results for the Sears Directors' Cup, which recognizes the top collegiate athletic programs in the country. Georgia finished second in Sears Cup standings in 1998–99 and third in 2000–01.
>
> Dooley led the athletic association's effort to donate some $2 million to the University of Georgia for the recruitment of [non-athletes], and funds have also been made available to the university for the construction and expansion of many facilities on campus.
>
> Dooley was also instrumental in bringing to Athens three sporting events (women's soccer, rhythmic gymnastics, and volleyball) of the 1996 Olympic Games and served six years on the advisory committee to the Atlanta Olympic Organizing Committee . . .

(The former coach/AD also provided $100,000 of his personal funds to seed and to personally lead a fundraising effort for endowment of the university's library. That leadership effort by Dooley has grown into an endowment now exceeding $4 million, UGA's fourth largest single endowment.)

Dooley's four decades in UGA athletics were not without tribulations. He was bruised in the 1980s when professor Jan Kemp ignited a national scandal and heaped scorn on Georgia's reputation with a lawsuit charging that she was wrongfully fired for speaking out against preferential treatment given to athletes. Kemp accused UGA officials of recruiting athletes who could run like the wind but were not as swift in the classroom, then putting them in watered-down "developmental studies" programs to keep them eligible to play football. She won more than a million dollars and her job back. Dooley was also criticized for his choice of Ray Goff as head football coach and Ron Jirsa as head basketball coach, both of whom he later had to fire. Dooley didn't actually hire Goff. He had taken a leave as coach and athletic director in 1988 to consider a run for governor. Goff was hired by President Charles Knapp before Dooley returned.

More recently, Dooley had to preside in his capacity as athletic director over the messy 2003 scandal involving head basketball coach Jim Harrick and his assistant coach son, Jim Harrick Jr., when the latter was caught giving players unearned grades so they could maintain eligibility. We will look at the Harrick controversy in more detail later.

The Kemp episode is well-remembered as a low point in Bulldog history and it especially burns in the memories of many who love UGA not for its football team but for its scholarly pursuits. The scandal cost then-UGA President Fred Davison and the two defendants—Virginia Trotter, vice president for academic affairs, and Leroy Ervin, director of the developmental studies program—their jobs, but when the dust-up was over, Dooley still had his. (Kemp returned to her teaching position in the developmental studies program for a time but then retired, and recently passed away.)

"Lest we forget," *Atlanta Journal-Constitution* columnist Mark Bradley reminded his readers in 2003, "Dooley was both the football coach and athletic director when the Jan Kemp trial convened, and somehow he stayed above the fray."

Of course, Vince Dooley had not yet even heard of Michael Adams. When he did, it was through one of his closest and oldest friends, Don Leebern. As it unfolded, the Dooley-Adams-Leebern triangle became one of the central elements in the dispute between Adams and the University of Georgia Foundation.

DONALD MELWOOD LEEBERN, JR., is the grandson of Lafayette D. "Fate" Leebern, who arrived in Columbus, Georgia, during the Great Depression and set about making a fortune in illegal liquor and gambling. Fate Leebern gained a measure of respectability in Columbus, where he ran a hotel and other legitimate businesses and where he founded a wine and liquor distributorship the day after Prohibition was repealed in 1938. That enterprise, the Columbus Wine Company Distributors, is said to have unloaded the first carload of legal liquor in Columbus following the end of Prohibition. Fate Leebern was shot dead in 1946 in the high dice room of the Southern Manor night club in Phenix City, Alabama, allegedly by Dixie Mafia gambling kingpin Hoyt Shepherd. Witnesses implicated Hoyt Shepherd in the murder, but his brother, Grady Shepherd, confessed and claimed self-defense. Both Shepherds were indicted, tried, and acquitted. After Fate Leebern's death, his only son, Donald M. Leebern Sr., ran the business until his own death in 1957, when Don Leebern Jr. took over the highly regulated but hugely profitable family-owned liquor empire while still a UGA undergraduate.

Today, the company that Fate Leebern began in 1938 is called Georgia Crown Distributing Company. An industry newsletter describes it as "a full-service beverage distributor, with wholesale operations doing business in Alabama, Georgia, and Tennessee, selling imported and domestic spirits, wines, beers and specialty products."

The company, like all liquor distributors in Georgia, operates as a monopoly thanks to a beneficent Georgia legislature. Georgia laws—largely unchanged since the 1930s—protect liquor distributors by requiring that retailers purchase through a wholesaler, rather than directly from distillers and brewers. To ship alcoholic beverages into Georgia, the producer must appoint a single distributor for a specified territory in the state. Once the producer chooses a wholesaler he cannot change wholesalers without demonstrating due cause and getting approval from the state Department of Revenue. Producers of alcoholic beverages are forbidden from owning a wholesale distributorship and wholesalers cannot own retail stores. Retailers are required to purchase from the designated wholesaler at whatever price the wholesaler sets. And once the alcoholic beverage is delivered to the retail store, it cannot be moved to any other licensed location, even to another store owned by the same retailer.

This three-tier system has long been criticized by consumer advocates as overly costly to consumers. A Georgia Public Policy Foundation study of the state's liquor laws concluded that the laws stifle competition. "They protect a monopoly controlled by a small number of wholesalers, who siphon off 18–25 percent of the cost to retailers, increasing prices for consumers, hurting producers such as small to mid-size wineries and making liquor distribution the most expensive in the packaged-good industry. There is no public policy reason why producers should not be able to sell directly to retailers, the public or grocers whether on the Internet or through other traditional sales methods." However, a state house legislative study committee looked into the liquor distribution system and concluded that it works just fine, a judgment that was a testament to the power of Georgia's liquor lobby and distributors like Donald Leebern. They give generously and they don't mind calling in favors.

Basically, Don Leebern inherited a cash cow and has grown it into a cash herd. He probably couldn't have done any better even if he had that degree in business administration that he never completed at the University of Georgia, where he played varsity football in 1957–59 under Coach Wallace Butts but didn't earn a diploma.

While at UGA, Leebern also courted and married a former Miss Georgia. Don and Betsy Leebern made a handsome couple, rich and rabid Bulldog backers. When Vince and Barbara Dooley arrived in Athens in 1963, they soon developed a close and powerful friendship with the Leeberns.

The Leeberns spent nights with the Dooleys and sat with Barbara when they attended Georgia's home football games. After Dooley left the sidelines to become exclusively the athletic director, the Leeberns joined the Dooleys in their sky box at Sanford Stadium. In turn, the Dooleys stayed with Betsy and Don Leebern when they went to Columbus or to their beach condo on St. Simons Island. The couples took trips together nearly every year to New York for the annual College Football Hall of Fame dinner. Their relationships extended to their children. Daniel Dooley and Donald Leebern III (Little Don) were roommates at UGA. The Leebern and Dooley daughters were in the same UGA sorority.

A career like Dooley's, spanning decades as head football coach and athletic director of an NCAA Division I power, is a magnet for attracting casual friendships. This was no casual friendship. Vince and Barbara Dooley have lots of friends in and outside of Georgia but few, if any, became closer to them than Don and Betsy Leebern.

"They weren't just acquaintances. We gave their son and daughter parties when they got married," Barbara Dooley recalls. "I thought they were really close friends. I considered them not just friends but close personal friends. He flew Betsy on his company plane up here with other close friends to celebrate my fortieth birthday. And there was nothing I felt like I could ask Don and Betsy to do for me that they wouldn't do it."

That cut both ways. Several times over the years, Dooley lent his considerable personal clout to Leebern's business interests. One instance was after Leebern created a new Georgia Crown division, Poland Spring Water Distributing Company, and began selling Perrier's Poland Spring bottled water. Quickly realizing the potential profits in bottled water, Leebern's company opened a plant in Dahlonega, Georgia, in 1991 and began marketing its own brand, Melwood Springs, "Georgia Crown's own private-labeled spring water." The problem was that Melwood Springs water doesn't come from a spring; it is pumped from a well in Dahlonega, just like city water. "Bottled well water" just doesn't have the cachet of "natural spring water."

Moreover, Perrier was threatening to quit marketing Poland Spring water in Georgia because new state agriculture regulations scheduled to take effect in May 1992 would not have allowed the product to be labeled as natural spring water. The regulation also would have affected Melwood Springs water. With Georgia Agriculture Commission Tommy Irvin about to put the kibosh on the whole venture, Leebern needed to do something—and quickly. He got hometown legislator Tom Buck of Columbus to introduce a bill in the 1992 legislature redefining natural spring water to include water that comes from wells. The bill easily passed in the state House of Representatives but was defeated in the Senate. Undaunted, Leebern, then a newly appointed member of the state Board of Regents, called on his friends at the University of Georgia.

Both UGA President Charles Knapp and Dooley lobbied for the legislation. Dooley's son Daniel was working for Georgia Crown at the time and

Knapp was an employee of the Regents. UGA spokesman Tom Jackson said Knapp and Leebern were personal friends and that Knapp's support of the legislation had nothing to do with his position at the university. After the full-court press by Dooley and Knapp, the Senate, which had voted 31–24 to defeat the bill two weeks earlier, reversed itself, voting 32–23 to approve the bill. Governor Zell Miller signed the legislation into law. Miller said he saw nothing wrong with the labeling or the lobbying. "In this age of where we want people to participate, there's no problem with anyone calling . . . no matter what position they hold," Miller told an *AJC* reporter. And as for the labeling controversy, Miller said he didn't see any difference between well and spring water. It can all be traced back to an underground source, he said.

THE LEEBERN-DOOLEY RELATIONSHIP, ENTWINED across personal, family, and UGA lines, held firm through the 1990s. In 1997, Leebern and another of Dooley's close friends, Sonny Seiler, personally called Dooley to give him a heads-up before the public announcement of the hiring of Michael Adams as UGA president. "You'll like him," Seiler predicted. "He has a real fondness for athletics." Leebern also mentioned Adams's fondness for athletics.

Like most Georgians, Dooley knew little about Adams and therefore had no concerns about his appointment. A self-described "good soldier," Dooley was confident that he would get along well with the new president. After all, he had served four previous presidents at UGA without conflict. Nevertheless, Dooley thought it was a good idea to reach out to the man who would be his boss during his final years at UGA, so he telephoned his congratulations and left his number. "He never returned my phone call," Dooley remembers. "This was a couple of days after he was named. So, I called him again in a couple of days and this time he took my call. I just congratulated him. That was the first time I talked to him."

Dooley wanted a close relationship with the president and tried to convince Adams that it was important to have good lines of communications. The best way to do that, Dooley felt, was for the two of them to have monthly meetings, just as he had done with previous presidents. Adams wanted no part of it.

Dooley hasn't said whether Leebern, in his heads-up call about the Adams selection, also explained that Adams was his personal choice, or that he had ramrodded Adams through the interview and hiring process. By then, Leebern had become the dominant personality on the Board of Regents. He was first appointed to the board in 1991 by Governor Zell Miller, then a Democrat. (Miller reappointed him in 1998 to another seven-year term; Republican Governor Sonny Perdue named him to a third term in 2005.)

Leebern has been a big contributor to the University of Georgia and to Georgia politicians. He has also been a lightning rod for controversy, not least due to his public flaunting of his relationship with Georgia gymnastics coach Suzanne Yoculan, with whom he lives openly on a $1.5 million estate outside Athens, though he is still married to Betsy Leebern, who maintains the family domicile in Columbus.

The Bulldog elite comprise a tight circle of friends and acquaintances where everybody knows everybody else. Barbara Dooley had heard rumors about Don Leebern's girlfriends for years but had always dismissed them. Some folks are jealous of anyone with Leebern's kind of money, she reasoned. "Anyway, if he was having affairs, he was being discreet about it, as far as I knew, and I assured everyone that he loved his wife, Betsy." That changed in early 2000 when Leebern began a very public affair with Yoculan.

Leebern began showing up at the Gym Dogs meets with his wife Betsy and their grandson. Surprised to see her friend at a gymnastics meet, Barbara wondered about Betsy's sudden interest in the sport. "She sort of rolled her eyes and said, 'Well, Don had to come.'"

Betsy Leebern soon stopped coming to the gymnastics meets and then she stopped attending UGA football games. She'd make excuses to avoid weekends with the Dooleys.

"She just wasn't going to tell me there was trouble," Barbara Dooley said. "And I was too stupid to realize what was actually going on. Betsy always made excuses during football season that Don could no longer come on Friday nights and they were just going to fly in for the game on Saturdays. Next she started making excuses why they would not go to New York with us as we had done for many years. It was a wonderful tradition to be in New York for the [College Football] Hall of Fame dinner with good friends, but it just ended. Things just started changing! The next thing that I hear is that he'd actually taken up with Yoculan."

One Sunday morning she awoke to a local newspaper article written by the late M. A. Barnes, announcing the engagement of Don Leebern to Suzanne Yoculan.

"I screamed for Vince and I truly almost fainted," she said. "I could not believe what I was reading. And I must have read it three or four times to make sure I was actually reading it right. It was the talk of the town and most people were shaking their heads and saying, 'What the hell is he doing?' He had given Yoculan an engagement ring and is still married to Betsy. And put it in our paper! I am still in denial at this point and kept thinking that just can't be true.

"Still even with this staring me in the face I thought our friendship was strong enough for me to call him and find out just what was happening. So, I called his telephone number. I said, 'Don, what the hell are you doing? I just read an article about your engagement. Are you totally out of your mind? You are setting yourself up for the biggest lawsuit this state has ever seen.' Well, he was silent for a minute and gave me an answer like, 'Mind your own business. I know what I'm doing.' At that point I realized our friendship was over and I needed to stay out of this mess. And so I told Vincent at the time, I said, 'Let me tell you something. I am drawing a line in the sand. This is against every principle in my body. Betsy is a good friend of mine and I will not condone any relationship like this.'"

Barbara Dooley said she began to avoid all functions where Leebern and Yoculan might be present. "Every time we'd get an invitation I wouldn't go. He would have to go by himself. And of course I would say I don't know why you're going.

"He said, 'Well, look, I'm the athletic director.'"

"I said, 'Yeah, and you should have fired her ass right away.' I said if that had been a male coach moving in with a married woman, the male coach would have been fired. The press would have been all over it. There's no way they could let that story alone. But it seems that it's totally different with a female. It's just amazing."

Barbara Dooley's sense of outrage wasn't felt at the highest levels of state government where money apparently talks more loudly than traditional morality, even in the heart of Baptist Bible belt.

Barbara Dooley has kept up with her friend Betsy vicariously through mutual friends and relatives. "She quit returning my calls a couple of years ago. I feel very confident that Don told her to stay away from me, and because he pays her bills . . . But her daughter came into our box during one of the games and literally had tears in her eyes and said she missed us terribly. She said, 'I just want you to know that we love you.' And I have to say, every time I get sick—and I've been sick a lot in the last three years—I always get flowers from Betsy. I always get a card from Betsy on my birthday saying I miss you and I love you. But she won't call me. I find it very interesting."

Vince Dooley was Yoculan's direct superior and tried to maintain a casual friendship with Leebern even after the couple moved in together and the affair became the topic of dinner conversations in Athens and Atlanta. Meanwhile, the athletics department was concerned about the NCAA watchdogs. The school was already in trouble with the NCAA for rules violations in the men's basketball program. The UGA Athletics Department's mission statement on integrity declares:

> By their very nature, athletics inevitably involve character development; for this reason, especially, we must conduct ourselves with utmost integrity. All programs and the activities on our behalf by alumni and friends must be consistent with the policies of the university and the athletic bodies which govern us. We are to be at all times honest and forthright in our dealings with each other, the public, and the media.

The question was whether Leebern's actions in living with a university system employee constituted a conflict, since the Regents have oversight of the entire university system.

Georgia's NCAA compliance coordinator, Amy Chisholm, wrote to the Southeastern Conference in July 2001 inquiring whether Leebern and Yoculan's living arrangement could be a violation of NCAA rules because of Leebern's role as an athletics booster:

Specifically, a head coach [Yoculan] is engaged to a representative of Georgia's athletics interest [Leebern]. The coach and representative have purchased a house together and will be sharing this house as of August. The coach would like to host meals for prospects and current student-athletes during official visits at their house without it being perceived as impermissible contact with an athletics representative. Although, legally at this time the representative is not considered a spouse . . . the NCAA has never legislated fiancés and other personal relationships.

Chisholm's letter didn't mention that the coach's fiancé was already married. A few days later Chisholm received a reply from Beth DeBauche, then SEC associate commissioner for compliance, informing her that such contact would, in fact, be an NCAA violation: "According to the NCAA Membership Services staff, the answer to this issue is no. The athletics representative's status is not changed by the fact he is engaged to the head coach. Accordingly, he cannot be involved in any recruiting activities." A fiancé should not be present at any recruiting meals or activities either on or off-campus, DeBauche replied. The upshot was that the SEC and the NCAA said that Yoculan could host recruits at her house but Leebern should not be present.

This novel situation posed increasing challenges for the man who was the coach's boss and the booster/fiancé's longtime friend. By coincidence, Dooley's relationship with Leebern began to sour just as Dooley was negotiating with Adams on a contract extension in 2001.

Riding the crest of her women's gymnastics team's SEC and national championships, Yoculan began angling for a promotion to become assistant athletic director. Her counterpart at the University of Alabama, Sarah Patterson, was an assistant AD and was using the title to aid in recruiting. Dooley ignored Yoculan's complaints, feeling it would have been unfair to elevate her over other coaches who had more seniority.

Afterwards, Leebern dropped by Dooley's office. Barbara Dooley recounts the conversation as her husband told it to her:

"'Buddy, I need a favor.' Of course Vince said, 'Sure, what do you need?' And he said, 'Well, you know, Suzanne really wants to be assistant athletic director.'"

Barbara Dooley said Leebern brought up that the Alabama gymnastics coach was an assistant AD and was flaunting it over Yoculan. Vince was against it but in his fairness to his longtime friend he said that he would look into it. Vince called the Alabama athletic director, Mal Moore, and found out that at one time Patterson had been an assistant AD with additional administrative duties, but that was no longer the case and she was no longer on the senior administrative staff. However, she didn't drop the title and used it to her advantage. Vince told Leebern all that, but Leebern still wanted the favor. Vince told him that he would do almost anything for him in light of their longtime friendship, but he could not compromise his responsibilities, especially since Andy Landers, Jack Bauerle, and Manuel Diaz, all with similar great coaching records as Yoculan, could make the same case to become an assistant athletic director.

"Vince stood on his principles on this decision and Don left there, and I'm convinced—Vince is not convinced, but I'm convinced—that Leebern left there that day and made a pact with the devil—Adams. Because Vince told him no, and I'm not sure anybody had ever told Don Leebern no," Barbara Dooley said.

6

VINCE DOOLEY AND MICHAEL ADAMS

enior faculty at Centre College say that while president there, Michael Adams had shown a keen interest in the school's athletic programs. He not only attended games but became directly involved with NCAA matters. That was considered a plus by some members of the Georgia search committee.

Vince Dooley felt certain that he would hit it off with the new president and began to reach out even before Adams arrived on campus, telephoning him congratulations from a hospital bed where Dooley was recovering from knee-replacement surgery. As previously noted, Adams didn't return the call. When Dooley called again and got through a few days later, the conversation was pleasant with Dooley offering congratulations and Adams saying he looked forward to meeting the legendary coach.

Dooley was satisfied that he would get along fine with the new president. "I'm a person that whoever is given the responsibility as president, my tendency is to go all out to support them," said Dooley. "I am a good soldier in that respect."

But Dooley and Adams were soon on a collision course which would reverberate across Georgia. Ironically, it was Adams's fondness for athletics that led to the dispute, and Dooley now recalls that he received early warnings of trouble ahead.

Shortly after Adams arrived at Georgia, Dooley made a presentation to the athletics board about adding sky suites at Sanford Stadium. Dooley said he didn't notice, but afterwards Dick Bestwick, the respected senior associate athletic director, commented on Adams's body language and red-faced expression as Dooley was speaking. Bestwick warned him after the meeting that he had better be wary of Adams.

"That was the first indication that this person was going to be different than any [president] I had dealt with. And I'm glad he was the fifth one and not the second or third one or I might have had a much shorter tenure at Georgia," said Dooley.

Bestwick later said Adams broached the subject of Dooley's retirement soon after arriving at UGA. "He asked me when Dooley was going to retire. I said, 'Why would the king want to abdicate his throne?'" Bestwick said Adams seemed disappointed with that answer.

Dooley recalled another early incident that gave him pause. In the fall of 1998 Uga owner and breeder Sonny Seiler asked Dooley to participate in a "changing of the dogs" ceremony at halftime of an upcoming Georgia football game. Dooley was to remove the collar from the retiring Uga V and ceremonially place it on the new mascot, Uga VI. A week before the ceremony, Dooley got a telephone call from Senior Vice President Tom Landrum saying that Adams wanted to participate in the ceremony. "Landrum said, 'Mike sees it as a great photo-op.' I said by all means but I thought to myself that the photo-op was typically political Mike Adams," Dooley said.

When the cast of characters assembled on the field at Sanford Stadium during halftime, Dooley said he wanted Adams as president to have a prominent part in the ceremony. Dooley suggested that he remove the collar from Uga V and ceremoniously hand it to Adams to then place on Uga VI. Adams nodded his approval of the idea. But when Dooley knelt and removed the collar from Uga V, Adams snatched it from his hand and displayed it for the cameras before Dooley could even stand up. It was a trivial matter, but Dooley was taken aback.

"Up until then, I had not worked for someone whose primary motivation in all things would be so politically self-promoting and ego-driven," said Dooley. "Prior to that incident, I had many people tell me about the ego and pompous attitude of [Adams], to which I'd paid little attention. But I have to admit that after encountering his display at the changing of the dog, I saw it firsthand."

Dooley also encountered Adams's famous temper early one morning in 2002 when he received an irate telephone call at home. Dooley recalls the testy telephone conversation thusly:

"Hello?"

"This is Mike Adams."

"How are you doing, Mr. President?"

"Not good."

"What's wrong?"

"I don't like what I read in the paper this morning."

"What did you read?"

"I don't like reading about an unauthorized stadium expansion."

Dooley said he explained, as the paper stated, that it was only a preliminary study but Adams replied that neither he nor any members of the athletic board had authorized the study "and this kind of unauthorized action upsets them."

Dooley said he was by this point in the conversation becoming irritated at Adams's abruptness. He reminded Adams, who chairs the athletics board, that he had brought the matter up at the previous board meeting.

"I have no recollection of that," Adams said.

"That's your opinion."

"My opinion counts."

"Mine does, too," Dooley responded.

After the conversation, Dooley said he researched the minutes of the athletics board and found reference to the study. He had a copy of the minutes hand-delivered to Adams's office later that morning. Adams never again mentioned the matter even though the two men sat together that very night at a dinner event.

Dooley said he tried to convince Adams that to have good two-way communications between the president and athletic director they needed to meet monthly. The arrangement had worked well with Adams's predecessors Fred Davison, Henry King Stanford, and Charles Knapp, but Adams rejected the idea.

"I think because I recommended it and it worked well with other presidents he didn't want that kind of relationship. In fact he told me once that under different circumstances he would have had me reporting to a senior administrator. But the fact is this kind of communication between president and athletic director has become standard procedure among universities and is highly recommended by the NCAA. He didn't want that. Now he does it with [Dooley's successor, Athletic Director Damon] Evans and I am pleased that is the case."

Adams's tendency of not following traditions established by former presidents also showed up in other relationships. For more than fifty years it had been a tradition of Georgia presidents to join the Athens Rotary Club. Presidents O. C. Aderhold, Fred Davison, Henry King Stanford, and Chuck Knapp were all Rotarians. This association served them well in establishing good relationships in Athens. Adams wanted no part of any local civic group, and his critics allege that this attitude was a major reason for a less than friendly "Town-Gown" relationship that developed.

Dooley said it became clear early on that Adams would use his role as chair of the UGA Athletics Board to make his presence felt more than most presidents in intercollegiate athletics. Soon after Adams's arrival, Dooley brought in two outside consultants to evaluate UGA's athletics program and to make recommendations for improvements.

Eugene F. Corrigan, former athletic director at the University of Virginia and Notre Dame and retired commissioner of the ACC, and Chuck Neinas, Big Eight commissioner and former executive director of the College Football Association, spent two days on the Athens campus in January 1999 interviewing administrators and coaches. Their official report, written by Corrigan and addressed to Dooley, generally praised UGA's athletic programs and facilities and particularly Dooley's tenure as AD. The report noted that a good relationship and direct access between the athletic director and the president was critical to both parties. The report said:

"It has always seemed to me that one of the main jobs of the AD is to protect the interests of the university (and the president) from all the sources both within and attached to athletics which can bring discredit to the institution. It allows the president to spend his time running the university—while always being aware of what is going on in athletics."

Writing privately to Dooley, Corrigan was more blunt. "In my conversations with Mike Adams I was struck with the fact that this guy from Pepperdine and Centre College seems to want to be involved more closely with football," Corrigan wrote. "I was quite direct with him and suggested that it was best to leave football issues to his AD (who knows just about everything there is to know about the game). However, he seems to want his board to know that he has contact with the football coach. I hope he heard what I told him, and more important, that he heeds the warnings. Mike should only talk to [head football coach Jim] Donnan at your request, and they both need to know that."

Corrigan offered his friend Dooley this advice: "Victory is wonderful, but hardly sustainable in a league as competitive as the SEC. Don't stay too long, because it can eventually only take away from the incredible accomplishments which you have achieved at Georgia. They should name the place for you."

Corrigan further noted that in his interview with Donnan, the football coach felt he was underpaid compared with other Southeastern Conference coaches. And not long after that assessment Donnan began agitating for a new multi-year contract.

Dooley had hired Donnan from Marshall University, a Division 1AA school in December 1995, a year and a half before Adams arrived. After a 5-6 season in Donnan's first year, the Bulldogs bounced back in 1997 to post a 10-2 record, losing only to Tennessee and Auburn and beating arch rival Florida 37–17.

Suddenly Jim Donnan was a hot commodity in the coaching ranks. The University of North Carolina, where Donnan had coached for several years under Vince Dooley's brother, Bill Dooley, came calling with a $1 million offer to coach the Tar Heels. So Dooley began working on a new contract for Donnan.

After negotiations with Donnan slowed, the impatient Adams did an end run around Dooley, the Athletic Board, and the Athletic Association lawyers who were negotiating the contract. Adams made an under-the-table verbal deal to pay Donnan roughly $250,000 should he be fired with three or more years left on his contract. The president specified that Dooley, the Athletic Board, and the Athletic Association's attorneys King & Spalding must not know about the deal.

Donnan's Bulldogs were 9-3 in 1998 and finished the season with a come-from-behind victory over Virginia. The team dropped to 8-4 in 1999 but came from behind to defeat Purdue in the Outback Bowl. It marked the first time since the 1981–83 seasons that Georgia had finished their season ranked among the top sixteen teams in the polls. However, Georgia lost its final regular season game to hated Georgia Tech.

When the Bulldogs finished the 2000 season with an 8-4 record and again lost the final regular season game to Georgia Tech, Adams let it be known he was unhappy. "Our special teams [stink]," he told reporters after the game. "We can't tackle. We don't stay in our lanes. We just don't cover."

Later that week Adams fired Donnan, implying that there were "off the field" problems with the football program without specifying what they were. Rumors swirled that some team members were into drugs. Donnan felt obliged to respond saying flatly, "We don't have any drug problems on our team."

(Donnan's successor Mark Richt couldn't say the same. In 2003 campus police were called to McWhorter Hall where they arrested five football players and one basketball player on charges of drug possession. In that case Adams, who had helped recruit Richt from Florida State University, saw fit to say nothing. Richt was winning even more football games than Donnan had and was 3-0 versus Georgia Tech.)

The dismissal of Donnan triggered the secret $250,000 buyout clause that Adams had been hiding from Dooley and the Athletic Association. In January 2001, Donnan's agent, Richard Howell, wrote Adams demanding that the university honor the agreement and pay Donnan. After Adams refused to discuss a settlement and weeks passed, Howell also contacted the Athletic Association attorney, Ed Tolley of Athens, and told him about the secret agreement. Tolley went straight to Dooley's office.

"Are you aware of this secret deal?" Tolley asked.

Not only was Dooley not aware of it, he could hardly believe what he was hearing.

After consulting with then-Chancellor Stephen Portch, Adams came to Dooley's office to explain. Adams acknowledged his "mistake," Dooley recalled. But he blamed Jim Nalley, a wealthy Atlanta car dealership owner and friend of Donnan's, who was acting as a go-between in the negotiations. "Adams told me if he wasn't trying to get a lot of money out of him he'd tell him what he thought of him," Dooley said.

The question then became what to do next, since the agreement hadn't yet been made public. Dooley set up a meeting. Attending the meeting were Dooley, his personal attorney Nick Chivilis, and Tolley and Floyd Newton of King & Spalding, who were representing the Athletic Association. Adams sent on his behalf Steve Shewmaker, executive director of the Office of Legal Affairs, the university's top lawyer and a personal friend whom he had brought to Georgia from Kentucky.

Shewmaker stunned everyone by suggesting the Athletic Association, which is funded by public donations, simply absorb the $250,000 without bringing the matter to the Athletic Association board, thus avoiding public exposure. This proposal smacked to the others as a cover-up and they quickly rejected it. They opted to bring the matter to the board for approval.

Shewmaker later told Deloitte & Touche auditors he didn't recall suggesting they keep the Donnan payment secret, but everyone else at the meeting remembered it that way.

On April 17, 2001, the Athletic Association executive committee met in the executive conference room at the Georgia Center for Continuing Education on the UGA campus. Adams, who chairs the Athletic Association Board, called the meeting to order and began the discussion of Donnan's contract. Rather than acknowledge a mistake, however, Adams implied the secret agreement was a misunderstanding.

According to minutes, "Dr. Adams said a verbal statement he made while Coach Donnan's contract negotiations were underway was taken as a commitment to extend the contract by six months should he be released from his duties before the expiration date of the contract."

The executive committee approved the payment unanimously and the full board approved it a week later.

Before the firing, however, Dooley, perhaps out of empathy for a fellow coach, had wanted to give Donnan another year to turn the team around or at least give him an opportunity to find another job. Dooley had met privately with Donnan and told him that he was going to recommend one more year but warned that he was not sure of the president's reaction to the recommendation.

As events unfolded, however, Adams then met with the Athletic Board members to get counseling. The board backed his decision to fire Donnan. Afterwards, Dooley, perhaps because of his many years as a football coach, felt obliged to make public his feelings that Donnan deserved another year to right the ship.

Some felt Dooley's comments were inappropriate. "I was on the Athletic Board and I favored firing Donnan," said Hank Huckaby, then a senior vice president. "When Vince came out and said he'd give him [Donnan] another year, I'd have fired him [Dooley] right then."

Huckaby said Donnan was fired for multiple reasons including suspicion of a lack of team discipline and "going 7-4 every year." Also, he said Donnan lacked good political skills.

Dooley said he felt it only fair to let it be known at the press conference that he had recommended another year with the decision ultimately resting with the president. "In good conscience, I had to tell the truth about what I had recommended, though, as I stated at the time, the president had the right to make the final decision."

In his autobiography written with *AJC* sportswriter Tony Barnhart and in subsequent interviews for this book, Dooley expressed his disappointment at being forced to retire earlier than he wanted. Other long-term coaches and athletic directors, like Bobby Dodd at Georgia Tech, Bear Bryant at Alabama and Darrell Royal at Texas, all had a say in their retirement, he said. Dooley said Adams wanted to put his own people in every position regardless of how proficient an individual might be at his job.

In his second year as president, Adams told Dooley that unnamed "key people" were not happy with Dooley as athletic director. "He said, 'You've done a good job here, Vince, but you never want to stay too long. And, you need to have something named after you,'" Dooley recalled in his autobiography. "My first thought was, now that's a crafty way to make a change. Is he thinking that I would want to resign in order not to stay too long and to have something named after me? Is he hoping that I will comply and gracefully retire on my own?" Soon, Dooley said he started hearing rumors, especially from his wife, Barbara, that Adams wanted to replace him. Dooley said he dismissed the rumors. He should not have.

As the rumors grew more persistent, Dooley wrote Adams a letter on December 15, 2000, asking for a four-year extension of his contract. Three days later the two men had a follow-up discussion on a flight to Tallahassee, Florida, to interview Mark Richt for the head football coach's job. Dooley said he offered a compromise of three more years as athletic director and two as a fundraising consultant after his retirement. It was an offer that Dooley didn't really want, but he proposed it in the spirit of compromise to avoid a controversy. And while in Tallahassee, Dooley said, Richt asked him, in Adams's presence, how long he expected to remain as athletic director. Dooley told him that he expected to remain for at least three years to help him get the program off to a good start. Adams said nothing at the time or on the return flight from Florida, Dooley said. However, on January 29, 2001, Adams responded with a "Dear Vince" letter expressing gratitude for Dooley's hard work in the search that resulted in hiring Richt. "I am pleased that you and I were 'in sync' with each other during the screening and interview process," Adams wrote. "Despite some media analysis to the contrary, I believe you and I were close to being 'in sync' with the decision made by the Athletic Board executive committee consensus to make a change in the leadership for the football program. In some ways, what we were probably talking about was timing and not the end result. This has been a trying time for all involved, and I look forward to beginning this new year with optimism and excitement for what lies ahead."

Adams's letter then got into the meat of the matter. "After much thought on the points you have raised in your letter regarding your future work here and on what direction I want to take on campus in the coming years, I have decided to offer you a contract of four years service, but I very much want to structure it so that you serve two years as Director of Athletics and two years as a Special Assistant to the President for Athletic Development," Adams wrote. Adams said he had discussed the arrangement with some "key people" including some members of the Athletic Board. While there was a multiplicity of opinion, Adams said, "I believe it is fair to say that most of the key people with whom I consulted believe this is a fair arrangement for the University of Georgia and provides the proper and well-deserved recognition of the important role you have played here and will continue to play."

Adams proposed that Dooley's contract become effective July 1, 2001. He would serve as director of athletics until June 30, 2003, and then transition to the job of special assistant to the President for two additional years. Dooley's compensation and benefits would remain the same.

"On a personal note, your usefulness and effectiveness in this contract extension will be enhanced if you feel like you are being treated fairly, and it is important to me that you indeed feel this way," Adams wrote. "It is my sincere hope that this arrangement will give you the opportunity to conclude your service to the University on a well-deserved high note. I think the arrangement described here is consistent with the one that Georgia Tech reached with Homer Rice and is significantly more rewarding financially than that agreement." Adams concluded by suggesting the two men get together to hash out any unresolved issues.

Dooley said Adams was flat wrong about the offer being more lucrative than Rice's contract. He was concerned with the two-year offer as athletic director. He wrote to Adams on February 1, 2001, stating his rationale for wanting three years, especially citing his commitment to Coach Richt, which was made in Adams's presence and with no rebuttal by the president at the time or afterwards. According to Dooley, they met February 6, 2001, and Adams offered to extend Dooley's tenure as athletic director to two and a half years with one and a half years as Special Assistant. Dooley asked for three years. Adams said "no," Dooley recalled.

"When I asked him why he gave me half of a year, Dr. Adams said it was not uncommon with faculty appointments," Dooley said. "When I reminded him that this was not at all a common practice in athletics, he basically said, 'Take it or leave it.' I told him I was going to take it, but I also said, 'I'm going to take the high road publicly but I'm going to tell you that I disagree with you and your decision. I don't think you're treating me fairly,'" Dooley recalled in his autobiography. Dooley later said that it was "vindictive Adams," once again, using the half year to justify the commitment that he made to Richt that was not questioned by him. In other words, Adams was covering himself by extending Dooley's contract a half year to cover the football season only and not the second half of the academic sports year. The following day, February 7, 2001, Adams wrote confirming their previous day's agreement but couching it as a three-year deal at an annual salary of $313,425.

"Consistent with our conversation yesterday, I am pleased that we have reached an agreement for your contract renewal as Director of Athletics for three years, commencing January 1, 2001. This new contract insures [sic] service at the University through December 31, 2003," Adams wrote. But Dooley's contract didn't expire until June 30, 2001, so the contract extension was really for two and a half years, not three as the letter suggested.

Dooley accepted the contract extension publicly with appreciation, but privately he was not happy. Adams had heard from some "key people" that the half-year part of the contract extension was coming across publicly as petty and vindictive, according to Dooley. But instead of going directly to Dooley, Adams addressed the issue in a Question & Answer interview with *Atlanta Journal-Constitution* reporter Tim Tucker. Asked if he would have a problem with extending Dooley's contract by six months to complete the school year, Adams said he would not. Dooley said that Adams called him the next day to discuss the interview and told him that Tucker had asked him an interesting question about an additional six months on the contract and he told Tucker that he would not have a problem with it. Dooley said he reminded Adams how adamant he was about not granting the six months in the contract discussions. But he told Adams he would gladly accept the additional time to round out a full year, if offered, but he wasn't going to ask. In June 2001, six months were added to the contract, which would then expire in June 2004. This didn't settle the issue as far as Dooley was concerned. By that stage in his career Dooley had signed numerous contracts, each followed by an extension. He insists that he saw this one as no different. Adams, on the other hand, felt differently. Anxious to get his own man in that important position, Adams wasn't about to negotiate another deal with Dooley. In early 2003, with eighteen months left on his contract, Dooley said he began thinking more about staying past his scheduled June 30, 2004, departure. He was in good health and was being encouraged by friends to stick around past his scheduled retirement. Dooley said that he wanted to finish the fundraising campaign that was off to a great start, and finish some projects that were in the initial planning stages with the stadium and the coliseum.

Adams and his top lieutenants felt Dooley was campaigning with prominent Georgians to pressure Adams for a new contract. "Adams gave Vince an extension and Vince accepted it," said Georgia Senior Vice President Hank Huckaby, who was treasurer of the Athletic Board. "But then he began almost immediately to get people to pressure Mike to extend his contract. Vince might have been able to pull it off but he went public with it."

Dooley said Huckaby is flat wrong.

"It's true that about a year and a half into the new contract and not 'almost immediately,' as Huckaby indicated, and after the encouragement of several people, I began seeking the counsel of some longtime friends about staying on." He went to Adams who told Dooley he would "think about it." About a month went by and Dooley had not heard from Adams.

Dooley said Huckaby is mistaken or misinformed about his going public with the request for an extension. Dooley said that former *Atlanta Journal-Constitution* sports writer Mark Schlabach, an aggressive reporter, called him about a month after he had made his request to Adams that he had heard that Dooley had asked to stay on. Dooley said he knew from experience that it's nearly impossible to keep such an issue out of news. Nevertheless Dooley said he was surprised when Schlabach called, and he asked him to hold the story for fear it would interfere with ongoing negotiations. Schlabach agreed but was understandably nervous about it, Dooley said. "Two more weeks went by without my hearing from Adams, and with rumors intensifying and the competition hearing rumors Schlabach, in good conscience, needed to run the story," Dooley said. And although he explained the situation to Adams and Tom Landrum, Dooley said it was obvious they didn't believe him. Schlabach told him that Landrum had called him to confirm Dooley's story, which Schlabach did, Dooley said. Nevertheless Adams was unconvinced and felt the leak came from the athletics office, telling Dooley that it didn't come from the president's office. Dooley isn't convinced.

"I know from experience that anyone he may have consulted with could have, even innocently, said things regarding the issue," said Dooley. "That is the way rumors get started and the media picks up on it."

By then, Adams had become convinced that many unfavorable stories about him had originated in the Athletics Department, Dooley said. And these prompted him to push Damon Evans, Dooley's replacement as athletic director, to make a change in the communications director in athletics. Dooley said that Claude Felton, widely regarded as among the very best sports information directors in the country, was targeted by Adams to be one of the staff members that Evans would replace. "While Damon agreed to let go some other staff members that Adams didn't like, he was smart enough not to let the best communications director in the business go," Dooley said. "If he had, it would have haunted him the rest of his career."

The press leak had obviously irritated Adams, but Dooley felt it was incidental. Dooley asked for a meeting with Adams after he had not heard from the president for over two months. He wanted to stem the public controversy that was stirring over his request for a contract extension. Dooley suggested a compromise in order to stifle the controversy. Adams responded that "we will stick with the original contract," Dooley said, and handed him a copy of a press release scheduled to be sent out immediately announcing the search for a new athletic director to be brought in six months before Dooley's scheduled retirement. When this was released Dooley still had almost a year and a half left on his contract. Dooley claims that "it was unprecedented and vindictive. Adams was pouring salt on the wound."

WHILE THE CONTROVERSY OVER Dooley's contract was raging, the men's basketball program was undergoing an NCAA investigation. The NCAA probe centered on basketball players who allegedly were given grades by assistant coach Jim Harrick Jr., without attending class and other violations. Harrick's father, head basketball coach Jim Harrick, was forced to resign on March 23, 2003.

Adams had personally interceded to bring Harrick to Athens. The two men had become acquainted when Adams was a vice president and Harrick was head basketball coach at Pepperdine University. Harrick later moved to UCLA where he coached the Bruins to a national championship in 1995. But, he was fired the following year for cheating on his expense account and had moved on to Rhode Island, where he was also having success as head coach of the men's basketball team when UGA went after him.

Harrick wasn't Dooley's choice to succeed Ron Jirsa as head basketball coach at UGA. "We didn't have him on our short list," recalled Dooley. "We didn't even have him on our long list to consider because of his past transgressions. We didn't know him; and he was beginning to get up in age." Dooley said Adams called him and started talking up Harrick. "Adams said, 'I knew him when I was at Pepperdine. He's a good coach.' I said, 'I know he's a good coach. That's beside the point.'" But Adams insisted that Harrick be added to the list of finalists and it became clear to Dooley that Adams wanted to give him top priority. And after Dooley's first choice, Delaware coach Mike Brey, cooled to the Georgia job, Dooley said he felt Harrick was the next best choice. In retrospect, Dooley said, it was apparent Brey had gotten "bad vibes" from Adams during his interview. He had been very interested in the job but decided to stay at Delaware, a program with a lesser classification and without the potential of Georgia. A few years later, Dooley said he visited Notre Dame and talked with Mike Brey who had then become Notre Dame's head basketball coach. Dooley said Brey told him, off the cuff, "I could have worked for you, but I could not have worked for that president of yours." Dooley said that he was somewhat stunned but later realized what had happened. Adams had shrewdly maneuvered the hiring of Harrick.

Dooley said that he became even more convinced of that after he received a copy of a letter that Adams had written to the father of a high school recruit on June 28, 2002, in which he took credit for hiring Harrick. "I think you know that I was instrumental in hiring Jim Harrick . . . I chair the Athletic Board, which recently approved a contract extension and a pay increase for him . . . Jim Harrick is a longtime friend and an excellent coach," Adams wrote.

At that time Harrick's team was doing well and Adams was quick to step out front and take responsibility for hiring him. That would not be the case a short while later.

Not long after his arrival in 2000, Harrick began recruiting talented but troubled athletes such as Tony Cole, a point guard who had left several colleges amid controversy. Cole was dismissed from UGA after female student accused him of sexual assault. After his dismissal from the team, Cole went on ESPN on February 27, 2003, with allegations that he received money and favors from the Harricks while at UGA and that he and two other basketball players were given "A's" in a "Coaching Principles and Strategic of Basketball" course taught by Jim Harrick, Jr., an assistant basketball coach.

Dooley and Adams made a joint decision to withdraw the basketball team from Southeastern Conference and NCAA tournaments. In a 2003 *Athens Magazine* article Dooley said, "We've had bruises, black eyes and strong winds of criticism, but we've always landed on our feet because we had a solid foundation of integrity as a base value."

The NCAA and the university both quickly began investigations. In April 2004 university officials—including Adams, Dooley, and Harrick—met with the infractions committee in Indianapolis. Harrick by this point had already been forced to resign and his relationship with Adams had soured. Dooley recalls Adams proudly opened the meeting with a ten-minute dialogue mostly about himself and his qualifications and his experience in intercollegiate athletics.

As they broke from the meeting, Adams walked past Harrick and made a light-hearted comment. Harrick was in no mood for levity. "You are the sorriest sack of shit I've ever known," he told a red-faced Adams. "If Adams had said anything back to him there's no telling what would have happened," Dooley said, but Adams wisely got out of the way in a hurry.

At the height of the Harrick controversy Adams called a meeting with senior UGA staffers Steve Wrigley, Hank Huckaby, and Tom Landrum. "I'm there with Damon Evans [assistant athletic director] and [sports information director] Claude Felton," Dooley recalled. "I guess everybody was looking to the president to set the tone of how this crisis was going to be handled. I was shocked and rather suspect others were as well, when Adams said, 'I want to cut his balls out,'" Dooley recalled.

Dooley said he thought to himself, "What in the hell am I listening to? What kind of leadership is that? Instead of him laying out an overall plan to address the crisis, his primary and only concern, at the moment, was to annihilate Harrick. I wanted Harrick to go and he needed to go, but I wanted us to find the best way of addressing the crisis for all concerned, especially the university. Adams wanted to make it as bad as he could on his old friend." The incident gave the school a black eye at a time it had been making progress in climbing the academic ladder.

After one staff meeting to consider how to handle the Harrick matter,

Dooley said Adams pulled him aside and said, "We both have a stake in this situation. Your legacy and my national reputation."

Typically, Adams's concern was more for himself than the university, Dooley said.

Perhaps the most embarrassing aspect of the NCAA investigation to university officials was the release of a final examination in a course on basketball taught by Harrick Jr. The questions included: "How many points does a three-point goal account for in a game?" "How many halves in a basketball game?" The university, which regularly makes the list of top party schools and had been trying to shake its image as a "football university," briefly became a punching bag for late-night TV hosts. "I don't know who was more embarrassed," quipped *Tonight Show* host Jay Leno, "the college president, the coach, or the six players who got it wrong." "It makes us look silly," Scott Weinberg, then chairman of the faculty's University Council, complained to the Associated Press.

The NCAA investigation, Adams's well-known role in hiring the renegade basketball coach, and the ongoing feud over Dooley's contract extension all came together. It looked as though Adams would be sucked into the vortex of a perfect storm, so widespread was the discontent both on and off campus. But to the media it looked like a sports story.

As tensions mounted, *Atlanta Journal-Constitution* sports columnist Mark Bradley weighed the situation. In a March 27, 2003, column Bradley determined that Adams, not Dooley, was on the hot seat and wondered if the president could survive.

"In his private moments," Bradley wrote, "Vince Dooley must delight in the knowledge that he, the old football coach, has outflanked university president Michael Adams, the old political operative. With the Georgia athletics department trying to ride out the tempest wrought by Tony Cole, the athletic director himself has managed to dance between raindrops. His rival, meanwhile, has gotten drenched . . ."

"Such a thing could happen again," Bradley continued. "Adams tried to run Dooley off two years ago, haggling over months in a contract extension, but this athletic director may remain long after the president is gone. Adams has come off looking scared and silly . . . Dooley, on the other hand, has seemed serious and statesmanlike."

Bradley misread the situation.

Unlike former President Davison, forced out in the Jan Kemp controversy, Adams lined up powerful backers including Governor Sonny Perdue, Chancellor Tom Meredith, and a majority on the Board of Regents, including Don Leebern (who would be reappointed by Perdue to a third term after Leebern made a $200,000 contribution to the Georgia Republican Party).

When Adams subsequently denied Dooley's request for a contract decision in June 2003, it stirred a firestorm. Many Georgia alumni and boosters were critical of Adams's treatment of Dooley, but many influential insiders saw the Dooley contretemps as simply another opportunity to express their profound displeasure with Adams's leadership and spending habits.

Seeing that the Harrick controversy was hurting the university, Dooley issued a statement asking the people of Georgia not to associate his name with issues that they may have with Adams's leadership. Adams seized the olive branch saying he would seek Dooley's advice, which Dooley said he did.

"He asked me what would make me happy," Dooley said. "I gave him my advice, not for me, but what I thought was best for the university. If you will give me just one more year then I think that most Georgia people will be very pleased with that and that you have extended an olive branch. And all it is, is just one more year, and I would be very happy with that and I think that many Georgia people would be. And it would help toward the healing."

Adams said he would think about it but later turned down Dooley's offer, apparently confident he had the power base to refuse the compromise. In his memoir, Dooley speculates that Adams used the time to line up support from "key people" not to grant a contract extension. Dooley said Adams frequently referred to unnamed "key people" during their contract discussions. As events have subsequently shown, Adams's "key people" certainly included Governor Sonny Perdue and Dooley's old friend, Regent Don Leebern.

Truth be told, Adams already had Perdue in his pocket by the time Dooley proposed his compromise. Dooley's contract extension wasn't denied by Adams until June 2003, but Perdue had already declared his support for Adams on March 12, 2003, two days after the president suspended Harrick.

Many of Dooley's close supporters, including his wife Barbara, believe that Adams conspired with Perdue and Leebern to end Dooley's career. Barbara Dooley didn't approve of Leebern's abandonment of his wife and she let Leebern and Yoculan know it. She is convinced that this and Vince Dooley's refusal to name Yoculan as deputy athletic director did in her husband.

Vince Dooley doesn't share his wife's view of the split with Leebern. After his contract was not renewed, he wrote a somewhat cryptic letter to the editor which he sent to several newspapers saying so, and forwarded a copy to Leebern with a "heads up" note:

> There have been a number of articles, editorials, and letters in recent in recent weeks regarding our gymnastics program and some have mentioned my relationship with Don Leebern.
>
> It is true that Don Leebern and I have been longtime friends since I arrived at Georgia over 40 years ago. It is natural that during a friendship over a long period of time, people will not always agree on various issues and thus we have not been as close as we once were.
>
> However, the assumption that the current situation was caused by Leebern's support of President Adams in his decision not to honor my contract extension request is absolutely false from my perspective. In fact, if I had been a Regent at the time, I would have supported President Adams's decision (despite privately not agreeing with that decision). The president has a right to make those personnel decisions and therefore I would expect all the Regents to support that decision—which they did—including several friends of mine.

Dooley consistently laid blame for his departure squarely on Adams, who had gained the power broker support that he needed. "He obviously wanted to make a change early on and waited for the right opportunity to make the move," Dooley said.

Regardless, it was the president's prerogative to make that decision, Dooley said. When the chance came, Dooley said he felt that Adams was not forthright. "He was constantly posturing, drawing from his political background. Had he been straightforward with me, more than likely, this situation would not have caused such an unfortunate controversy for the university."

The issue was not whether Adams had the authority to remove an athletic director; that was a university president's call. But as we have seen, the events leading up to Adams's decision had already left a bitter taste in the mouths of Dooley and his close supporters, and the infighting was about to get much worse.

An opinion poll commissioned by the Atlanta-based *Insider Advantage* internet newsletter in May 2003 found that 64 percent of Georgians held a favorable opinion of Dooley while only 18 percent felt the same way about Adams. Nevertheless, on June 10, 2003, four days after Adams shut the door on Dooley's career at UGA, the Regents met to formally respond to the developing schism. At the beginning of the Regents meeting, chairman Joe Frank Harris, a former Georgia governor, read a statement.

Please allow me to take a moment of personal privilege as your Chair to comment on a current issue that has generated a great deal of attention. I'm speaking of the publicity surrounding the University of Georgia and its athletic program.

First, let me recognize the extraordinary contribution of Vince Dooley to the University of Georgia in a career spanning four decades. He has established a legacy envied by athletic programs across the country. We deeply appreciate all Mr. Dooley has done and will continue to do for UGA and the state of Georgia.

In February 2001, President Michael Adams and Mr. Dooley both agreed on the term of service of Mr. Dooley as UGA's athletic director. The president has decided to honor the agreement and the Board of Regents unanimously supports the president's commitment. Let me just add another personal comment. Chancellor, members of the Board, I want to take this moment and personally salute President Adams for his leadership at UGA. We point with great pride to the progressive and positive positions President Adams has taken to move UGA to new academic heights. We are proud of Michael Adams and of the record he has established. He has our unanimous support. The statement stands on its own. President Adams is here today. We just want you to know we appreciate the leadership you are providing and you have this Board's unanimous support.

It has never been explained how the Regents arrived at such a sweeping conclusion having not met officially in public or private prior to Harris reading the statement. It should be noted, however, that no Regent stepped forward to challenge Harris's assertion of "unanimous support" even though it set the Board of Regents on a path of supporting Adams almost unconditionally. The chancellor and Board of Regents had been backed into a corner and felt they had little choice but to support their president.

While Adams apparently had Meredith's tacit support for his decision not to extend Dooley's contract, the timing apparently caught even the chancellor by surprise.

Former long-time Regents spokesperson Arlethia Perry-Johnson recalled that Chancellor Meredith was upset when she told him by telephone of Adams's action.

"I was going to a conference in north Georgia when I got a call from (UGA spokesman) Tom Jackson that the release was going out that afternoon. When I called Meredith he was not reacting very positively. I got the impression that some discussion taken place that I was not privy to when Tom Jackson told me the news release was going out. When I called Meredith he wasn't pleased with that and indicated that he had not given his support for that action. I think he was surprised. This was not a strategy he would have pursued," said Perry-Johnson.

She said it wasn't that Meredith disagreed with Adams's not extending Dooley's contract. Rather, it was Adams's announcement that he'd formed a search committee for Dooley's replacement that seemed to upset Meredith. "The action [to replace Dooley] was agreed upon. I think it was how it was done that left a bad taste. The news release focused a lot on the search committee. That was a concern to Meredith."

7

THE UGA FOUNDATION

Tension was mounting in early 2003 between President Adams and both the faculty and the UGA Foundation even before Georgians reacted to news of Dooley's forced retirement with the same enthusiasm they gave General Sherman's army as it approached Atlanta. But Dooley's dismissal on the eve of the university's embarking on a $500 million capital campaign sent many Foundation trustees over the edge.

As one big contributor after another called to cancel their pledges, more than five hundred people asked that their names be removed from the university's fundraising list. Two-time Heisman Trophy winner Herschel Walker quit the fundraising campaign, and then hundreds of people sent the school checks for 34 cents after Atlanta businessman John Withers launched a campaign to show solidarity with Dooley and Walker, who wore number 34 when he played for Georgia.

Web sites and even billboards called for Adams's head. Sixty thousand people signed petitions urging the Board of Regents to fire Adams and keep Dooley. Leaders of the effort delivered the petitions to the Regents' offices in a wheelbarrow.

Gary Pollock of Greenville, South Carolina, withdrew a $6 million pledge, enough to pay Dooley's $300,000 salary until the year 2023. However, Pollock, a 1982 Georgia graduate who operates a staffing business, said his decision to withdraw the pledge had nothing to do with Dooley's firing.

"In my opinion Dr. Adams has now put our University at great risk," Pollock wrote in a letter to UGA Foundation officials. "Apparently, Dr. Adams either did not do his homework or he is making decisions based on his agenda instead of [what's in] the best interest of the University of Georgia.

My decision is not one of a simple protest as 'an ignorant football fan' versus the Board of Regents or the academic 'elite,' including Dr. Adams, toward his latest decision not to extend Mr. Dooley's contract. It is a decision based on my complete loss of confidence in Dr. Adams's perceived overall management ability, integrity, and behavior as president of the University of Georgia."

Some influential UGA Foundation members were already unhappy with Adams. They confided that over the five years of Adams's tenure to that point, they had often found the president arrogant, quick-tempered, and intolerant of their ideas. They also saw him as a reckless spender of the Foundation's money. A few had been conducting ad hoc meetings to discuss their ongoing problems with the president.

Dooley, they said, was never a topic of those discussions. "Our concerns were centered on Adams and his moral deficiencies and management style. There were a significant number of us who simply had grave concerns about this guy's integrity," says Billy Espy, a Foundation member who attended the meetings. "We didn't know the depth of the animosities until the [Dooley] fuse was lit."

Shortly after Adams's decision not to extend Dooley's contract, Shell and Wyck Knox met with Adams and UGA Foundation chairman Jack Rooker. Adams made a pitch for contributions to the recently announced capital campaign. The Knoxes are longtime friends of Vince and Barbara Dooley, and Shell Knox brought up the issue of Dooley's contract.

"I said, 'Mike, why do you want to alienate a whole group of people over someone so highly respected?' He looked me straight in the eye and said, 'I appreciate your point of view and I disagree with it. I do what I want and it's time for a change.'"

UNIVERSITY FOUNDATIONS ARE POPULAR with higher education administrators because they not only raise vast amounts of money but they also invest and manage the money in ways that directly benefit their affiliated institutions. Investment profits from cash given to the University of Georgia would accrue to the state general fund. But investment profits from gifts to the University of Georgia Foundation stay with the Foundation. More than 90 percent of Foundation gifts are earmarked for specific scholarships, professorships or programs. Also, foundations have more leeway on how they can spend money. They can entertain, buy alcoholic beverages, and even pay bonuses to state employees that the university itself could not. Foundations operate as private corporations and are viewed by the Internal Revenue Service as public charities. Thus, contributions to the Foundation are tax deductible. They receive gifts and pledges, manage investments of assets and distribute endowment gifts for scholarships and other purposes, all to support the university.

Foundations also have a responsibility to the donors to ensure that their gifts are properly used. This aspect of the UGA Foundation's responsibility was not fully understood or appreciated by UGA officials and the Board of Regents, according to the late Atlanta attorney Griffin Bell, former U.S. attorney general and counsel to the Foundation, who was interviewed several times for this book prior to his death in January 2009. And that, not Vince Dooley, said Bell, was at the heart of the dispute between President Adams and the Foundation.

"These people furnishing money were worried about how it was being used," said Bell. "It seemed to me they had some right to question the use of the money. Otherwise they wouldn't be carrying out their duties as trustees. This became a big thing. I think if you go back to the root of the problem, you'll see that neither the Regents nor the university officials fully appreciated the role of the Foundation trustees. These people had certain duties. They have a fiduciary capacity. I don't think anyone ever recognized that."

IN HIS EXHAUSTIVE 1948 history of the University of Georgia, Thomas Walter Reed recognized the importance of the UGA Foundation.

> Nothing it has accomplished in its more than a century of existence has been of greater importance than the organization by the Alumni Society of the University of Georgia Foundation. There is an element of permanency about it. Its work goes on every day and hour and week and month. It has no intention of ever stopping that work.

When Reed wrote those words more than sixty years ago, the UGA Foundation had amassed a whopping endowment of $250,000. The Foundation made its first grant in 1945—a $600 salary supplement for legendary history professor E. Merton Coulter, who taught at UGA from 1919 to 1958.

Today, there is a much greater expectation that foundations go out and raise money, says a different Reed, University of California Chancellor Charles Reed. "That gives people the discretion to go out and hire the named professor, the superstar professor. They used to say the difference between a good and a great university is fundraising."

Because of the additional demands on state funding for such things as K-12, health care and the criminal justice system, legislatures have told universities they must help themselves.

"It's a three-legged stool," Reed says. "The first leg is state support. That's adequate but never what it once was and adequate will not build great universities. The second leg is that the people who benefit have to pay. That's tuition and fees. It used to be students paid 10 to 12 percent. Today they pay 25 to 40 percent. And the third leg of the stool is private fundraising expectations."

Reed points out that before the 1970s, public universities didn't raise much private money. Fundraising was thought of as something private institutions did. Nowadays, public university administrators are constantly on a nationwide scavenger hunt for private contributions. Presidents and deans are expected to spend a great deal of time mining private money to support their schools. Wherever alumni are, there is likely to lurk a university fundraiser.

"The great public universities all have major fundraising programs. Michigan and Ohio State have offices in Naples, Florida, that they man year-around," Reed said.

MICHAEL ADAMS'S PERCEIVED ABILITY to generate private contributions was the aspect of his resume most often cited by his supporters as an argument for choosing him over seemingly more academically qualified candidates for the UGA presidency. As vice president for university affairs at Pepperdine University, he had led a $100 million fundraising effort that reached its goal eighteen months ahead of schedule. And Centre College's endowment had more than doubled during Adams's tenure as its president.

Even Foundation members who were cool toward or actively opposed to

Adams's hiring in 1997 nevertheless believed that he would be a good fund-raiser for Georgia. What they didn't anticipate was how proprietary Adams would feel toward Foundation funds.

When Adams arrived, the Foundation had few rules about the president's spending of privately raised money in accounts over which he had direct control. These "president's discretionary funds" were used to pay for such things as country club memberships, entertainment, and transportation. If a UGA president asked for money it was assumed to be in the best interest of the university and was generally not questioned by the Foundation. Adams's predecessor, Charles Knapp, had been a frugal caretaker and the Foundation has seen no reason to require strict rules governing the president's spending.

Adams, however, brought a different attitude. He quickly spotted the money centers that were under his control and began using them for airfare that appeared personal, dinners at expensive restaurants for himself and his staff—even a graduation party for his son's law school class. This outraged some members of the Foundation and prompted them to tighten rules on how money was spent. Adams and the Foundation board had been cranky with each other on this and other issues almost since his arrival on campus. The Foundation board never turned down a request for payment of Adams's expenses. But their oversight was a source of constant irritation to the president. This tension was exacerbated after Gerald McCarley, a CPA, retired from his firm in 1999 and volunteered to set up an internal auditing process for the Foundation. As described earlier in Chapter 5, the new audit process soon began to flag questionable Adams expenditures and led to the revoking of his Foundation-issued credit card.

Adams himself acknowledged in a 2003 letter to Chancellor Meredith that concerns by some key Foundation members about his spending habits predated the Dooley decision:

> For example, two years ago at a Fall Foundation meeting, I was presented with new operating guidelines for expenses by a trustee substituting for Finance Chair Wyck Knox who was absent from the meeting. I had been given no opportunity for comment or discussion before the meeting and did express some concern to him about that at that time. But realizing the

level of concern that he had raised and that the trustees had raised, I readily accepted the provisions of the new guidelines and took additional personal measures of my own.

Nothing could be further from the truth said Mike Marshall, the unnamed trustee Adams was referring to in his letter.

"I went to [Adams] and said, 'Let's walk up to the finance committee meeting together.' We were across the campus in another building. I said, 'Are you aware of the guidelines we've set forth for the handling your expenses?' I think he said he hadn't seen them, but he gave every indication that he had. He bowed up like he tends to do when he's angry. I said, 'Let me go over them with you, because I don't want you to be blind-sided.' They're mild, but we feel that we need some guidelines in place, and these were recommended by our internal auditor [Gerald McCarley]."

Adams's immediate reaction was, "We need to get rid of that goddamn Gerald McCarley."

Foundation members, especially some of those most directly involved with its finances, had thus been struggling for several years over what to do about Adams. The decision to ungracefully show the door to the legendary Vince Dooley was no more popular with Foundation members than with the public, and it was having an immediate and drastic negative impact on fundraising. In any case, the failure to extend Dooley's contract was the last straw for the Foundation trustees.

Some wanted an up or down "no-confidence" vote on the president. Others thought that was premature and would add validity to the widespread portrayal in the media that the burgeoning controversy was simply an academics-versus-athletics dispute. Foundation members were particularly rankled by that characterization for two reasons, first because they had been working hard for two decades to raise Georgia's academic reputation, and secondly because Adams had involved himself in athletics affairs to a greater extent than his predecessors, asserting his influence on everything from the selection of coaches to the budgets for various Bulldog sports teams.

In fact, even as he publicly professed concern for academics over athletics, Adams's uncommon interest in the university's athletics programs had raised anxieties among Vince Dooley's supporters, some of whom were Foundation members.

Adams also had significant critics within the faculty, and the faculty grievances had nothing to do with Dooley.

There is a common and widespread public misconception, apparently also held by Adams, that having successful athletic teams increases a university's fundraising capacity. However, this isn't necessarily the case. An intensive study by the Andrew W. Mellon Foundation of the relationship between college sports and other aspects of university activities debunked this commonly held assumption. The study found, for example, that having a winning football team doesn't have a positive impact on giving rates in the Division 1A private universities or Ivy League institutions.

Moreover, most large universities heavily subsidize their athletics programs. Money-making sports such as men's football and basketball subsidize but don't completely offset the costs of other sports. Only six of the 119 NCAA Division 1 athletics programs had remained in the black over the last decade, according to NCAA president Myles Brand.

NEVERTHELESS, AS CRITICISM OF Adams mounted, the beleaguered president appeared on ESPN-TV's "Outside the Lines" program on June 30, 2003, and suggested that nothing short of control of the university was at stake.

"This has now become about what element is going to control the University of Georgia, the academic side of the house or the athletic side of the house," he told an ESPN reporter.

Responding to Adams's comment, Dooley told the *Red and Black* campus newspaper, "Nothing is farther from the truth. Academics will always be the forefront in and the top priority of any college or any university."

Nonetheless, Adams, whose doctorate in political communications makes him an expert in spin, had unearthed the perfect response to his critics. His characterization of the dispute—hearkening back twenty years to the Kemp affair—would become the master narrative for journalists covering the Adams-Dooley-Foundation controversy as it unfolded publicly over the next two years. Foundation trustee Wyckliffe Knox remembers almost as a moment of destiny the exact time he learned of Adams's comments to ESPN.

"On July 1, I picked up the *Atlanta Journal-Constitution* and in it Adams is quoted as saying this is all about academics versus athletics," Knox recalled. "I was dumbfounded. Adams had seized on the opportunity to change the subject to athletics."

Knox would have been more than dumbfounded if he and other Foundation members had realized the extent to which they had already been backed into a corner by Adams. The immediacy of the Regents' statement on June 10, 2003, was an indication that although Adams had alienated Foundation members over what they saw as his cavalier handling of their money, he had been steadily solidifying his political support elsewhere. That support began with Regent Don Leebern and extended through Leebern to the governor's office. Though Leebern and Adams seemed an unlikely pairing, Leebern had taken an early liking to him. Whatever it was Leebern saw in Adams, he pushed him for the presidency and was his chief defender each time Adams stubbed his toe. Leebern even spent generously from his own wealth on Adams's behalf, underwriting a $51,000 a year stipend (funneled through the Foundation) to Mary Adams for, essentially, serving as first lady of the university. In return, Adams presumably turned a blind eye to conflicts occasioned by Leebern's personal relationship with an employee of the UGA gymnastics coaching staff.

Griffin Bell observed, however, that Adams's initial support from the Regents might have been more complicated than it seemed. "The Regents I talked to felt like if anything happened to Adams it would make it look like the football crowd got rid of him," Bell said. "And they were more worried and they wanted to get Dooley off the campus. And they thought if they got that over with they could deal with Adams later. That was the best protection Adams had was the Dooley problem. He had other problems too. The faculty was against him."

Adams cleverly used the academics versus athletics argument to win support for himself, Bell said. "Then, the newspapers bought into it. Everybody bought into it. Who is in favor of the athletics program running things?"

BY MID-2003, FOUNDATION TRUSTEES had been squabbling with Adams for years over his spending of university money for items they considered personal in nature. More damning, some of the Foundation members who had the closest dealings with Adams said they no longer trusted or believed him. Dooley's dismissal just when the Foundation was kicking off a $500 million fundraising drive was the final insult that triggered a revolt among the Foundation trustees.

Boxed in by Adams's political maneuvering, the Foundation leaders ultimately hit upon the idea of a forensic audit in an effort to expose what many considered unethical or perhaps even illegal use of Foundation funds by the president.

They could not have foreseen what a self-inflicted blow they were about to strike.

8

THE DELOITTE & TOUCHE AUDIT

F orensic audits are by their nature often controversial. More an investigation than an audit, they're usually ordered up when there is suspicion of misconduct or abuse of office. Seeking to expose certain of Michael Adams's actions and activities as improper, with risk of financial repercussions, Foundation leaders compiled a list of grievances that they felt were worthy of closer examination. They reasoned that if the public knew what Foundation members knew, there would be outrage and the Board of Regents would be forced to take action. But realizing they could not control the independent-minded Regents, the Foundation trustees decided on an indirect approach. They asked their long-time legal counsel, the King & Spalding law firm, to engage an outside auditor, hoping that the arms-length nature of an independent investigation would prove or disprove the serious concerns of a growing number of the Foundation's trustees.

In July 2003, a month after the Dooley decision, King & Spalding hired the fraud and forensic investigations unit of Deloitte & Touche to investigate. The big national auditing firm was charged with looking into seven specific issues, all of which had been publicly aired although not in great detail. The issues to be explored were:

- Adams's expenses paid by the Foundation;
- Adams's compensation as supplemented by the Foundation;
- Mary Adams's stipend, as passed through the Foundation;
- Adams's $250,000 side agreement to former football coach Jim Donnan;
- the unauthorized purchase of an Ecolodge in Costa Rica;
- an Alumni Center construction project;

- other findings that might emerge.

The review was headed by J. Donald Fancher, then Deloitte & Touche's regional managing partner of forensic services.

The report, completed in October 2003, concluded that Adams had mishandled Foundation money. It also found fault with the lax oversight of spending by the Foundation trustees, a point that would be driven home again and again by Adams's supporters.

Taken as a whole, the Deloitte & Touche investigation casts Adams as a self-dealer who took advantage of his position and of weak oversight by Foundation trustees. It was a portrait so unflattering that even Adams himself claimed he "hardly knew the Dr. Adams the report seems to describe."

The report accused him of using Foundation assets to benefit himself, his friends, and his family members. It also called into question Adams's honesty in dealing with the Foundation, suggesting he lied about a job offer at Ohio State University in order to get a salary increase from the Foundation.

It was a bold indictment that might, in a different political climate, have forced out a university president immediately. "Faced with an audit that damning, from an accounting firm as respected as Deloitte & Touche, no CEO in America could have survived twenty-four hours," observed one Atlanta business executive who read the audit. But as matters had developed throughout the summer of 2003, it didn't really matter what the audit report found: the Regents, chancellor, and governor were already committed to their president's survival.

Nonetheless, following are summaries of the key findings of the Fancher audit in the seven exploratory categories listed above.

Expenses of President Adams

In 1999 under the direction of Gerald McCarley, a team of internal auditors reviewed cash disbursements quarterly and issued reports to the Foundation board, which also meets quarterly. McCarley's group questioned Adams's use of a Foundation credit card to pay for personal expenses, dinners, and golf outings that were unrelated to his job. Though Adams has never earned less than $280,000 a year at Georgia, he used the Foundation credit card for personal travel and would eventually file an expense report and sometimes reimburse the Foundation. This method sometimes resulted in the Foundation paying additional interest because of delays in filing expense reports.

In April 2001, the internal auditors questioned a $13,490 charge from January 2001 to charter an airplane to take Adams and two university executives and their wives to George W. Bush's inauguration in Washington. The trip was unprecedented and because of Adams's Republican Party ties, it had the aroma of a political junket. Moreover, Adams was listed as a passenger on the flight when officials would later learn that he was not on either leg of the flight; Adams himself took a commercial flight to Washington on January 19, and returned January 23 on a different charter, at an additional cost of $2,422.50.

The internal auditors' recommendation was to "remind executives of the University that they are spending donor contributions and the travel policy of the Foundation."

Foundation CFO Cindy Coyle first noticed the expense, forwarding a copy of the reimbursement request to UGA Vice President for External Affairs Kathryn Costello, who was also executive director of the Foundation and reported directly to Adams. The request was ultimately approved for payment but resulted in policy changes that increased restrictions and provided for regular review of expenditures of funds that support the president's office.

Adams maintained the inauguration trip provided him and other senior university officials with a good opportunity to visit the Georgia congressional delegation. University officials claim that contacts made in Washington on the trip "helped secure $10 million for funding of a new campus building and $1.5 million for a new Marine Institute facility on Sapelo Island."

The D&T report also cited Adams for spending $10,000 in Foundation money for food and beverages to host a commencement luncheon for the 2002 law school class that included his son, David. The luncheon, at the president's house, was "by invitation only" and not all the faculty and students were invited.

The Foundation could find no other instance where Adams hosted a luncheon for a particular UGA college or school. The facts that the event was "invitation only" and that his son was a member of the class raised additional questions as to whether this was a personal expenditure. The timing and circumstances for having this event "do not appear justified," auditors concluded. When confronted, Adams wrote a check to the Foundation for $10,000.

Another questionable charge cited in the report was $2,255 to charter an airplane for a trip to Winter Haven, Florida, to deliver the eulogy at the funeral of Robert McLeod, president of Centre College from 1938–45. McLeod had long retired before Adams arrived at Centre College in 1988. But Adams had said he wanted to connect with presidents who preceded him, according to James H. Evans, former chair of Centre's board of trustees. Adams had thus invited McLeod back to Centre and developed a relationship with him, Evans said. But auditors questioned how this trip benefited UGA, said the expense appeared personal to Adams, and said that Foundation funds shouldn't have been used for the trip.

The auditors concluded that Adams, his staff, and even some members of the Foundation Board seemed to mistakenly believe that the president's discretionary funds were Adams's to do with as he pleased. That is not the case, auditors said. The only difference between the president's discretionary funds and any other funds is that Adams was given authority to determine how the money was to be spent to further the Foundation's purposes, not to benefit individuals, auditors concluded.

The audit report also found that Adams "knowingly provided inaccurate and or incomplete documentation to the Foundation" when he handed out free tickets to football games to personal friends and listed the friends as major gift prospects.

Adams Compensation

Auditors also found that Adams had misled Foundation trustees to win himself a substantial pay increase in 2002. In 1998, his first full year at Georgia, Adams earned $281,498, about a third of which was paid by the Foundation. However, shortly after coming to UGA, Adams began expressing to a number of people his view that he was underpaid. In 2001, the Foundation provided $200,000 in deferred compensation that he would receive if he stayed at Georgia until October 2007.

In 2002 Adams let it be known that he had received an offer to become president of Ohio State University, his alma mater. He said OSU would pay him $850,000 to $1 million a year. Adams told auditors he seriously considered the job but ultimately decided to stay at Georgia, partly for personal reasons and partly because of a promise by Foundation chairman John W. Rooker that the Foundation would supplement his state-paid salary to a level of approximately $600,000 a year.

Rooker made good on the promise. He signed a February 14, 2002, resolution giving Adams an annual salary supplement equal to 49 percent of his state-paid salary, approximately $160,000 in annual deferred compensation, a $40,000 annual longevity supplement, a leased automobile, and a $500,000 life insurance policy. The four-page document titled "Resolution of the Trustees of the University of Georgia Foundation, Inc." states that it was approved by the Foundation Executive Committee and adopted by the full Foundation Board of Trustees on February 14.

In fact, the resolution was never voted on by either the Executive Committee or the full Foundation Board. In fact, said trustee Billy Espy, "No member of the Foundation Board knew this document existed." Former Foundation Secretary Rachel Conway, who signed the resolution along with Rooker, said it was prepared by Senior Vice President Tom Landrum, at that time the chief of staff to President Adams. Conway said she never questioned its authenticity. Auditors suggested there was a deliberate act to conceal Adams's pay increase from the faculty and staff. "Apparently there is some concern as to how the faculty and staff of UGA would react to Dr. Adams receiving significantly greater raises, bonuses, etc., than the faculty and staff," the report says.

There is evidence, however, that the Foundation Executive Committee was aware of the plan to increase Adams pay since the Committee had named an ad hoc compensation subcommittee to make recommendations.

Auditors also suggested that Adams turned a deliberate blind eye to a mistake in the formula for computing his deferred compensation package that would have caused him to be overpaid. The deferred compensation plan is based on two incentive formulas that would reward Adams for growth in gifts to UGA and the Foundation's endowment. One component of that formula is a minimum threshold to be raised before the formula kicks in. In computing that threshold the ad hoc committee made a $7.4 million error, the effect of which was to lower the gift threshold by that amount.

"Why," auditors ask, "did someone not notify the ad hoc compensation committee of their error? Given the magnitude of this incentive amount and the personal nature of this to Dr. Adams it appears improbable that this calculation would not have received a fair amount of scrutiny by Dr. Adams."

That wasn't the only time Adams overlooked a payroll mistake in his favor. In January 2003 Adams received a $12,000 increase in his state salary without authorization from the chancellor and Board of Regents.

The unauthorized increase came about as the result of a 1998 Board of Regents action that temporarily allowed the university to provide a tax-deferred annuity for the president until the Regents established a permanent executive retirement plan. In October 2002 the Regents created a new retirement plan and the university began making payments to the new plan. At that point Adams should have stopped receiving the $12,000 in salary that paid for the annuity.

State Auditors blamed the mistake on inadequate communications among the president, senior vice president for Finance and Administration, and the Human Resources Department. The president's office didn't inform HR and Budget personnel that the president should no longer receive that salary increase to fund his tax deferred annuity, they said.

When confronted, Adams reimbursed the state by a payroll deduction in December 2004, as he had done previously with the Foundation.

Adams worked tirelessly to get the Foundation to supplement his salary, according to several Foundation and former UGA staffers. The Deloitte & Touche report suggests he wasn't always up front in these efforts. Adams claimed that Ohio State offered him $850,000 to $1 million a year and that he helped steer the job to UGA Provost Karen Holbrook after he turned it down. Both assertions were "flatly refuted" by James Patterson, chair of the Ohio State search committee.

Patterson confirmed that Adams was a finalist but that Ohio State didn't make an offer approaching $850,000. In fact, Patterson said compensation even reaching $600,000 was "out of the question." Patterson also denied

that Adams had anything to do with Holbrook getting the position, telling
auditors she was interviewed before Adams. (Independently of the Deloitte
& Touche audit, the *Columbus Dispatch* reported in October 2003, citing an
unnamed source, that the OSU presidential search committee had recommended two candidates to trustees. One was UGA Provost Karen Holbrook,
who was hired as OSU president. The other recommended candidate was
not Adams, the source said.)

Adams wrote two letters turning down the alleged OSU offer. One dated
July 1, 2002, was addressed to Dr. Jan Greenwood at A. T. Kearney, Inc.,
of Alexandria, Virginia, the company that assisted Ohio State officials in
the search for a new president. Adams expressed his gratitude to the OSU
presidential search committee but took himself out of the running saying,
"I am convinced that now is not the right time and this is not the right opportunity for me." That letter didn't state explicitly that Adams had been offered the job. However, on July 18, Adams wrote to James F. Patterson, who
headed the search committee, specifically turning down the job offer. "As I
mentioned to you by phone today, I must respectfully decline your offer to
become President of The Ohio State University," Adams wrote.

Skeptical auditors and Foundation members wondered whether Adams
was turning down a job that was never offered by OSU in order to boost his
value and salary at UGA. Adams has claimed to have documentation of the
OSU offer, but six years later, the proof has not been produced.

The $250,000 Donnan Side Deal

Supporters and detractors alike describe Adams as an impatient man
who, once he makes a decision, finds delay almost unbearable. Few incidents
demonstrate that impatience more than Adams's deal to extend former head
football coach Jim Donnan's contract.

As previously described, Donnan had been recruited and recommended
by Dooley and hired by Charles Knapp. He did well at Georgia and received
other offers, including a $1 million a year deal at the University of North
Carolina.

Donnan then began negotiating a new contract with UGA and in December 1997 Adams and Dooley agreed to a multi-year deal with a $650,000

annual salary. At the time it was agreed that the Athletic Association would guarantee some aspects of the contract but not the exact number of years. Negotiations dragged. By July 1998 some players, coaches, and alumni were questioning the delay. Jim Nalley, a wealthy Atlanta automobile dealer, Foundation trustee, and friend of Donnan, went to Adams about the matter. Adams told Nalley to "get the deal done" and if Donnan was fired they would deal with compensation later.

Incredibly, Adams specified that the deal was to be verbal and kept secret from Dooley and Athletic Association lawyer Floyd Newton of King & Spalding. Dooley and Newton, who were completely unaware of the side agreement, were shocked when Donnan and his agent suddenly seemed to relinquish their demands for a longer term.

Two years later, in December 2000, after an 8-4 season with losses to arch-rivals Florida and Georgia Tech, Adams went over Dooley's head to fire Donnan, who had compiled a 40-19 overall record at Georgia.

Weeks later Donnan's agent wrote Adams a letter reminding him of the agreement and asking his assistance in getting payment. Adams and Nalley had discussed the possibility of Nalley paying for off-the-books supplement or "passing the hat" among boosters to raise the money but soon learned that it would be a NCAA violation to do so. The Athletic Association Board of Directors then voted to pay Donnan $255,250 in April 2001.

At the time Adams told reporters that he felt agreeing to the additional six months payment was necessary to complete the deal. He acknowledged that he had no authority to commit Athletic Association money without board approval.

"In hindsight, I probably would have handled it differently," Adams said.

The Stipend to Mary Adams

Deloitte & Touche auditors found payments to the president's wife troubling in both the amount and the manner in which the matter was handled.

Mrs. Adams had held a position at Centre College and Adams felt his wife should be reimbursed for her efforts on behalf of the University of Georgia.

Adams suggested to then-Foundation chairman Jim Nalley that she be put on the Foundation payroll. Nalley thought that a bad idea as did other members of the Foundation Executive Committee.

In 2000, Patrick Pittard succeeded Nalley as chair of the Foundation and in casual conversation over dinner with their wives, Adams again brought up the subject. He mentioned that the UGA Veterinary School wanted to hire Mary Adams but she was prevented from taking the job because of UGA's nepotism rule. Pittard subsequently told auditors he came up with the notion of a Foundation stipend.

At about that time, the Foundation received a contribution from a donor that established a restricted fund for discretionary use by the university president. Although not named in the report, the generous donor was Regent Don Leebern. In effect, Mary Adams went on Leebern's payroll but with a twist. Because she was paid through the Foundation, Leebern could claim a tax write-off as a charitable contribution.

The Foundation Executive Committee, which has authority to make financial decisions, approved paying Mary Adams a $2,500 per month stipend, $700 a month car allowance, and reimbursable expenses of up to $800. Sometime later in 2000, at the Adamses' request, Pittard agreed that the $800 expense allowance would be placed in Mary Adams's supplemental retirement account. The net effect of this, auditors said, was to guarantee Mrs. Adams an additional $9,600 in annual income. This put Mary Adams income at $48,000 per year, according to the D&T report, all from the Foundation's "Leebern Fund."

Foundation officers told auditors they remember approving payment of $30,000 to $40,000. An article in the Atlanta newspaper on October 20, 2000, states that Mary Adams's stipend would be $30,000. The article quotes Pittard as saying that she is "an extraordinary fundraiser" and would be working as a development officer.

D&T concluded that Pittard violated Foundation procedures by agreeing to put the $800 per month into a retirement account without getting Executive Committee approval.

The auditors also concluded that the Foundation Executive Committee erred in approving a $30,000 honoraria to UGA Senior Vice President Henry

Huckaby—one of Adams's staunchest defenders—for working a six-month stint on Governor Perdue's transition team. While the FEC had good intentions in rewarding Huckaby, auditors concluded that Huckaby's work on the transition provided no benefit to UGA or the Foundation. Huckaby offered to return the honorarium but the offer was turned down.

The Alumni Center

Plans were already underway for a three-building, $8.6 million Alumni Center when Michael Adams became president in 1997. Six years later, when Deloitte & Touche auditors looked into the matter, the price tag had ballooned to $75 million. And the university had spent $1.4 million in architectural fees with nearly nothing to show for it.

What happened is a tale of intrigue, mismanagement, and finger-pointing. And auditors put the blame squarely on Adams's micromanagement of the project.

Campus architect Danny Sniff told auditors that Adams got involved to the level of deciding which trees were to be cut down and which ones left. Others told auditors of Adams requiring them to move a wall two or three times.

The project was moving forward despite some environmental problems with the site and in 1999 a selection committee chose Michael Dennis & Associates of Boston from among six firms to design the three building complex. Board of Regents regulations require a local architect to be involved and the committee chose the Atlanta firm of Jova, Daniels and Busby.

Adams didn't like the design offered by Dennis and in the summer of 1999 told Sniff to end Dennis' work on the project. At that point the firm of Jova, Daniels and Busby took over as sole architect. Their designs were not well received by the building committee and weren't shown to Adams. During 2001 Sniff brought in a Baltimore firm, Ayers/Saint/Gross. Their designs never made it past the review stage, auditors said.

By that time the UGA Real Estate Foundation, a subsidiary of the UGA Foundation, had taken over as project manager and responsibility transferred from Sniff to Jo Ann Chitty, executive director of the UGA Real Estate Foundation. A Real Estate Foundation committee conducted another search for a design architect. A selection committee that included Mary Adams chose Collin Cooper Carusi of Atlanta to do the work. Adams approved the choice.

During this time it became clear that the site chosen for the center was too small for the building now being discussed. Perhaps more importantly, auditors said environmental problems were uncovered that forced them to relocate the building to Central Campus near the football stadium. A parking garage and bookstore was added to the design.

When the design was finished, an Alumni Association committee endorsed it. Adams, however, considered it mediocre. By that time the president's opinion was being influenced by Pittsburgh architect Al Filoni, whom Adams knew from his days at Centre College. Filoni had designed a campus master plan and the two men had hit it off.

According to D&T auditors, Filoni was stopping by Sniff's office regularly making critical comments about the Collin firm's design. Finally, Adams ordered the Collin design to be sent to Filoni in Pittsburgh so he could create a design that would please Adams.

Filoni went to work, auditors said, often meeting ex parte with Adams on the design, Sniff and Chitty told auditors. This was significant, auditors said, because until Filoni arrived Adams never met with architects. Adams and others visited Filoni in Pittsburgh to view his work on the design. They liked it and made arrangements in February 2003 for Filoni to present the design to the entire Real Estate Foundation board.

At that meeting Filoni quoted a price of $50 million for the project. Chitty and then UGA Foundation Chair Jack Rooker, who is in the construction business, had done their own analysis and had a real estate specialist look at the design. Their conclusion was that it would cost $75 million. Chitty ordered Filoni to cease work. Today the Alumni Center remains an unfulfilled promise.

The D&T auditors pointed the finger at Adams as the one person who had the final say over every design. The only one he liked was that of his friend Al Filoni, they said.

Adams also violated purchasing procedures when he hired Filoni without going through proper purchasing procedures. But UGA officials told auditors that Filoni wasn't named as the design architect and was only acting as a consultant even though he clearly expected to get the job. Filoni was paid about $75,000 for the work he did for UGA (he was paid by the UGA Foundation after the university refused to pay).

"We note as have others that bringing in an old friend, no matter how talented and accomplished, raises eyebrows even to the most casual observer," auditors wrote. "At a minimum Mr. Filoni should have been required to pursue the normal bidding process. For Dr. Adams to single-handedly put Mr. Filoni to work on the design and terminate the Carusi firm simply does not appear proper. In short, it creates an appearance of impropriety on the part of Dr. Adams to have proceeded in this manner."

The Ecolodge

Adams is a strong advocate of foreign studies programs. He created major programs at Centre College and at Georgia. UGA students began using a facility in San Luis, Costa Rica, for study in the late 1990s. In 2001 faculty learned that the facility might be sold and become unavailable to students. There was immediate interest in the university purchasing the 170-acre site. Negotiations with the owner began almost immediately.

In March 2001, Kathryn Costello, UGA senior vice president for external affairs and executive director of the UGA Foundation, traveled to Costa Rica to assess the property.

Negotiations were soon underway and Costello agreed on a price of $895,000. The Foundation Executive Committee approved $40,000 as earnest money toward the purchase. On October 1, 2001, Costello informed the Foundation Executive Committee that the earnest money had been paid and that the balance of $855,000 would be due in thirty days.

Then began a sequence of events that auditors said resulted in the Foundation purchasing the property without approval of the Foundation Executive Committee. It also resulted in the firing of Costello.

On October 4, the FEC met and questioned whether the financing plan outlined by Costello had been reviewed. They decided to refer the matter to the Foundation Investment Committee.

On October 18, the investment committee referred it to the UGA Real Estate Foundation.

By the end of October UGA Real Estate Foundation President Jo Ann Chitty had reviewed the proposed Ecolodge budget and concluded that it wouldn't generate a positive cash flow without debt and "will definitely not" with debt. That message gave the FEC pause. In November 2001 an extension was negotiated to allow the Foundation to study the transaction more closely. The Foundation agreed to forfeit the $40,000 deposit.

By the end of November Adams challenged Costello and others that if they could raise $500,000 he would commit another $500,000 in Foundation funds, a promise that he had no authority to make, according to auditors. By that time the FEC was losing confidence in Costello to run the upcoming $500 million capital campaign.

On December 7, 2001, the FEC met to discuss the Ecolodge and other matters. FEC member Billy Espy and others remember reaffirming the position that the project should not go forward until it was approved by the Real Estate Foundation. The committee also went into executive session where they decided to ask Chair Patrick Pittard to inform Adams that they had lost confidence in Costello.

That message was delivered to Adams within a couple of days, auditors said. Costello said the message was delivered sometime before she approved the unauthorized Ecolodge purchase. She was to receive eighteen months of full salary and another $70,000 to continue working on fundraising for the Foundation, Costello said. Her last day was to be March 1, 2002.

On December 11, Costello e-mailed Ecolodge faculty Milton and Diana Lieberman, who were assisting in the purchase effort, telling them of Adams's commitment of $500,000 in Foundation funding. She made it clear in the e-mail that she wasn't authorizing the purchase at that time, however, saying she wanted to touch base with senior UGA officials, including Adams.

Then a week later, on December 17, 2001, Costello gave authorization to go forward with the closing, although she told auditors that she didn't realize it at the time. Following logic or reasons she has never explained, Costello had countermanded the explicit directive of the Foundation Executive Committee. Given that she was in the meeting when the directive was given, her actions beg the question of whether she was acting on her own or following orders, say still-dumbfounded Foundation members.

In any case, Costello took responsibility for the unauthorized purchase of the Ecolodge, calling it an "error in judgment." But she also said she never would have done so had she thought Adams was opposed to it. Meanwhile, she continued to work on raising money for the Ecolodge through January and February 2002. The efforts included the unauthorized borrowing of $100,000 from a personal friend at 15 percent interest rate and obligated the Foundation to repay the loan; the unauthorized loan allowed her to close the deal.

On February 21, 2002, Costello wrote Adams that his challenge had been met and that they had $500,000. Adams on February 25 said that the purchase was subject to approval by the Real Estate Foundation, apparently unaware the purchase closing had already occurred. He instructed her to resign from the Costa Rica corporations that held title to the Ecolodge assets.

Auditors concluded that Costello was at fault in making the unauthorized purchase of the Ecolodge. But they said Adams failed to properly manage her and had received information that she was having difficulties in her personal life. And they said Adams had no authority to issue a challenge that promised $500,000 in matching funds from the Foundation.

One of the most intriguing issues that auditors uncovered was a telephone conversation between UGA Senior Vice President Steve Wrigley and fundraising consultant Charles Witzleben regarding employment of Costello. Adams asked for Costello's resignation after her role in purchasing the Ecolodge in Costa Rica became public in late February 2002. Costello accepted responsibility for the unauthorized purchase but told Deloitte & Touche auditors that she never would have purchased the property had Adams explicitly told her not to do so.

On December 7, 2001, the UGA Foundation Executive Committee had expressed a lack of confidence in Costello to lead the upcoming capital campaign. Costello was an employee of UGA but as the Senior Vice President for Development she was a fundraiser for the Foundation and ultimately for UGA. The executive committee asked Pat Pittard, then chair of the Foundation, to relay their lack of confidence in Costello to Adams, which he did.

After Adams passed the bad news along to Costello he talked to Witzleben about the Foundation's lack of confidence in her. Witzleben had worked with

Adams as a fundraising consultant for Centre College. Witzleben, who was also friends with Costello, met with her after her meeting with Adams. They talked about her resigning and Witzleben urged her to talk with Adams, whom he said would probably help her out in some way.

Two months later in March 2002, after Costello had been fired, Witzleben said he received a telephone call, while in Raleigh, North Carolina, from then-UGA Vice President Steve Wrigley regarding Costello's employment. According to the Deloitte & Touche audit report, Wrigley, former executive secretary in Governor Zell Miller's office, asked if Witzleben would consider putting Costello on his payroll "with the Foundation directing Ms. Costello's payments through Mr. Witzleben's firm. This would occur by having Mr. Witzleben bill the Foundation back for the increased expense of having Ms. Costello on his payroll."

When Witzleben responded with an emphatic "No," Wrigley asked if he would think about it for a few hours. Witzleben said that if he thought about it for a few hours the answer would not just be "No, but hell no." He told Wrigley he considered his request insulting to him and his company and that he would never agree to such an arrangement.

Witzleben said that Wrigley began the conversation by stating that he had been asked to make the telephone call and seemed uncomfortable doing so. Wrigley acknowledged to auditors that he made the call to Witzleben asking if Costello could work for his firm. But Wrigley didn't recall Adams asking him to make the call or billing UGA Foundation an additional fee to pay her salary. Wrigley was then a vice president at UGA and Adams was his direct supervisor. So if Adams didn't ask him to make the telephone call, who did? That question remains unanswered.

Adams had a different recollection. He was adamant that Witzleben actually called him and said Costello had called and asked if she could work for Witzleben's firm. Adams said Witzleben told him that in light of recent events that it would not be possible for him to employ her. Additionally, Adams told auditors that he never asked anyone to call Witzleben on Costello's behalf.

When asked about the alleged conversation with Adams, Witzleben insisted that he had never telephoned Adams about hiring Costello. Costello also insisted that she never called Witzleben and asked for a job, auditors said.

The divergence of memory was so acute that someone had to be lying and the Deloitte & Touche auditors pointed a finger at Adams. Witzleben's version of events was much more credible, they said, citing a number of reasons.

First, auditors said Witzleben was a disinterested party and didn't come forward to volunteer the information to auditors and in fact didn't even want to talk to them, expressing a strong desire to be left out of the report. He considered Adams a friend and had worked with him as a consultant in Kentucky.

And at the time the conversation with Wrigley took place Witzleben was being paid for his consulting work with UGA. He stood to lose those fees as well as future business.

"His comments, which do not reflect favorably on the Adams administration, could be viewed very negatively by some of these trustees and thus impact Mr. Witzleben's business elsewhere in Georgia. Finally, D&T found Mr. Witzleben's recollection of this conversation and several other events as being much more precise and detailed than that of Mr. Wrigley or Dr. Adams, both of whom confessed to a poor recall of any topic dating back to 2001 and 2002 when the Ecolodge transaction occurred," auditors said. Moreover, auditors said they had to press Wrigley to get him to admit making the telephone call to Witzleben.

Wrigley's official response was that he didn't immediately recall the conversation with Witzleben and denied that he had to be pressed for the information.

UGA management also said Deloitte & Touche erred in asserting that Wrigley asked Witzleben to put Costello on his payroll and to pay her salary through his firm using Foundation funds. In fact Witzleben's consulting contract was paid with state funds, not by the Foundation. State money was the only option for retaining Costello as a consultant, they said.

In a brief interview shortly after the Deloitte & Touche audit was made public, Witzleben said the D&T report about his conversation with Wrigley is accurate in everything except where the money to pay Costello would come from.

"I was asked if I would be open to putting Kathryn Costello on my payroll. I didn't really give a damn where the money was coming from. I wasn't interested in the arrangement," Witzleben said. "I think quite frankly Steve was asked to call me. He began the conversation by saying 'I think I know the answer to this question before I ask it but I've been asked to call,'" Witzleben said.

There is another reason for believing Witzleben. He had told the same story to UGA Foundation trustee Billy Espy in confidence just weeks after the telephone call took place. The conversation between Espy and Witzleben occurred during the Foundation's May 22–24 spring meeting at Sea Island on the Georgia Coast. Espy was head of the Foundation's Development and Public Affairs Committee at the time and was working closely with Witzleben in the planning of the capital campaign. They met privately at the Beach Club at 10:30 A.M. on Thursday, May 23, to go over a presentation before the full Foundation board the next day.

"Charlie and I were working very closely together," Espy recalled. "I like Charlie a lot. So we planned between various other committee meetings to visit about what we would do the next day. We met at the Beach Club and there was nobody else around. We were just having a cup of coffee. He said I want to tell you something in total confidence. That's when he told me of the telephone call he received."

Espy was appalled. When he returned to Atlanta he wrote a memorandum to himself detailing the conversation:

> When together on 5/23/02, in confidence, Witzleben recounted the following to me. During the first week of March 2002, Witzleben was driving in his car in Metropolitan Raleigh when he received the following call from Wrigley at around 5 P.M. The details of the phone conversation as provided by Charlie were as follows:
>
> Wrigley: "Charlie this is Steve. I have a question to ask and I think I know the answer—but I have been asked to make this call. Would you employ Kathy Costello as a consultant to your company and we will simply increase the fees to cover her costs."
>
> Witzleben: "Steve, not no, but hell no."

Espy said he kept Witzleben's confidence until the Foundation hired Deloitte & Touche to conduct the audit. At that point, Espy called Witzleben and told him that he was going to violate the confidence. He said Witzleben would have preferred not to have been brought into the controversy.

Espy said he and other members of the Foundation Executive Committee never believed that Costello would have made the Ecolodge purchase without Adams's tacit approval. Espy believes Wrigley's subsequent overture to Witzleben was an effort to get "hush money" to Costello for her taking full responsibility for the Ecolodge purchase. And Espy interprets the way Wrigley began the conversation with Witzleben—about being directed to make the phone call—as a signal to Witzleben that he knew what he was asking was inappropriate if not illegal and that it wasn't his initiative. Furthermore, Espy says, Wrigley didn't have the stand-alone authority to make such a request of Witzleben as he did in the call.

FOUNDATION LEADERS FELT THE audit report was, if not a smoking gun, at least a road map for a criminal investigation. Some members of the Foundation boldly predicted that Adams wouldn't be around to collect the deferred compensation promised by the Foundation in 2007.

Atlanta attorney and UGA alumnus Robert Miller, a retired former partner in King & Spalding, fired off letters to Georgia Attorney General Thurbert Baker demanding an immediate investigation.

"I know something about this type of report," Miller said in an interview. "I was chairman of the board of directors of a New York Stock Exchange Company. If this report had been written about a senior executive of a private corporation he would have been summarily fired. No questions asked and probably in less than three hours."

But Adams's situation proved quite different.

The Deloitte & Touche audit report began with a standard disclaimer: "Such services do not constitute an engagement to provide audit, compilation, review or attestation services prescribed in pronouncements on Professional Standards issued by the American Institute of Certified Public Accountants."

The language is meant to distinguish these investigations from standard audits. Forensic audits aren't intended to count paper clips or balance the books. Critics nevertheless seized upon this verbiage to ridicule the report as unprofessional and biased; an allegation that went unanswered by the auditors at the time. Years later Fancher, who is no longer at Deloitte & Touche, explained the auditors' reasons for remaining quiet.

"The report was intended to be objective," Fancher said. "It wasn't received that way in my mind because of the politics surrounding the situation. But nonetheless our effort was to be very objective and to present as much of the info as we could. But obviously the president and his lieutenants came back with a very derogatory and one-sided response to everything."

"I think they were lies, quite frankly," Fancher said of the direct responses. "But many other issues they skirted and never really addressed."

Rather than get into a public dispute with the president of the state's flagship university, Fancher said Deloitte & Touche executives and corporate attorneys decided to ignore Adams's responses. Fancher said it was up to the Foundation trustees and the Board of Regents to determine what to do with the information.

9

REACTION TO THE AUDIT

In retrospect, the Foundation's "smoking gun" turned out to have fired a blank. Instead of forcing the Regents to take the Foundation trustees' concerns seriously, the Deloitte & Touche report caused the Regents to dig in their heels. By instigating a forensic audit, Foundation trustees felt they were being good stewards of the university's funds. But the Regents and Chancellor Meredith saw the audit as interfering in their internal affairs.

On October 24, 2003, Chancellor Meredith accepted the Deloitte & Touche document, grimly vowing to carefully consider its contents. "We'll be reviewing that report over the next few days," Meredith said. "We should have a response, I would expect, by the middle of next week." At the same time, without having read the report, Meredith assured reporters that Adams's job was not in jeopardy.

The Regents were caught in a trap partly of their own making. If they allowed Adams to be forced out, it could be perceived that they were not in control. And that, many of them felt, would cause long-term damage to the university. The Regents' response was to condemn the audit; for the second time in six months they handed the UGA president an unconditional pardon.

The very day they received the Deloitte & Touche document, Meredith and Regents vice chairman Joel Wooten Jr. wrote a memorandum to the Regents urging them to circle the wagons around the beleaguered president. "We are in receipt of the report from the UGA Foundation regarding President Adams . . . You will receive a copy very shortly from the UGA Foundation," the memo stated. "We strongly encourage you to keep this report confidential and not discuss it with anyone . . . It will be imperative for the Board of Regents to be unified in their position and response . . . If you are contacted by the press please refer the caller to the chancellor so we can speak with one voice on this important matter." Adams received a copy of the report the same day, according to a subsequent letter he wrote to Meredith.

On October 27, three days after being handed the document, Meredith convened a strategy session of the Regents executive and compensation committees at the Regents headquarters in Atlanta. Attending the meeting were former governor and Regents Chair Joe Frank Harris, Vice Chair Wooten, and Regents Donald Leebern, Patrick Pittard, and Glenn White—all strong Adams backers—along with Adams and members of his senior staff. The group emerged from behind closed doors after two and a half hours but took no official action that day.

Two days later, on October 29, the full Board of Regents met for four hours behind closed doors. When they emerged they issued a biting assessment of the Deloitte & Touche audit and lectured Foundation members on their behavior.

"The Regents find the report offensive in a large number of ways," their statement said. The Regents said the Deloitte & Touche report was flawed by: numerous significant factual errors; assumptions not based on facts; selective use of information; lack of understanding of a complex research institution's operations; hearsay; statements attributed to unidentified sources; and inappropriate conclusions.

The Regents complained that they and the chancellor had been given short notice to review the report and prepare a response.

"Since neither the chancellor, the Regents, nor President Adams was given the opportunity to see the report prior to its distribution last Friday, there has been no opportunity to prepare a response until this late date. No reasonable explanation was provided for this unusual approach," the Regents said.

Meanwhile, the Foundation had released the report to the public three days after giving it to the Regents. For their part, Foundation leaders felt they had good reason for doing so because for some weeks the Foundation had been locked in a legal battle with the media over its right to conduct its business in secret. Foundation attorneys had argued that as a private corporation they were exempt from the state's open meetings and open records laws. But Attorney General Thurbert Baker had issued a stern notice that the Foundation was conducting the public's business and must obey the open government laws. And once in the hands of the Regents, the report was certainly subject to the Open Records Act, which has a three-day trigger.

Nevertheless, the failure of the Foundation trustees to give the Regents and Adams advance notice of the audit and an opportunity to review the report had irritated the Regents. "For such a report to be submitted by Deloitte & Touche and for the report to be accepted by the Foundation and forwarded to the Regents without giving the President of the University an opportunity to respond or even to see the report is neither reasonable nor fair and has no place in the world of academia," the Regents stated.

Their irritation extended beyond the timing of the report and into its content and even the general principles of university governance. To the dismay of the Foundation trustees, the Regents gave Adams such a blanket endorsement that it would be hard for them to retreat from it into a discussion of any serious complaints. The Regents stated that Adams had made mistakes but that they were relatively few and were readily acknowledged. And in a sweeping generalization, they said the president had always acted in the best interest of the university. The Regents said:

> The UGA Foundation has the potential to be an extraordinary resource for the University. However, its responsibility goes beyond managing assets. It not only must actively raise private resources, but its members must also give of their time and assets in a way so as to serve as a positive model and catalyst for others to give. If and when Foundation members have questions regarding the president's activities with Foundation funds, it should meet with the president or the chancellor privately and specifically address those concerns in a professional way and not in the manner demonstrated with the D&T report.

Further, the Regents turned the tables on the Foundation, saying its own internal procedures and practices contributed to some of the "concerns and confusions." They urged Foundation members to look outside its membership for counsel to improve their procedures and governance. They found the reports submitted by Adams and senior management to be "far more credible that the report submitted by Deloitte & Touche." The Regents reiterated their "total and complete support for President Adams" and urged the Foundation to "close this chapter and now move forward and be about the business of raising private funds for the University."

And they issued a not-so-veiled invitation to unhappy Foundation members to walk away. "Individual members," they said, "will have to decide whether or not they desire to continue as a trustee."

In a letter to Foundation trustees Chancellor Meredith said Adams had provided "a more than adequate response" to concerns raised by the audit.

> The issues raised in your report have been taken seriously. They have been held to the highest level of scrutiny and inquiry by all of those responsible for the effective governance of the University System of Georgia.
>
> Accordingly, the members of the Board of Regents and I have received and fully evaluated President Michael Adams's responses to the Deloitte & Touche report, as well as the requested response filed by senior administrative staff at the University of Georgia. I now ask all of you to do the same. In order to provide a fair and balanced hearing to the various issues and concerns expressed in your Deloitte &Touche report, the president's extensive response and the institution's management response, all must be given equal time. That is what the Board of Regents has done. President Michael Adams has provided a more than adequate response to the concerns we have asked him to address. He has the Board of Regents' and my full support as he continues to provide leadership to the University of Georgia.
>
> In order to allow this great university to continue to flourish, we must resolve to bring to closure the issues that have plagued the reputation of our state's flagship higher education institution for several months. Our board will bring closure to this issue today with the public distribution of the Deloitte & Touche report, their formal response to the report, and the formal response documents received from President Adams and the senior management team.
>
> With these public statements, let us vow to join together, for the continued progress of one of this nation's great universities. I stand ready to be of assistance in whatever way possible.

Individual Regents were even more biting. Adams's original Georgia patron, Donald Leebern, called the report "an assassination attempt of Mike Adams for honoring an [Dooley's] employment contract." Regent Timothy Shelnut of Augusta told the *Atlanta Journal-Constitution* that "It looks to me like the report is an indictment of the Foundation."

THE REGENTS WEREN'T THROUGH. They wanted no more challenges and set out to restrict the Foundation's authority.

Since 1996 the Board of Regents and the UGA Foundation relationship had been governed by a three-page memorandum of understanding signed by then University President Charles B. Knapp and Shell H. Knox, who was then chair of the Foundation. The document set forth the purpose of the Foundation and laid out the relationship between it and the university. The Foundation would raise and manage assets to benefit the university. They would share administrative staff to reduce costs. The Foundation would make any audit reports available to the university president.

Now, on the heels of the Deloitte & Touche report, in an effort to ensure more institutional control, the chancellor and the Regents required all schools in the system to come up with new operating agreements. As we shall see, this requirement eventually led to UGA's disassociation from the UGA Foundation. It also led to a policy change that ended the practice within the University System of Georgia of foundations providing direct supplemental pay to university presidents, a practice that many felt gave the UGA Foundation a sense of entitlement to challenge Adams's tenure.

Some Foundation trustees accused the Regents of not bothering to read the document before issuing a statement endorsing Adams. The truth is that the Regents already knew much about what was coming. In addition most were convinced that the Foundation had no business meddling in their affairs. They saw it largely as a personnel matter and seized on every opportunity to discredit the audit report.

To understand the Regents thinking, it's helpful to understand how the Regents operate as a body, said Arlethia Perry-Johnson, who spent eleven and a half years as the Regents' spokesperson.

"There is a cohesiveness and high degree of camaraderie," she said. "Conflict is an anomaly. They felt that their authority was being challenged, and they felt it important to communicate their governance role in no uncertain terms. And that role at its core in addition to setting policy is the hiring and firing of the chancellor and presidents. So when you heard the debate being discussed in terms of being about academics versus athletics they wanted to convey that at their core, they felt that a lot of the people who had taken sides were linked in many ways to the athletics aspect of it because of the profile that Dooley had at the beginning."

She said the Adams dispute further galvanized the Regents, who then wanted to emphasize that any review of Adams's performance was the responsibility of the chancellor and themselves. They saw the audit as an attempt to embarrass Adams by airing dirty laundry that belonged both to him and to the Board of Regents. Their reaction was that the Foundation is supposed to be a cooperative body working on behalf of the University of Georgia and at the behest of the Regents, she said.

Perhaps even more so than the members of the UGA Foundation, the Regents are well-connected. The eighteen members are appointed by the governor to seven-year terms and are, by Georgia's Constitution, an independent agency of government. They oversee thirty-five state colleges and universities with a combined enrollment of 260,000 students.

Created in 1931 by government reorganization during the administration of Richard B. Russell, the Board of Regents brought public higher education under a single governing board. The board meets monthly and behaves generally like a board of directors of a corporation. It takes cues from the University System chancellor who acts as an executive officer. Regents appoint the chancellor as well as college and university presidents. Only the Board of Regents can fire a chancellor or president.

The Regents' much-touted independence has its origin in the 1941 Eugene Talmadge episode described previously in Chapter 2. Talmadge's heavy-handed control over the Regents to enforce segregation led to an accreditation crisis, and in the backlash to the election of the young reformer Ellis Arnall, who promised to remove the University System from political interference. One of Arnall's first acts as govenor in 1943 was to sign legislation creating a constitutionally independent Board of Regents. Nevertheless, Georgia governors have retained significant influence over the Regents, down to Sonny Perdue, the incumbent at the time of the Deloitte & Touche report.

One of Perdue's then-recent appointees to the Board of Regents was Pat Pittard, the wealthy chairman, until he was relieved, of Heidrick & Struggles, Inc., an executive recruiting firm. Pittard had struck up a strong friendship with Adams while serving earlier as a UGA Foundation chairman. Documents suggest that he played a key role in 2003–05 as an emissary between the Regents and Perdue, keeping the governor informed of developments inside the Regents' meetings.

For Pittard, the issue was simply one of control. A Terry School of Business distinguished alumnus and a big contributor to UGA, Pittard's views were partially colored by his recollections of the past scandals involving athletics. After the Jan Kemp affair drove former UGA President Fred Davison from office, Pittard's head-hunting firm had handled the search for a new president, Dr. Knapp. And that made his decision to support Adams easy, Pittard said.

"We heard over and over after Jan Kemp how UGA was an academic wasteland," he said. "Top academics were leaving. It was beyond awful." President Charles Knapp, who served between Davison and Adams, toiled for a decade to bring the university back to respectability, Pittard said. "And we were about to do it all over again."

In Pittard's mind, it didn't matter who was right and who was wrong. "The point was the president decided it was time for a change," he said. Like many Adams supporters, Pittard has no doubts that the controversy was about the athletics side trying to control the university.

"Their storyline changed after meeting with a PR firm," he said. "The laughter was so loud that it hit the state capitol. Everybody's trying to put a happy face on this pig."

OUTSIDERS FAMILIAR WITH FORENSIC investigations, as well as insiders familiar with Adams's tenure as president, had reactions that were very different from those of the Regents.

After reading the report and Adams's responses to it, former FBI Special Agent Oliver Halle of Marietta, an expert on white-collar crime, wondered "how the hell this guy could have could still be president." Halle, an attorney and author of *Taking the Harder Right*, a book about ethics, anti-corruption and fraud prevention, conducts seminars for corporations and government agencies.

Halle said he saw nothing in the report that rises to the level of a federal crime. Adams just comes across as a petty chiseler, Halle said. "The overall pattern of the guy is a nickel-dimer. It seems he's always looking for a way to justify his actions—talking about his wife working uncompensated. To hear him tell it, he's a victim. Like other chiselers he bellies up when you have irrefutable evidence, like the law school party. He bellied up and said it was a mistake and I'm sorry. By then he'd been there five years. He had to know the rules. I don't think it passes the red-face test," said Halle.

Much of the faculty had become disenchanted with Adams long before the Dooley crisis and the UGA Foundation audit, said biology professor Barry Palevitz. The faculty largely viewed him as aloof and unapproachable—a CEO type who wasn't interested in day-to-day instruction, said Palevitz.

"Mike had a hard act to follow" after the popular Charles Knapp, adored on campus for his give-and-take with the faculty, said Palevitz. "Knapp was a faculty's president. He cared about academics and the day-to-day running of the university. Adams installed a campus provost to deal with the academic side of things."

Dooley's dismissal simply provided a spark that ignited smoldering embers of unrest, Palevitz said. "It was simmering and the whole Dooley thing was a catalyst. Not that the faculty rose up in support of Dooley. That's not what it was all about. It was over the bad publicity and the embarrassing fight with the Foundation."

"This was not about athletics. If the newspapers put it in that context they were woefully wrong," Palevitz says. "The faculty was upset at the portrayal in the media as a war between academics and athletics with the president standing up for academics. That was flat out wrong. The faculty got angry that it was being portrayed that way."

After the Foundation's audit was released, Professor Nancy Felson, the UGA Faculty Senate President at the time, and other faculty leaders began meeting with Adams seeking answers to the questions that had been raised.

For example, Felson said Adams gave a "long and convoluted narrative" about the OSU job offer. "My comment to him at the time was, 'Well, if it's true why don't you just bring out the evidence and put it out in the open.' He said he had the evidence in a file cabinet. I said if there's evidence in writing, I'd like to see it . . . We didn't see it."

Felson said she began with an open mind about Adams, but as the faculty senate gathered information from reading and talking with Adams, she became concerned that Adams wasn't coming clean. "It was like when a kid is caught with his hand in a cookie jar and he tries to explain," she said.

The faculty senate ultimately took a poll in February 2004 of the faculty of UGA's largest college, the Franklin School of Arts and Sciences, about Adams's performance. Some 64 percent of the faculty participated, and of those, 70 percent gave Adams a "no confidence" vote, 15 percent abstained, and 15 percent expressed confidence in the president.

The survey also asked whether the faculty senate should express an opinion on Adams's leadership; 74 percent responded in the affirmative. The subsequent faculty senate statement was another searing indictment of the UGA president, questioning not only Adams's "extravagant spending" but his moral fiber:

STATEMENT OF THE FACULTY SENATE

An enlightened leader of a great university should be the best representative of the deeply held values of academic life. Such a leader must represent these cherished values for the entire community, whatever the changing climate in politics and social mores, whatever the priorities of the marketplace. Such a leader should embody the ideals of the honor code required of all students.

The Faculty Senate of the Franklin College of Arts and Sciences recognizes that President Adams has made many positive contributions to the University. We acknowledge that a number of the difficulties faced by the University stem from the current economic climate, over which the president has no control, and we thank him for his efforts to mitigate the effects of hard economic times. We do, however, have serious concerns about the direction in which the University has moved, and continues to move, under President Adams's leadership.

Many faculty members perceive or fear an erosion of academic excellence—in research and teaching—in large part as a result of the values and priorities of his administration; they see an imbalance between efficiency and profitability on the one hand and quality and depth on the other. Many characterize the president and his administration as repeatedly implementing policies that have major impact on the faculty, with little or no faculty input. Examples include the proliferation of administrative positions prior to the budget cuts, the sequestering of retired faculty lines by the Provost's office, the recent increase in teaching loads, the tuition return policy for study abroad programs and the creation of new colleges by removing departments from Franklin College.

As one respondent to our poll states: "I am disturbed by the apparent need of President Adams to operate like the CEO of a corporation. In my opinion a president of a flagship academic institution should be more like a leader and exemplar to the faculty."

Many members of the faculty are outraged at extravagant expenditures by the president. Some of these came to our attention as a result of the Deloitte & Touche report. Widespread knowledge of these matters both inside and outside the University community is embarrassing and demoralizing to the faculty. The majority of the faculty members who have read the D&T report find the written and public responses of the president unconvincing.

Faculty members are also distressed by the questionable decisions that have plagued the University in the athletic realm, for which President Adams bears substantial responsibility. A series of events including the resolution of the previous football coach's contract and the scandals ensuing from the choice of a basketball coach with a record of NCAA violations at two prior institutions, has distracted attention from the University's positive achievements and debased its academic reputation.

The University of Georgia is a great institution, one that the citizens of Georgia can be proud to support. The faculty of the Franklin College of Arts and Sciences provides students with a superior education and carries out innovative research in a wide variety of fields. Nevertheless, as a body of faculty committed to the future of the university, we believe that major problems exist because of the leadership of President Michael F. Adams.

Individual faculty members, who were not required to give their names, were even more stinging in their comments. Typical of the 331 faculty members who gave Adams a "no confidence" vote were these:

"Leadership is not a word that I would associate with Michael Adams."

"There is an extreme lack of trust and confidence in the leadership of President Adams."

"Dr. Adams's behavior shames the entire faculty and administration."

Still others condemned what they called his profligate spending, his imperial presidential style, and his ethical and moral lapses.

The Faculty Senate statement and survey received little notice in the media and had even less impact.

Adams was out of town when the survey results were released. He issued a statement that seemed calculated to dismiss the seriousness of the faculty's "no confidence" vote, saying he would take the results as "constructive criticism."

"As we grow in mutual understanding of our concerns and those we face together as an institution, I trust that confidence in our direction and decision-making processes will grow," Adams said.

American Council on Education attorney Sheldon Steinbach correctly predicted at the time that the vote would have little impact on Adams. Usually, presidents have the support of their employers—in this case the Board of Regents—by the time a grievance has reached a vote, he told the *Atlanta Journal-Constitution*. "A vote of no confidence is the last card that a faculty has to play," Steinbach said. "In twenty-first century academe it carries significantly less weight than it did fifty years ago.

Felson said reaction to their "no confidence" vote was disappointing. "We were disheartened," she said. "It was treated as a trivial thing. We based our no-confidence vote for the most part on the feeling that he was exploiting the system. And he was self-aggrandizing. Some people felt he was aloof, non-academic. He was treating the place like he was the CEO."

"There was a lot of stuff. Some of it would have been the faculty being disgruntled. But we didn't think the members showed that that was primarily what it was about. We felt that there was a sense of outrage which is very rare at the university because it's such a passive faculty for the most part. But each of the people in Faculty Senate that year was asked to study the matter and bring it up to their constituents and try to form an opinion.

"We had never met the Board of Regents so we didn't know how they would take it. But the chancellor didn't take it seriously."

University of Georgia law professor James F. Ponsoldt, a former prosecutor in the U.S. Justice Department, said the Deloitte & Touche report should have been referred to the attorney general for review.

The report reflects institutional failure resulting from a lack of oversight by the Board of Regents and the Foundation, he said. He compared Adams spending for the law school party to the former Tyco International CEO Dennis Kozlowski's spending $200 million for a Mediterranean toga party to celebrate his wife's fortieth birthday. Kozlowski was sentenced to federal prison for diverting corporate funds for his private use. His defense, Ponsoldt said, was that funds were used for corporate purposes that also benefited him and that the Tyco board of directors tacitly approved of his conduct as additional compensation. Ponsoldt sees similar failure at UGA where the Foundation members deferred to spending practices that led to abuses.

Ponsoldt, who retired after twenty-eight years at UGA, blames the new "corporate culture" at UGA. "They bring in the CEO types. It seems the main criterion for success is how much money you can raise. The corporate culture allows corruption to occur. There's no questioning allowed. Just give the CEO what he wants," he said.

Dick Bestwick, former head coach at the University of Virginia and a respected former assistant athletic director at UGA, sent the Regents a letter blistering them for ignoring the auditors' findings. "It is incomprehensible to me that you would take issue with the objectivity of a Deloitte & Touche audit, but give credence to what Mike Adams and his five sycophants have to say as being 'objective,'" Bestwick wrote. "Any close observation or anything said or claimed to have been done by Mike Adams has to be viewed with a great deal of skepticism. Honesty and integrity are two virtues sadly lacking in Mike Adams's character."

Atlanta attorney Robert Miller was among the most vocal in calling for further investigation of the allegations. A UGA and Yale Law graduate, Miller had given almost $180,000 to his alma mater, most of which went to provide support for summer study abroad for UGA honor students.

A corporate lawyer for thirty-one years, Miller served on the audit committees of publicly held companies and was thoroughly familiar with forensic audit reports. In a carefully-worded letter to then Foundation chairman John W. Rooker, Miller offered his own detailed assessment of the Deloitte & Touche audit, and of Adams's and UGA management's response to it.

Miller called the hiring of architect Al Filoni "an end-run" on the state's bidding rules for hiring architects. The Foundation paid Filoni $74,000 for developing plans for the new alumni center after University officials refused to pay the invoice. Adams and senior management's response that Filoni was hired as a consultant and not as an architect doesn't wash, Miller said. Filoni in fact developed a design for the alumni center. Neither Adams's nor management's response explains why, if Filoni's hiring was proper, the university refused to pay him.

Adams explanation for charging the Foundation to charter an airplane to attend the funeral of a friend and former Centre College president was "mushy" and doesn't come close to be an acceptable reason for spending donors' gifts.

Charging the Foundation for a party for Adams's son and some other graduates of the law school was more than an error in judgment, as management claimed in their response. It raises questions about the integrity of those involved, Miller said.

The university's senior managers blamed a lack of clear guidelines for any misuse of Foundation monies. "Do not misunderstand the message being sent by UGA management," Miller warned. "Paraphrased, it is 'Your failure to have very specific rules gives us the opportunity to push every issue to the limit and perhaps beyond. If money is improperly spent, it is your fault for not having tight enough rules.' Management makes no mention of things like integrity and propriety," Miller wrote.

The telephone conversation between fundraising consultant Charles Witzleben and Senior Vice President Steve Wrigley should be referred to the attorney general for further investigation. Because, he said, if the auditor's opinions are correct, a senior UGA official was advancing a scheme to defraud the Foundation.

Miller urged Rooker to seek a refund of $2,255 spent to charter an airplane for Adams to attend former Centre College President McLeod's funeral and of the $74,000 paid to architect Al Filoni.

"That's knee-jerk," said Miller. "That's not rocket science."

Miller was astonished by the Regents' response to the report.

"No board of directors having received this report would ever have issued such whitewash. I'm convinced they never read a word of it," he said.

Miller didn't limit his criticism to the Adams administration.

"The Foundation," he wrote "has not been a good steward of the money entrusted to you by alumni like Mary Helen [Miller's spouse] and me . . . The sloppiness, the failure to follow sound practices and the inherent conflict in having Foundations expenses approved by an executive director who was also the president's chief of staff are hardly the way you ought to have looked after the $400 million entrusted to you as fiduciaries for the benefit of the University of Georgia.

"In the trustees' defense, I suspect many of you never dealt with an administration that makes undocumented, unapproved $250,000 promises or engages in end-runs on established procedures like what seems to have happened in the architect Filoni matter. It is a sad commentary that in this day and time a Foundation trustee—much like a corporate director—has to design controls and processes on the assumption people will try to abuse the system."

Upon learning about Adams's unauthorized verbal agreement with Donnan, the Foundation should have acted immediately to tighten controls over Foundation spending.

Foundation members who had pushed for the audit were equally miffed at the Regents reaction to it. "When you read the comments of the Board of Regents one has to be astonished," said Billy Espy. He pointed out that the Regents made not a single effort to meet with Foundation trustees, their lawyers, or Deloitte & Touche. Instead, they simply issued a statement damning the report. Espy said he met with one Regent several months after

Deloitte & Touche issued its report and discovered that he hadn't read a single page of it.

Wyck Knox, the Foundation's treasurer and a leading critic of Adams, said the Regents simply misinterpreted the trustees' intent. "We were trying to protect the contributors' money," he said. "It appeared as though we were trying to bully and run the Regents and we weren't," he said. "Tom Meredith said that several times to me. You're doing an audit of our president and you're not involved. You know, you're overstepping your bounds here. But what they forget is that it was they who insisted that we pay all that money and he was misusing it. And they wanted us to sit there and do nothing?"

Public relations guru C. Richard Yarbrough, a former Bell South vice president and Olympics spokesman, said it all might have turned out differently had the Foundation leaked the critical audit report to the media instead of giving it to the Regents.

The Foundation's big mistake, Yarbrough said, was in not seeking public approval for what it was doing. "They had some pretty good information," he said. "But to carry it to the Board of Regents and just give it to them, they wasted a lot of effort. They should have talked to people in the media and got a full head of steam developed before turning it over to the Regents."

CHANCELLOR MEREDITH ASKED ADAMS for a written response to the allegations in the report and directed him to assign his senior staff to respond to the Deloitte & Touche audit.

Three days later, Adams responded in fourteen pages of self-pity, apologia, and counterattack. It included an admission by Adams that indeed he wasn't perfect. He complained about the short time in which to respond to a report that took forensic auditors three months to prepare. He worried about the negative impact on the university and the cost of conducting the investigation. He suggested his right of "due process" had been violated then abruptly switched gears, offering to do whatever can be done not only to respond to this report, but to respond to whatever alterations in substance or style that might be needed. After all, nothing less than the future of Georgia's flagship university was a stake, Adams said.

He then launched into an attack on the Deloitte & Touche report as a biased product instigated by vengeful friends of Vince Dooley. Adams was surprised, he said, that auditors accepted as fact information gained from confidential sources. The report turned up nothing illegal or even unethical in his behavior, Adams insisted.

Adams admitted making mistakes but pointed out that auditors found "the majority of expenses have complied with all policies and procedures." Adams seemed to be saying that following the rules most of the time should be sufficient.

He acknowledged using the Foundation's skybox at Sanford Field to entertain personal friends and relatives during football games but said he wasn't aware the Foundation was paying the university for the tickets.

His spending of $10,000 in Foundation funds to throw a graduation party for his son's law school class did give the appearance of impropriety, Adams acknowledged. But when it was called to his attention, Adams said, he repaid the Foundation. "This expense was a mistake on my part and I apologize," Adams said.

On the issue of salary, Adams said Ohio State University offered him $600,000 in direct compensation, a house, two cars, and a stipend and travel reimbursement for his wife, Mary, to accompany him on university business trips. This put the total compensation "into the range" that Deloitte & Touche reported with such a degree of skepticism, he said.

Regarding Mary Adams's stipend at UGA, Adams said that since their arrival in Georgia, Mrs. Adams has worked practically full-time. As a first-year empty nester she was happy to do so for a year or two. But as demands increased on her, it seemed appropriate that she receive a stipend. There was an agreement with the Foundation chair that if the arrangement was deemed inadvisable it could be stopped on an annual review basis.

It wasn't about the money, Adams insisted. "Our main interest was not the income, but the validation, that came from some simple arrangement that indicated value to what was being done." That high-minded explanation rang hollow considering the amount of effort Adams put into obtaining the stipend and the circuitous manner in which he went about it.

In response to the Alumni Center fiasco, Adams dismissed it as "a challenge that seemingly just can't get solved."

He was asked about his support for a new Alumni Center by a member of the search committee on the last day of his interviewing for the president's job in 1997, Adams said. He indicated support for the project but would need to make a full analysis of the sites.

After becoming president, Adams said, the issue of where to build the center was brought to him. He had "instinctive misgivings" but acquiesced to both the plans and the site for the Center. He sought to avoid an argument with the Alumni Association early in his tenure. But as things progressed, Adams said, he became less and less satisfied with the scope and direction of the project. It was his decision to bring in his friend, Pittsburgh architect Al Filoni, to review the plans and make recommendations. Until he read the report Adams said he thought the university and not the UGA Foundation paid Filoni's $74,000 fee and he believes the university should repay the Foundation. University officials refused to pay Filoni apparently because he was hired by Adams without following proper purchasing laws, according to Deloitte & Touche.

"I did make some mistakes with the planning of the newest Alumni Development Center proposal because we tried to put too much in the building and thus escalated the cost beyond anything that was reasonable. There was also considerable opposition by prominent alumni to the bookstore being in the center and I have agreed they were right."

Adams acknowledged that there had been previous misgivings by some Foundation trustees two years earlier about his spending and that he was given new spending guidelines. He expressed reservations about the tighter restrictions placed on him but "realizing the level of concern," Adams said, he readily accepted them.

Adams had asked for and received the Foundation's permission to end mandatory audits of the president's discretionary funds soon after he became UGA's president, a move that auditors said was a mistake. Adams said he had no personal or philosophical objections to audits of his discretionary accounts but felt other internal and external controls were sufficient to prevent misuse.

SENIOR MANAGEMENT'S RESPONSE WAS even more dismissive of the report. The five senior executives, Provost Arnett Mace, Hank Huckaby, Steve Wrigley, Tom Landrum, and Steve Shewmaker also accused the auditors of bias while maintaining that they had made every effort "to respond with complete objectivity and on a factual basis." Adams's critics found this assertion laughable given that all of the men worked directly for Adams and four of them figured prominently in the report. Some of their observations did help clarify events while others seemed like exercises in hair splitting.

For instance, management's response to an auditor's assertion that one of Adams's first acts as president was to "stop the mandatory audits of the Foundation accounts over which he had control" was not true, they said. They cited the minutes of the Foundation's finance committee in 1997 and 1998. The 1997 minutes reflect that the president's funds were audited in 1997 but that in future years such audits would be done "if requested by President Adams." The Finance Committee minutes reflect that the audits were discontinued in 1998.

"To reiterate, there is no factual basis to indicate that Dr. Adams stopped the mandatory audit of Foundation accounts in his office . . . The audit scope continued unchanged for FY 97 and the finance committee voted to exclude the funds from the FY 98 scope. Such action was the prerogative of the finance committee, not President Adams," senior management said, suggesting that auditors got it wrong.

In fact, a fair reading of the audit suggests senior management set up a straw man. The sentence directly following the one cited by management states that "Dr. Adams requested and was granted approval from the Foundation finance committee to discontinue the mandatory audit of these accounts." They were reinstituted in 2001 after Foundation officials began questioning Adams's use of Foundation credit cards and his chartering of a private airplane for a trip to President Bush's inauguration.

Management dismissed as unimportant the fact that Foundation executive committee never approved a February 14, 2003, $40,000 pay supplement, $168,000 in deferred compensation and $1,800 life insurance premium. The compensation package was reviewed and approved by the full Foundation board on May 3, 2003, after the mistake was discovered.

What the response doesn't say is that Chancellor Meredith had informed the Foundation that the Regents, apparently believing the February 14 resolution was legitimate, had already approved that level of compensation for Adams and considered their action legally binding on the Foundation.

As for the personal use of football tickets, senior management blamed the lack of clear written guidelines other than a form for listing tickets assigned and for what purpose. "Without the benefit of clearly written procedures and given the intertwined nature of the role the president plays at the University, there exists a gray area for deciding what constitutes an institutional interest benefit when a game day ticket is assigned. In virtually all cases where Dr. Adams's immediate family members were given free tickets he had the value reported as a fringe benefit and paid taxes on them," they said.

By declaring the tickets as a fringe benefit and paying taxes, Adams clearly knew they were a personal perquisite and not a benefit to the university. However, the D&T report, named twenty-nine individuals—Adams friends and family members—who were given free tickets that were classified by Adams as business-related or major gift prospects.

The Donnan side agreement was an old issue and no Foundation money was involved, management noted. Adams and Shewmaker vigorously denied D&T findings that they wanted to conceal the $250,000 payment to Donnan from the Athletic Association board. They noted that it was ultimately approved by the Athletics Association Board of Directors, after it was discovered.

As for the Huckaby honorarium for working in Governor Sonny Perdue's transition office, management pointed out that UGA depends heavily on the state for financial support. "Responding to the governor's request is obviously a benefit to UGA and is within the scope of its public service mission," they said.

In conclusion, management found the report contained factual errors and "is not the result of a straightforward process. In addition to outright errors, the report contains numerous instances of subjective judgment that Mr. Fancher is in no position to make," they said. The assertion that Adams focused on his compensation to the exclusion of other issues is "a totally inaccurate depiction of Dr. Adams."

They called the D&T report "a compilation of subjective opinions and judgments. "Management respectfully submits that the Board of Regents should not accept the D&T report as credible on the issues it attempts to address," they said.

AMIDST THE BACK AND forth, many prominent UGA supporters worried that the squabbling would damage the university's fundraising campaign. Foundation trustee Otis Brumby Jr., publisher of the *Marietta Daily Journal*, was one of the few to spy a silver lining. He said the controversy might cause some who felt Adams was treated unfairly to dig deeper in their pockets. Most of the commentary ran the other way.

"Without question, this circumstance is going to impact the university's ability to raise money," Tom Cousins, an Atlanta business leader and honorary chairman of the campaign, told the *AJC*'s Maria Saporta. "It's not just the Dooley issue. Several people have expressed a lack of confidence in the leadership of the university. So long as that attitude exists on the part of the university's major supporters, it would adversely affect any campaign."

"The campaign is absolutely dead, and it's dead as long as Michael Adams is at the University of Georgia," echoed Atlanta insurance executive David Boyd. Boyd said he would not fulfill a six-figure pledge to the campaign until Adams is gone.

And Atlanta real estate developer Richard "Bo" Means, in a letter to Wyck Knox, said he was "embarrassed and ashamed" by Adams and his spending.

"I still have $350,000 to give, but I'm holding it back right now," Means said. "It's no one issue. It's all of them. Adams wants complete control, and I have no faith in him. He needs to be out. He needs to either resign or be let go."

As we shall see, neither scenario came to pass.

10

THE BREAK WITH THE FOUNDATION

If Foundation trustees were blindsided in June 2003 when Adams managed to turn criticism against him into an "academics versus athletics" issue in the news media, they had seen nothing yet. The initial news story in the *Atlanta Journal-Constitution* about the Deloitte & Touche report carried the headline: "Audit targets UGA Foundation oversight, spending by Adams." The headline and story gave the same emphasis to the Foundation's lack of oversight of Adams's spending as it did to Adams's alleged misuse of funds. His critics on the Foundation were incredulous.

The tit-for-tat theme was quickly picked up by Adams's supporters even though the issue of Foundation oversight was covered tangentially in only a few pages in the forty-six page report. Regent Timothy Shelnut of Augusta called the report an indictment of the Foundation.

Adams even had support within the Foundation. *Marietta Daily Journal* publisher and Foundation trustee Otis Brumby Jr. called the audit more an indictment of Foundation procedures than of the president's practices. Former Foundation president John "Jack" Rooker, who was criticized for approving a pay raise for Adams without proper authorization by the Foundation board, became one of Adams's staunchest backers.

Adams's critics on the Foundation believed the audit should have prompted a criminal investigation by Attorney General Thurbert Baker's office. Instead, they were stunned to find themselves on the defensive.

Foundation leaders initially let anger and egos take over. Their first reaction was to threaten to cut off the Foundation's $300,000 supplement to Adams salary.

The audit report had recommended that the Foundation reduce the number of its trustees—a number which had increased over the past few years at

Adams's urging for fundraising purposes. Auditors felt the trustee structure had thus become unwieldy. The trustees did as recommended, but they went a step further by removing Adams as a voting member of their executive committee and by barring all UGA administrators except the president from voting positions on the Foundation board.

Then the Foundation put the president's luxurious Buckhead townhouse up for sale. This 4,500-square-foot condo off West Paces Ferry Road in one of Atlanta's most elegant neighborhoods had been purchased several years earlier at Adams's urging. He persuaded the trustees that UGA officials needed a "front door" in Atlanta to entertain and occasionally to spend the night while in the capital on university business. He argued that some of the condo's cost could be offset by charging university officials $100 for overnight stays and $250 for fundraising events. Not surprisingly, the investment turned out to be a bust. Overnight stays were rare and event bookings were even rarer. University officials said the property turned out to be unsuitable for their use because of a lack of parking. In 2002, the townhouse hosted just one reception and recorded receipts of $250. Revenue for the year from nightly rentals totaled $0, while expenses came to more than $145,000. From 1999 to 2003, the cost of operating the townhouse exceeded revenues by more than $500,000.

Meanwhile, Chancellor Meredith, who was having his own problem getting the Regents Foundation to meet a promise to supplement his own salary, threatened litigation if the UGA Foundation cut Adams's pay. He said the Regents had already approved Adams's new salary based on the Foundation's own Valentine's Day 2003 resolution.

Foundation trustees quickly caved in to Meredith's pressure and on February 13, 2004, voted unanimously to give "good faith consideration" to paying whatever the Regents recommended as a salary supplement for the president. The vote was another victory for Adams. His critics on the Foundation said they just wanted to put the controversy behind them and move forward to support the university.

Adams called the decision "good for the university." The headline in the *Atlanta Journal-Constitution*, "UGA President Prevails," was followed by a subhead, "Meeting closed in defiance of opinion by state's attorney." Three weeks later, in March 2004, Foundation trustees folded their tent and promised to comply with the attorney general's open meetings ruling. Henceforth, the Foundation said it would make all meetings open to the public.

Despite his troubles at Georgia, Adams found himself on a list of potential candidates to replace University of Tennessee President John Shumaker. Ironically, Shumaker had resigned after coming under fire for spending $500,000 on improvements to the president's home, more than $165,000 for tailgate parties, and more than $34,000 on personal expenses, including travel on the UT airplane. The lapses seemed minor in comparison with some of the accusations against Adams. Investigators cleared Shumaker of any criminal wrongdoing.

IF THE UGA FOUNDATION trustees hoped that settling the issue of Adams's pay would satisfy the Regents, they were again mistaken. Negotiations between the Regents and the Foundation were not going smoothly. By late March 2004, the Foundation's concession on Adams's supplemental pay had been forgotten in a dispute over the Foundation's proposed bylaws revisions.

A March 30, 2004, letter from Senior Vice Chancellor Corliss Cummings to Foundation Chair Lynda Courts questioned trustees' motives in removing senior UGA administrators as voting members of the Foundation. She wrote:

> The Foundation is a cooperative organization of the Board of Regents created in 1937 to strengthen, support and assist the University of Georgia and the president of the University. Foundations are an integral part of the higher education partnership that is needed in this state in order for higher education to thrive. It is critical that any changes in the by-laws encourage a spirit of partnership and continue to recognize the leadership of the University in setting the direction of the Foundation. No foundation should ever have its own agenda.
>
> . . . The revised by-laws specifically prohibit a board of Regents employee—other than the president—from serving as a trustee. Failure to have senior administrative staff of the institution bring their knowledge, skills and expertise to the table is troubling. If the Foundation exists to provide

support for the University, then surely the University's voice would be sought in all discussions.

And in bold type, this missive:

> In general, there is no reference to the UGA Foundation being a Cooperative Organization under Policy 1905 of the Board of Regents.

Cummings concluded by sounding a hopeful note along with a veiled warning:

> I am confident we all want a Foundation which is viewed as beneficial to the university and acting always in the best interest of the institution. All would be well served if ample time is given for representatives of the Foundation and the Regents to have the time to adequately discuss these proposed by-laws and reach accord. No chance should be taken to produce additional negative publicity and endanger the signing of a memorandum of agreement which is required under Policy 1905 of the Board of Regents.

However, on April 27, 2004, the Foundation adopted new by-laws that removed Adams as a voting member of the Foundation's executive committee. A month later, on May 25, the Board of Regents retaliated, giving the Foundation a ninety-day notice that it would no longer be considered a cooperative organization. In other words, the Board of Regents was about to disassociate the University of Georgia from the University of Georgia Foundation.

"We don't have that sense of cooperation [with the Foundation]," Regents Vice Chairman Joel Wooten Jr. told the *Atlanta Journal-Constitution* after the May 25 meeting. "This board has spent a lot of time on this [that] we could have spent on different issues."

Governor Perdue, who had said little publicly about the quarrel up to this point, now stepped forward. He had already made up his mind to support the Regents' decision to disassociate the Foundation and perhaps had even helped orchestrate the action. E-mails make it clear that Perdue was far from the carefully managed detached persona he portrayed himself as in the media. An exchange of e-mails from the governor's office to the chancellor's office beginning just before midnight on May 25, 2004, reveals the governor's involvement.

Perdue's press secretary, Dan McLagan, e-mailed John Watson and Jim Lientz of the governor's office a copy of the *AJC* article about the Regents' decision along with this message:

> We will probably have to address this tomorrow along the lines we discussed. While the Regents Comms person committed to giving us an early look at whatever they released, they did not do so, leaving us to hear about it from a reporter. Given this vacuum, the Governor's decision not to address the issue was exactly the right call. [Perdue had declined to comment that evening when contacted by reporters.]

The next morning Lientz, the governor's chief operating officer, e-mailed Chancellor Meredith:

> Tom — not a good thing that the communications were not executed as should have been.

Meredith responded a few minutes later:

> I don't know what happened. It was all set up. The governor knew what the board was going to do. Pittard called him and reported back to the board before it took action. I will check on the breakdown with Dan!

The next day Perdue broke his silence. "I believe [the disassociation] was a responsible action aimed at preserving the academic integrity of our flagship university as well as the University System as a whole," Perdue said. "It is evident to me that the Regents felt that they had exhausted all other means of reconciling a situation that had become untenable."

THE REGENTS' PRE-EMPTIVE STRIKE caught Foundation trustees, who were preparing for their annual meeting at Sea Island, completely off guard. When the Foundation trustees had relented in February 2004 on paying Adams's salary supplement, the *Atlanta Journal-Constitution* announced that the crisis was over. "UGA president prevails; Foundation members halt effort to get Adams fired," read one headline. The article quoted Foundation member Billy Payne, who had called for Adams's ouster, as being pleased with the decision not to try to punish Adams by cutting his salary. "We fought over this compensation issue so much, I'm glad someone else will review it," Payne said. "The Regents are better equipped to deal with it."

But this fight was about more than Adams's salary.

Joel Wooten, soon to be the Regents' chairman, had expressed his frustration in dealing with the Foundation trustees over Adams's salary. Those frustrations grew over the next several months even as representatives of the Regents and the Foundation trustees tried to negotiate an end to the hostilities.

Trustee James Blanchard, CEO of Synovus Financial Corporation, was representing the UGA Foundation in the talks, primarily with Chancellor Meredith and Regents Vice Chair Wooten. Blanchard said the talks had been positive and he thought the two entities were nearing a resolution of differences. In fact, he thought he had reached a good faith agreement with his fellow Columbus, Georgia, resident, Joel Wooten.

Blanchard felt betrayed by the May 25, 2004, action by the Regents. It wouldn't be the last time.

Wooten, however, said he felt the talks had stalemated and that the idea of disassociation just "evolved" as the Regents were discussing new guiding principles for UGA cooperative organizations. He said the Regents kept asking themselves whether the Foundation was living up to the sixteen principles and most of the Regents agreed that it was not. "One thing led to another" and by the end of the meeting the Regents had voted unanimously to pull the plug on the Foundation, Wooten said.

Minutes of the May 25 meeting do not entirely support Wooten's recollection. There is no mention in the minutes of any vote on the issue, much less a unanimous one. Regarding the issue, the meeting minutes state:

> The Regents then took up the issue of presidential compensation and had
> a discussion about salary supplements for presidents. They discussed national

and market data on presidential compensation. They further discussed the System's historical practice of allowing cooperative organizations to supplement salary and recent problems associated with the University of Georgia Foundation, Inc.'s (the "UGA Foundation") payment of supplements.

There was additional discussion of the UGA Foundation and the Guiding Principles. Some Regents expressed concerns about accreditation and academics at UGA. This discussion led to the Regents' directing President Adams to give notice that UGA would terminate its memorandum of understanding with the UGA Foundation and no longer recognize it as a cooperative organization. The Regents further directed President Adams to send a letter to Lynda Courts, Chair of the UGA Foundation, saying that the Board had directed President Adams to send the letter beginning this process.

The Regents then discussed what would replace the UGA Foundation. They concluded that they needed to explore options regarding the establishment of a new foundation and that they should consider a 90-day reorganization period.

WHILE FOUNDATIONS SOMETIMES SQUABBLE with governing boards of universities, this move was unprecedented in higher education and caught the Foundation flat-footed. It was, in effect, a slap to the head of Foundation members and it got their attention.

Realizing they could not win in a head-on fight, members of the Foundation began a quiet campaign to settle their differences with the Regents. They again chose Blanchard as their point man. A UGA Law School graduate, Blanchard built Synovus Financial Corporation into a $30 billion company and is one of Georgia's most respected businessmen.

Blanchard and new Foundation Chair Lynda Courts began meeting with Meredith and Regents Vice Chair Joel Wooten. Griffin Bell, former Governor Joe Frank Harris, Augusta attorney Wyck Knox, and real estate developer Tom Cousins sometimes joined in the effort.

Bell, the elder statesman at King & Spalding, had been called in earlier to help settle an internal dispute among Foundation trustees over what to do about Adams's expenditures.

Meredith produced a list of "demands" necessary to get the Foundation back in the Regents' good graces, including a $300,000 deferred compensation package for Adams and a board of trustees that would be friendlier toward the president.

Blanchard presented the demands at the Foundation's specially-called June 30, 2004, meeting. According to Foundation minutes, Blanchard told his fellow trustees that to resolve the dispute the Foundation would have to pay $300,000 into Adams's deferred compensation account, contingent on Adams and the Regents signing a release of liability for any further payments for 2003 and 2004.

In addition, the Foundation would have to modify the existing deferred compensation agreement with Adams to provide that all amounts payable under the deferred compensation agreement are due and payable upon Adams ceasing to be employed as president of the university rather than in 2007 as originally provided.

Was this a signal that the Regents were willing to dump Adams? Foundation trustees certainly thought so.

Trustees Knox, Read Morton, and David Boyd, vocal critics of Adams, withdrew themselves from consideration for officer positions.

The trustees voted to restore Adams's deferred compensation and to make it payable upon his departure as president. They elected new officers who were seen as more friendly to the president and they agreed to allow the university to use the UGA trademark, which the Foundation owned.

Blanchard was ecstatic, saying he hoped the actions would end the controversy and restore the Foundation's standing as a cooperating partner with UGA. "I'm setting today, June 30, as a new era," Blanchard said. "I fully expect the Regents will also take the high road."

As THE DOG DAYS of summer 2004 approached, the dispute between the Foundation and Regents appeared to be heading for a happy ending. Foundation executive members quickly agreed to several of Adams's suggestions for new committee chairmen who were friendly toward the president.

On August 4, 2004, the Regents voted to rescind its May 25 directive to sever ties with the Foundation.

"You can count on us to be your friend, your ally and your partner," Blanchard told the Regents.

"This is a new beginning," Regents chairman Wooten said.

In November 2004 Blanchard wrote Meredith:

> We believe the Foundation has done everything you asked us to do with respect to our entire agenda pursuant to our discussions. We are still awaiting instructions on how to handle the $303,000 compensation for Dr. Adams for 2005. We have yet to receive instructions on the proper approach.

Negotiations continued until April 2005 and Blanchard and members of the Foundation's executive committee felt everything was moving smoothly toward a solution. They had spent months working with Meredith and Wooten to develop an acceptable operating agreement. Blanchard and Foundation president Lynda Courts had spent hours working out the details of the document that would guide the Foundation.

Only one issue remained unresolved—a memorandum of understanding between UGA and the Foundation outlining the relationship between the the two entities. The Foundation missed an April 12 deadline imposed by the Regents for signing off on the memorandum.

Foundation Chair Courts felt this was a minor issue because the Foundation had essentially agreed to all of the Regents demands. She faxed a letter to Chancellor Meredith notifying him that the executive committee would meet that day to approve the agreement and the full Foundation board would take up the issue at its May 26 meeting.

"That's the fastest we can get together," Courts said. "It was not a desire on our part not to cooperate. I don't know what we can do, other than pass it by executive committee Wednesday afternoon and present it to the full board when we meet in May."

But the Regents were having none of that. When they met on April 20 Wooten called them into executive session ostensibly "for the purpose of discussing personnel and compensation issues," according to the official minutes. When they emerged two hours later, Wooten reconvened the meeting and announced that the Regents were directing Adams to send a notice to the Foundation that it would no longer be recognized as a cooperative organization. Minutes of the meeting read, in part:

> At approximately 10:30 A.M. on Wednesday, April 20, 2005, Chair Joel O. Wooten, Jr. called for an Executive Session for the purpose of discussing personnel and compensation issues. With motion properly made and variously seconded, the Regents who were present voted unanimously to go into Executive Session. Those Regents were as follows: Chair Wooten, Vice Chair J. Timothy Shelnut, and Regents Hugh A. Carter, Jr., Connie Cater, William H. Cleveland, Julie Hunt, W. Mansfield Jennings, Jr., James R. Jolly, Donald M. Leebern, Jr., Elridge W. McMillan, Martin W. NeSmith, Doreen Stiles Poitevint, Richard L. Tucker, and Allan Vigil. Regent Patrick S. Pittard attended the Executive Session via conference call. In accordance with H.B. 278, Section 3 (amending O.C.G.A. § 50-14-4), an affidavit regarding this Executive Session is on file with the Chancellor's Office . . .
>
> At approximately 12:30 P.M., Chair Wooten reconvened the Board meeting in its regular session and announced that the Board of Regents was directing President Michael F. Adams of the University of Georgia ("UGA") to send a notice to the University of Georgia Foundation, Inc. (the "Foundation") communicating that the Foundation would no longer be recognized as a cooperative organization of UGA.

The Regents had apparently voted in executive session—a violation of the Georgia Open Records Law—or did not take a formal vote, which seems unlikely. Adams and his top staff were reportedly jubilant, giving each other "high fives" when the Regents' decision was announced.

Wooten explained that the Foundation was thumbing its nose at the Regents by not meeting the deadline for signing the memorandum of understanding. He said that thirty-three of the state's thirty-four institutions had already signed such memorandums—a statement he knew or should have known wasn't true. At least a half-dozen schools, including Georgia Tech and the Medical College of Georgia, had not inked agreements when Wooten made the statement. Thus, the sole reason cited by Wooten for the Regents' action on April 20, 2005, turns out to have been a sham. But the media never picked up on it and no one stepped forward to correct the record.

Atlanta attorney and Foundation trustee Read Morton, who was negotiating the agreement on behalf of the Foundation, said everyone on the executive committee knew Georgia Tech and MCG had not signed. But he said by then the Foundation simply wasn't being heard in the media. "Their PR machine was working overtime and we were totally ignored," Morton said.

Trustee executive committee member Wyck Knox said he had always understood that UGA was treated differently than Georgia Tech and MCG on this issue. Moreover, the UGA Foundation's executive committee, which was to meet April 20 to approve the memorandum of understanding, had full authority to bind the Foundation to the agreement. The full Foundation's approval would have been a mere formality.

"So what Wooten said is just not true but rather a smokescreen to justify what they wanted to do, get rid of the Foundation and start a new one," said Knox. "I do think what the Regents said for their justification for 'firing' UGA Foundation was a sham and it was all orchestrated by Adams who was present with his closest staff at the Regents' offices when the action was taken. The irony is that the firing resulted in UGA Foundation becoming stronger than ever since we were freed from the conflict of interest in having the UGA president dominate or influence the spending policy. Make no mistake, UGA Foundation continues to support UGA fully, but now resources are devoted to academic support and faculty support."

Regent Pittard, a former chair of the Foundation, said the Board simply got tired of dealing with the issue.

"I know Jimmy Blanchard was trying to broker a deal. He worked very hard. But deadline after deadline continued to be missed for all kinds of strange and unsubstantiated reasons," said Pittard.

And in an interview more than a year after the split, Pittard repeated the false assertion that only UGA had failed to sign the memorandum of understanding. "We meet monthly so each month we asked for the memorandum of understanding. All the other foundations in the state signed it. Everyone except the UGA Foundation. Finally the board of Regents said that's enough. That's it. Maybe the politics within the Foundation were such that the people who would agree to sign it couldn't deliver."

If the Foundation had grievances with Adams they should have taken them to the chancellor, said Pittard.

Two former Regents said that after the first separation vote in 2004, Regents meetings were "governed" by the dispute with the Foundation. More important issues took a back seat. Leebern was the strongest personality on the board and kept stirring the cauldron of conflict. Some Regents felt the very survival of the board was at stake.

Just like the Foundation, the Regents split into factions. Those who wanted to cut ties to the Foundation and those opposed, they said. However, unlike the Foundation, the Regents always presented a united front in public.

"It was presented [at Regents meetings] as though we were letting the Foundation run the board of Regents. That we were sacrificing one of our employees. I remember Don Leebern saying Mike has worked so hard and look at what they're doing to our boy," a Regent said. "I consider it all pettiness that never should have happened."

People familiar with the negotiations said Blanchard, Wooten, and the chancellor agreed on a deal that would give Adams a respectable time, perhaps a year, to step down as UGA's president. That deal fell through, however, when Meredith fell out of favor with the governor and the majority of Regents.

"I think somebody wrote a check they couldn't cash," said former UGA vice president Hank Huckaby.

One former Regent said the board no longer functions independently as required by law. "It's run by the governor. The new chancellor was hand-picked by the governor. It wasn't really a board appointment," the former Regent said.

Perdue interviewed all three finalists for Meredith's replacement causing some critics to accuse the governor of improperly meddling in the Regents business.

The Regents ultimately chose Erroll Davis, the former CEO of Alliant Energy in Wisconsin. David Perdue, the governor's cousin, is on the board of directors of Alliant.

THE DISPUTE TOOK A toll on everyone involved, said Arlethia Perry-Johnson, former long-time spokesperson for the Board of Regents. "Seeing friendships crash and burn. Relationships that had been fostered over the years disintegrate. Those were the things that were difficult. Seeing a well-respected member of the board reduced to tears. Those were the things that were very trying," she said.

The Regents action hit Blanchard like a sucker punch and he fired off an uncharacteristic e-mail to Wooten and Meredith the next day.

"The recent actions of the Regents are an abomination and the act of bully," Blanchard wrote. "Consider me an adversary, rather than an ally. The system of governance of our University System is broken and I intend to be a part of the effort to fix it."

Wooten shot back with his own e-mail saying that it was the Foundation trustees who were being bullies.

"Despite the Foundation's public statements that it would be a 'cooperative organization' a certain group of trustees never stopped their efforts to frustrate the administration of the University of Georgia," Wooten wrote.

Bell, who had persuaded Foundation trustees to present the Deloitte & Touche audit report to the Regents instead of going directly to the state attorney general, said he met with Meredith several times and felt they had an agreement that would settle the dispute.

"I think we made peace and it never came to pass," Bell said. "I finally decided he was not the last word. I think somebody on the Regents was but I never did find out who it was. I know there was great celebration on the Regents when they expelled the Foundation. They expelled the Foundation and the way I saw it they had no good reason to do that. All they had to do was make peace. And we just got the back of the hand is what we got."

The unflappable Blanchard felt he had been double-crossed.

Throughout the summer of 2004, Blanchard, Wooten, Meredith and others worked secretly on coming up with a solution to end the controversy. The Foundation essentially agreed to meet all of the chancellor's and Regents' demands including Adams's pay supplement.

"[Wooten] made the commitment that they were going to get rid of Adams. They wanted us to pay something. Pay this and pay that. We agreed to do it and Adams was going to be gone and they flat did not deliver on what they promised us they were going to do," said Wyck Knox.

Knox believes he has figured out what happened though he has no proof. "The governor in all that period was trying to get rid of the chancellor. And the chancellor got the rug cut out from under him because the governor and his forces were trying to get rid of Tom [Meredith]. And Tom was trying, on the face of it, to get rid of Adams. But the Adams forces made a deal with the governor and Don Leebern and they got rid of Tom instead of Mike. Bottom line, the chairman and the chancellor didn't have the votes to deliver on what they promised us they were going to deliver."

"We now know we made a mistake in who we were dealing with and Griffin Bell had told us that early on. He had said, 'You know, I'm not sure this guy can deliver.' We should have done business with Leebern if we wanted to get the job done. That's what we should have done and we didn't."

Blanchard's angry e-mail was so unlike him that friends said he must have felt betrayed by the process. He has steadfastly refused to talk about the matter.

To an e-mail request for an interview, Blanchard politely refused:

> I played a very sensitive role on behalf of the Foundation and don't want to discuss the facts, circumstances and developments with respect to the UGA Foundation issues. You may have noticed that I have not discussed this with any of the newspapers or other reporters along the way and really don't want to start now. Thanks for your acceptance of my position.
>
> Best wishes,
>
> Jim Blanchard

After separating from the UGA Foundation, the Regents moved quickly to start a new private fundraising outfit, dubbed the Arch Foundation.

Meanwhile, the UGA Foundation voted not to disband and continues to manage an endowment of about half a billion dollars for the university. Last year, despite being declared a non-cooperative organization, the Foundation generated revenue of $75 million, all for the support and benefit of the university, according to finance officials. All the Foundation trustees serve without compensation.

11

THE KASWAN IMBROGLIO

The year 2003 wasn't pretty for UGA President Michael Adams as revelations about decisions he made in the case of former veterinary professor Renee Kaswan are proving increasingly clear. Kaswan is the inventor of Restasis, a medical breakthrough for the treatment of dry eye, with the potential of $300 million or more of annual revenue. Instead, the UGA Research Foundation headed by Adams sold short and it may have cost Georgia more than $200 million in patent revenues.

On top of that, the announcement in June 2003 of his decision to end Vince Dooley's career triggered an explosion of public rancor. Then in October, the Deloitte & Touche audit brought into question Adams's judgment as well as his ethics.

Moreover, the state was in an economic lull, and lagging tax collections had caused Governor Sonny Perdue to order across-the-board budget cuts that reduced the university's funding by $52 million in 2003. The Board of Regents ordered a 15 percent increase in tuition—the largest increase in two decades. And there was talk of another 5 percent budget reduction the next year. Politicians expressed concern that the state's lottery wouldn't produce enough profits to fully fund the popular HOPE Scholarship program, which pays the tuition of virtually all incoming UGA freshmen.

Adams considered the situation desperate enough that he wrote a column in the *Atlanta Journal-Constitution* warning of the dire consequences of more budget cuts. "While money is not the sole determinant of quality in higher education, Georgians must recognize that there is no such thing as cheap excellence," he wrote. And he noted that Georgia isn't alone. Nearly every public university in the country faces the same financial worries. Government funding for public universities had been dwindling for years. The nation,

Adams said, is "dangerously close" to a higher education system that offers top quality only in its private institutions.

But there was a ray of economic sunshine just over the horizon. The U.S. Food and Drug Administration—the FDA—in a surprise decision on Christmas Eve 2002, had approved Kaswan's invention for widespread use. The giant pharmaceutical company, Allergan, Inc., which held the license to produce Restasis, had begun marketing it in April 2003.

Restasis promised prestige and profits for the cash-strapped university because UGA held the patents and was poised to reap hundreds of millions in royalty payments from Allergan.

Although she had left her teaching position at the veterinary medicine school in 1996, Kaswan had continued to push the FDA and pharmaceutical companies to bring her product to market. Kaswan too, was in for a big payday. Her contract with the UGA Research Foundation would pay her 35 percent of the royalties paid to UGA by Allergan.

It should have been a glorious conclusion to a thirty-year effort. Instead, it turned into a financial and legal nightmare that embroiled the university in an ongoing legal battle and cost the school $220 million in royalties. None of this was an issue in the Adams-UGA Foundation contretemps or the resulting Deloitte & Touche audit. But how it happened is a story of intrigue, manipulation, and another secret deal orchestrated by President Adams, who also chairs the university's research foundation.

THE RESTASIS STORY BEGINS in the 1980s when Dr. Renee Kaswan, then in her final year as a veterinary student at the University of Georgia, began experimenting with a treatment for "dry eye" in small animals. The painful condition can lead to eventual blindness.

The only treatment at the time was an operation to reposition the salivary duct from the mouth to the eye, allowing the animal to, in effect, spit in its own eye for lubrication. While assisting her professor in the surgical procedure, Kaswan wondered if anyone had done a biopsy to try to discover the cause of dry eye in animals. Not that he was aware of, her professor said. They decided to send a sample of a diseased tear duct to the laboratory. The lab result suggested the condition was caused by an autoimmune response where an organism attacks its tissue. This was also known to be the usual cause of dry eye in humans.

Kaswan made an instant decision to focus her career in ophthalmology. She persuaded the university to create a residency program in the field and to make her its first student. Here, she felt, was a chance to enter uncharted waters and possibly to find a cure for a common and painful condition afflicting thousands of animals and people worldwide.

She reasoned that if dry eye was caused by an autoimmune response and the response could be interrupted, then perhaps the condition was reversible. She knew that immunosuppressant cyclosporine was commonly used to prevent organ rejection in transplant patients. Perhaps it could also reverse the autoimmune response that caused dry eye in animals.

While using cyclosporine eye drops to treat a dog for corneal inflammation, Kaswan noticed the drops caused an increase in tear production. She mentioned this observation to Dr. Keith Green, director of ophthalmic research at the Medical College of Georgia, who was taking Sandimmune, an oral cyclosporine, following a kidney transplant. Green said he'd noticed excessive tear production since his surgery but hadn't connected it to the cyclosporine.

Intrigued, Kaswan tried the drops on three more dogs with the same positive results. And when the university's famed football mascot Uga IV, developed dry eye in 1985, his owner, Savannah lawyer Sonny Seiler, brought the bulldog in for treatment. The treatment cured Uga IV and he returned to the sidelines and completed an illustrious 77-27-4 mascot career that included Vince Dooley's last game as head football coach. Without the treatment Uga IV would have gone blind.

In 1988 the university licensed KB Visions, a company owned by Kaswan, to market her product for veterinary use. She sublicensed it to Schering Plough, which marketed the treatment as Optimmune. Another seven years passed before Kaswan won FDA approval of Optimmune for widespread use on small animals.

Kaswan now had a nice steady income from royalties from Optimmune, and she operated an animal hospital in Atlanta. However, she continued her efforts to gain approval for a product that could be used to treat dry eye in humans. A self-described "noodge" who sometimes irritates people with her insistent behavior, Kaswan wasn't winning friends at the UGA Research Foundation or with the pharmaceutical companies.

Zealously protective of her patent rights, Kaswan used her private company, KB Visions, to file suit against pharmacy compounding companies that were producing her invention without paying royalties to the university. Kaswan was trying to protect patents which the university held and felt she was doing the university a favor. Initially, the university favored Kaswan's aggressive tactics in defending the patents. The university's own lawyers sent out hundreds of "cease and desist" letters to compounding pharmacies that were distributing a generic version of Optimmune. Eventually, university attorneys asked Kaswan to write the letters directly to the pharmacies. And in the 1990s it authorized her to sue pharmacies that were not licensed to use Optimmune and who were not paying royalties to Kaswan and the university. But when the pharmacy companies responded to her by challenging the validity of the patents, university officials panicked and intervened on behalf of the pharmacies. Kaswan maintained these were standard legal responses by the pharmacies and that the patents were never in danger and time has proven her right. Nevertheless, university officials sided with the pharmacies and against Kaswan. She claims university officials were just trying to intimidate her into going away. Her aggressive tactics had become a bothersome.

While working to get FDA approval for Optimmune, Kaswan had been simultaneously pressing Sandoz Pharmaceuticals, the original licensee, to complete human testing and gain FDA approval for human use. Between 1988 and 1992 she wrote 139 letters to the company prodding them to move faster. In 1993, she helped the university recruit and license Allergan to take over the study on humans from Sandoz. She collaborated with Allergan scientists on the human testing and when that effort faltered she talked university officials into pressing the company into giving her project a higher priority.

Still, they seemed to be making little progress and in 1999 the FDA held up Allergan's application for human eye drops. Frustrated with the bureaucracy, Kaswan began negotiation with the university's Research Foundation to assign her control of the patents so she could pursue an effort to win FDA approval. Negotiations dragged on for eighteen months until in late 2002 officials at the Research Foundation agreed in writing to assign her the patents. Assigning the patent rights to Kaswan meant that she would receive 75 percent of any future royalties should the product ever meet FDA approval. Draft contracts initiating the rights transfer were being completed when the FDA surprised everyone by approving Allergan's Restasis product for use on humans on December 24, 2002.

That's when things began to get ugly. Seeing an opportunity for a new and significant income stream for the cash-strapped university, university officials immediately reneged on their promise to assign her the patents, informing her of the decision on January 6, 2003. Kaswan and her attorneys argued that the patent assignment to her was a "done deal" and threatened legal action.

Kaswan was hoping to avoid long legal entanglement. She appealed in a letter to research vice president Gordhan L. Patel to a sit-down to discuss a solution that would be agreeable to all. But the university was adamant. Patel responded in a January 13 letter telling Kaswan that, in effect, there was nothing to talk about "given the lawsuits in which the validity of our patents is challenged and the threats of future litigation." A copy of the letter was sent to Adams.

UGA then initiated a pitched legal battle against Kaswan and her company. They hired the Atlanta law firm Sutherland Asbill & Brennan to represent the research foundation. The university then intervened on behalf of three compounding pharmacies in lawsuits that KB Visions had filed, one of which university officials had authorized in writing. In February 2003, research foundation lawyers opposed KB Visions' motion seeking a summary judgment in federal court that the patents, which were held by UGA, were in fact valid. This legal maneuver preventing a declaration of validity gave the university cover to continue legal claims against Kaswan and her company.

University lawyers initiated lawsuits against Kaswan over minor violations of the veterinary license. They accused her of not properly reporting quarterly income and not providing proper sublicensing agreements although Kaswan said she had reported the information in the same way for a decade. They filed suit in federal court accusing Kaswan of invoking, without permission, the university's name in patent enforcement letters to companies who were using her veterinary medicine, Optimmune, without paying royalties to her and the university. The university acknowledged that the letters were identical to letters the research foundation had itself previously sent to pharmacies in an effort to enforce its patents.

Kaswan had left the veterinary school in 1996 to found a veterinary hospital in Atlanta and was dependant on income from the hospital and on the royalties from Optimmune. She was understandably defensive of the patents and felt the university should share her concerns. But UGA officials had bigger fish to fry. A 1993 agreement between Allergan and the Research Foundation required the company to pay the university 7 percent of its net sales through the end of 2009 when the patent was due to expire. If the company was able to get the patent extended for an additional five years (which it did), the royalties would drop to 5 percent.

In April 2003 Allergan had began marketing Restasis for dry eyes in humans. The product, according to Allergan and UGA, had potential annual sales of $300–$500 million. Sales at that level would produce annual royalties of between $21 million and $35 million. It almost certainly would be the most profitable patent in the history of the of the UGA Research Foundation. And with government support for UGA dwindling, the cash-strapped university was keen to exploit the invention.

Even before Restasis hit the market Allergan approached the university with an offer to buy out the royalty agreement with a one-time payment. But first, they wanted assurances from the university that UGARF had full authority to negotiate the buy-down agreement and that it would be kept secret from Kaswan. UGA agreed and the two sides began meeting.

Allergan officials noted the university was hurting for cash and also reminded research foundation officials that there were no guarantees that its patents would hold. Besides, company officials said, there was another product seeking FDA approval that could compete with Restasis. Accepting a deal would guarantee UGA a big payday immediately and remove uncertainties about the patent validity and the level of sales and royalties. Company negotiators brought up budget stresses affecting the university at the time.

"It was," one observer said, "like waving a small carrot in front of a hungry rabbit."

Allergan offered a one-time payment of $13.8 million.

The university said "thanks but no thanks" and countered with a $47.6 million offer.

On August 29, 2003 the research foundation's executive committee, made up mostly of senior university officials, met to consider another Allergan offer—this one for $22 million in lieu of all royalty payments. The executive committee, which Adams heads, has full authority to act on behalf of the entire research foundation board of directors. In 2003 the executive committee consisted of Adams as president; UGA Vice President for Research Gordhan Patel, executive vice president and chair; UGA Provost Arnett Mace, vice chairman; UGA Senior Vice President Henry Huckaby, financial vice president and treasurer; chemistry professor Charles R. Kutal; F. Abit Massey and Jane Willson. Five of the seven members answer directly or indirectly to Adams.

Again the executive committee said "no" to Allergan's offer. Committee members noted that Allergan's offer was based on sales of $200 million a year even though the company itself had projected $300 million to $500 million in annual sales. Moreover, the offer was based on a five-year period when they fully expected to get a five-year extension on the patents. But even without the extension, university officials noted that royalty payments would exceed Allergan's offer. Finally, they said an agreement would have to include indemnification for patent infringements and "other claims" that might be brought against the university. University officials recognized the potential for legal problems if they excluded Kaswan from the negotiations. They wanted money for legal expenses and indemnification if Kaswan won a lawsuit.

Negotiations between Allergan and the research foundation continued through the summer and Allergan kept sweetening their offers. Finally, on November 20, 2003 Allergan made another offer to executive committee. They bumped the lump-sum payment up $1 million to $23 million to cover the cost of legal expenses if Kaswan sued, which everyone considered likely. It also included $15 million in milestone payments. Allergan agreed to pay the university research foundation the $23 million within 30 days of signing the agreement and another $5 million the first year that sales hit $275 million and an additional $10 million when net sales hit $375 million. The agreement cut UGA's royalty from 7 percent to 2 percent through 2009, and eliminated the provision for an additional five-year payment at 5 percent through 2014. The committee decided to call a meeting of the full board the next day, November 21, to vote on the offer.

One board member wondered whether it was ethical to exclude Kaswan before agreeing to the deal. A Sutherland Asbill attorney advised against it, saying that Kaswan would probably try to get a temporary restraining order if they told her about deal before it was signed. In that case Allergan may withdraw the offer, he said. If they waited, she would probably sue but in either scenario the attorney said the university would probably win. The board then voted unanimously to accept the agreement.

Kaswan was dumfounded when she learned of the Allergan deal. Her attorney had been negotiating with Sutherland Asbill & Brennan lawyers all through the summer and fall to settle their disagreements.

"We even scheduled a mediator for December 16. We each paid him $10,000. All the while they were negotiating with and closing on their deal to sell my royalty stream to Allergan for an up front payment. UGARF had no intention to mediate. It was simply a distraction. Although attorneys for UGARF were asked direct questions about their interactions and communications to Allergan as late as November 2003, they lied about the subjects of their meetings in depositions to conceal the deal from me. I thought they were negotiating in good faith, but they were simultaneously doing the Allergan buy-down deal," said Kaswan.

The university's public relations machine, which cranks out hundreds of "good news" stories each year about the most inconsequential of campus activities and discoveries was eerily silent about the agreement—the largest single royalty payment in the school's history.

Kaswan was told of the agreement on December 12, 2003. She knew immediately it was a bad deal for the university. On December 15, 2003 she filed a lawsuit in Athens-Clarke Superior Court in an effort to stop the deal. Not only had she been the most actively involved in pushing her invention to market but she shared a financial stake in the deal. Moreover, she was more knowledgeable of the potential market value of Restasis than anyone at the university. That the university would exclude her from negotiations was not only unwise but personally hurtful.

Financial analysts hired by Kaswan for her court case project that UGA will receive $72 million from the deal. It's a nice payday. But under the original agreement, the university would receive $294 million in royalties. The secret deal will cost UGA some $222 million based on current projected sales. The figures are largely unchallenged by the university.

The lawsuit has been slowly winding its way through the court for five years, much of it under a veil of secrecy. In an e-mail response to my request to open the files, Superior Court Judge David Sweat said depositions and exhibits remain sealed because "they have not been used by the court." Thus, documents that may reveal the duplicity, perjury and unethical behavior remain under seal by order of the court.

In April 2007, Judge Sweat granted summary judgment in favor of the research foundation after sorting through dozens of motions and hearing months of legal arguments. Kaswan's contract with the university gives the institution complete control over the patent and had the authority to negotiate the deal without informing the inventor. The fact that the university made a bad deal with Allergan is relevant, Sweat said in his summary judgment, which is not under seal.

At the hearing on summary judgment, Kaswan's attorney Foy Devine pointed out that Allergan acknowledged in internal memorandums that it would have been willing to pay the university up to $71 million, more than three times the amount of the contract. In one exchange with Kaswan's attorney, Foy Devine, Judge Sweat left little doubt about what he thought of the university's actions.

> The Court: But you're—They made a bad deal.
> Devine: Pardon?
> The Court: UGARF made a bad deal.
> Devine: They not only made a bad deal, your honor, and they made a horribly bad deal.
> The Court: That doesn't make it illegal.
> Devine: Not in . . .
> The Court: It may be stupid.

Nevertheless, Judge Sweat ruled against Kaswan's claim that the research foundation and Allergan conspired to commit fraud. He said the university's policies vest wide latitude in how it administers patents and inventions created by the faculty and staff.

"No doubt many of the university faculty and staff may be dissatisfied with those provisions that limit their ability to direct development of products that may become commercially viable based on the inventions," Sweat said, "but these agreements leave little question that the employees assignment of the patent vests the decision making authority to the University of Georgia Research Foundation."

Adding further insult, Judge Sweat ruled that the university could withhold part of her share of the royalties to pay for the legal costs of the research foundations. Essentially, Kaswan is paying the research foundation's legal bills as well as her own. Nevertheless, Kaswan vows not to go away.

Adams brushed aside the entire episode as not rising to the level of "institutional concern."

In a sworn deposition in the federal suit on August 13, 2003, Adams claimed to have learned of the possible lawsuits a couple of months earlier at a research foundation board meeting. As for Kaswan, who was named UGA's "inventor of the year" in 1998, Adams's first full year at Georgia, Adams said he didn't recognize the name at the time. However, court documents suggest otherwise.

Judy Curry, the research foundation's legal counsel, wrote Adams January 21, 2003 regarding the FDA approval of Restasis. "You may have heard the news that Allergan's dry eye product, Restasis, has received FDA approval," Curry wrote. "This is very good news because UGARF holds the patent on which the product is based and will receive royalties on sales thorough the life of the patent . . . Based on annual gross sales of $100 million, UGARF's royalties would be about six million. As you know the inventor on this product is Dr. Renee Kaswan."

In March Curry again wrote the president updating him on legal action the research foundation had taken against Kaswan. Both letters were marked "attorney client privileged."

Kaswan is convinced that Adams orchestrated the deal to make himself look good without regard for the long-term damage to the university. "Even if it weren't a horrible financial deal for the school long-term, such treatment of a researcher and inventor will damage the school's reputation and make recruitment of top researchers more difficult," she says.

"Michael Adams lies so smoothly and automatically it's frightening," Kaswan said. "What he did in this situation was so underhanded that it's hard for people to conceive that a president of a major university would behave this way. It is deeply disturbing that UGA's defense in the Restasis buy-down case, which cost the university over $220 million, hinged on the legal argument that the school's Intellectual Property Policy, which all employees are required to sign as a condition of employment, is so severely one-sided that the inventor has no rights," Kaswan said. "UGA lawyers claimed the UGA Intellectual Property policy evades even the usual requirements for good faith and fair dealing inherent in all other employment contracts."

12

THE ATTORNEY GENERAL

Under Georgia law, the office of the state attorney general is charged with prosecuting public corruption cases. However, the office has no investigators and relies on fact-finding from the Georgia Bureau of Investigation or local authorities. On the release of the Deloitte & Touche report in October 2003, Attorney General Thurbert Baker immediately announced that his office was reviewing the audit report. Baker said he would make a determination about whether to file criminal charges but gave no timetable.

Months passed with no report. Inquiries to Baker's office by news reporters got only an official "no comment," although reporters were assured privately that the AG's office was looking into the matter and would soon have a public pronouncement. Reporters took the attorney general at his word and waited.

One prominent UGA donor, Atlanta attorney Robert W. Miller, soon grew weary of waiting. As described in Chapter 10, Miller had written UGA Foundation Chairman Jack Rooker a few days after the audit was released urging Rooker to seek refunds of apparently misspent Foundation monies and to refer the matter to the state's attorney general. Rooker did not respond.

Between February and June 2004 Miller fired off a series of letters directly to Attorney General Baker, seeking follow-up investigations of the audit findings. Miller wanted the attorney general to look into payments to architect Al Filoni; payments committed by President Adams to former football coach Jim Donnan; and the alleged solicitation of a job for Kathryn Costello by UGA Senior Vice President Steve Wrigley. Fundraiser Charles Witzleben had told auditors that Wrigley urged him to hire Costello and conceal her salary within other billings. There were contradictory accounts of the conversations involved, but Miller wrote Baker that if the auditors were correct, Wrigley had advanced a criminal scheme to defraud the Foundation or the university.

"I believe this serious allegation should be investigated by you so that the conflict in statements can be resolved by use of your subpoena and other investigative powers and appropriate action, if warranted, can be taken," Miller wrote.

By this time, the media had bought into Adams's and the Regents' storyline that the dispute was all about Vince Dooley. Miller, however, was not a football fan and he was frustrated by what he saw as an ongoing whitewash of serious allegations. In a February 27, 2004, letter to Baker, Miller sought to separate his concerns from the Dooley controversy:

> I have not written this letter because of actions taken or not taken with regard to Vince Dooley. Indeed, I am weary of the Board of Regents, the University System Chancellor and the *Atlanta Journal-Constitution* claiming mindlessly that expressions of concern over misuse of Foundation and other funds by the University's administration come solely from angry Vince Dooley supporters. What I am is a citizen and UGA alumnus who thinks the attorney general should exercise his authority, investigate some serious allegations and take appropriate actions.

In a separate letter, Miller also noted that Baker's office had acted quickly on a complaint by the Atlanta newspaper about the Foundation closing its meetings by ordering that its meetings be open to the public:

> I trust and assume that you and the Department of Law will act with comparable promptness to investigate the matters described in my letter to you earlier today. Those matters go to the substance of funds used by Dr. Adams and the university administration and deserve at least equally prompt action.

Miller received a puzzling response to his letters from Assistant Attorney General Samantha M. Rein on March 11, 2004. She essentially told him that the attorney general and assistants are prohibited from representing or giving legal advice to private individuals: "As a result, our office is unfortunately unable to assist you in this matter."

An incredulous Miller shot back a March 13 letter noting that the attorney general's duties include prosecuting public corruption cases and conducting special investigations in questionable activity concerning any state agency or department, which is precisely what he had urged Baker to do.

On April 30, Deputy Attorney General Michael Hobbs finally responded to Miller, acknowledging that he had "raised important issues" and promising a full review of the Deloitte & Touche findings.

"Please be advised that I am now in the process of reviewing the Deloitte & Touche report, the response to the report provided to the Board of Regents by management at the University of Georgia, as well as the Board's October 29, 2003 statement in response to the report," Hobbs's letter states. "Thank you for bringing your concerns to the attention of this office."

It was the last Miller ever heard from the attorney general.

DESPITE A STATEWIDE UPROAR, Miller was apparently the only citizen who wrote to the attorney general seeking an investigation. Nevertheless, Baker expressed interest, publicly at least, in delving into the auditors' findings. He identified three areas of interest in the report that merited "review." They were the same three items that Miller had mentioned.

One was the $74,000 payment to Pittsburgh architect Al Filoni, hired by Adams, without authorization and without a bid process, to review the plans for a proposed new alumni center. Adams's excuse was that he hired Filoni, a personal friend, as a consultant and not as an architect, and therefore he didn't have to go through proper bidding procedures. However, when the university refused to pay Filoni, presumably because of how he was hired, the UGA Foundation ended up footing the bill.

A second area of interest, Baker said, was the secret side agreement that Adams struck with football coach Jim Donnan without getting the Athletic Association Board's approval. That agreement, which Adams insisted be kept from even the athletic board's attorney, cost the university $250,000 when Adams subsequently fired Donnan. Then Athletic Director Vince Dooley and Floyd Newton, the athletic board's attorney, claimed that UGA Legal Affairs Executive Director Steve Shewmaker wanted them to make the payment without bringing it to the Athletics Board. Shewmaker denied that allegation.

The final and most intriguing issue that Baker claimed he was looking into involved the previously described conversation Adams's assistant Steve Wrigley had with fundraising consultant Charles Witzleben regarding the possible employment of Kathryn Costello.

In May 2004, Baker told the *Athens Banner-Herald* that his office was not yet calling the review a full-blown investigation, saying it was still in the "fact-finding phase" and was being reviewed by lawyers who specialize in issues pertaining to UGA. If a basis was found for the allegations in the audit, it could become a full-blown investigation, Baker said. He added that there was no timeline for completing the review which could turn up anything from a minor glitch in the system to human error to criminal wrong-doing.

A year after Baker's statement to the Athens newspaper, the *Atlanta Journal-Constitution* printed a brief story which quoted Russ Willard, the attorney general's spokesman, as saying Baker "still has the matter under review." Meanwhile, obliging and compliant news media waited for word from Baker's office that never came.

SHORTLY AFTER I BEGAN research for this book in early August 2006, I filed a request under Georgia's Open Records statute for all documents in the attorney general's possession regarding the Deloitte & Touche audit. I also asked for any investigative files, preliminary or otherwise, in the attorney general's office. I got a prompt e-mail reply from Russ Willard stating that the records I was seeking were exempt from release under a section of the Open Records Law (OCGA 50-18-72(a)(4)) that allows active investigative files to be kept secret. I called Willard to discuss the matter and he assured me that indeed there was an open investigation. That was almost three years after the attorney general had said in October 2003 that his office was reviewing the Deloitte & Touche findings. I was, to say the least, surprised that Baker's office claimed its work on the matter was still active.

There was simply no way a three-year investigation of the UGA president could have escaped everyone's attention. The only logical conclusion was that the investigation had been shelved, yet Baker didn't want to release any documents.

At the same time, Baker had been a consistent supporter of open government. He had sided with the media in forcing the UGA Foundation, a private corporation, to open its records and meetings to the press, citing its public purpose. Was the great defender of open government hiding behind an exemption in the law to avoid handling this hot potato? There had to be another answer.

In the summer of 2006 Baker was in the middle of a hotly contested reelection campaign and he wasn't looking to make enemies, especially not politically powerful ones. Baker has been attorney general exactly as long as Michael Adams has been president of the University of Georgia; both assumed their present posts in June 1997. Baker was appointed by Governor Zell Miller to fill out the unexpired term of Republican Mike Bowers who resigned to run for governor. Baker was reelected to four year terms in 1998, 2002, and 2006.

The first African-American attorney general of Georgia since Reconstruction, Baker is a Democrat in an era of Republican domination in Georgia. Since the mid-1990s, Republicans, abetted by party-switching Democrats, have taken control of both of Georgia's legislative chambers and the offices of governor, state superintendent of schools, insurance commissioner, and other statewide offices. The most notable party switcher, Governor Sonny Perdue, was formerly in the Democratic leadership in the state senate before changing parties to run for governor.

Baker ran a "tough on crime" campaign in 2006 against Republican Perry McGuire. Baker claimed he pushed for tougher laws against violent criminals and aggressive enforcement of Georgia's death penalty.

Baker showed little inclination to push for more open government when he was sworn into office in 1997, telling a reporter who asked about the issue that he was more interested in Medicaid fraud and domestic abuse. Baker suggested there was little he could do about local government secrecy anyway because his office lacked jurisdiction to prosecute local officials who violate open government laws. And he declined to write a letter reminding local governments to familiarize themselves with Georgia's open meetings law, saying it would be too time-consuming and unnecessary.

However, after Governor Roy Barnes, whom Perdue defeated in 2002, a strong advocate of open government, threw his weight behind stronger open government laws, Baker quickly signed on. He created a open-government mediation program in an effort to work out conflicts between the press and local officials. He published a guide to open government for state and local officials. And his opinions consistently sided with transparency in government, which won him the hearts and minds of most media.

In 2003 Baker was rewarded with the Charles L. Weltner Freedom of Information Award given by the Georgia First Amendment Foundation, a nonprofit that pushes for transparency in government (I am a member). The award honors Georgians who, in the opinion of the First Amendment Foundation, have done the most for requiring government to conduct its business in the open.

Before Zell Miller appointed him attorney general, Baker served nine years in the Georgia House of Representatives. He was Governor Miller's choice for floor leader in the House, and in 1993 helped guide the popular HOPE Scholarship program through the legislature.

Although he stood up to Perdue by defying the governor's wishes in handling a redistricting case, Baker certainly wasn't searching out new enemies in 2006. And his strong ties to Zell Miller, and Miller's close relationship with Perdue and Adams, raise questions as to whether the attorney general took a pass on the Deloitte & Touche investigation for political reasons.

Baker, now an oddity among statewide officeholders due to both his race and his party, won 57 percent of the statewide vote to handily beat Perry McGuire in 2006. Baker also trounced McGuire in fundraising, collecting about $3 million in campaign contributions to McGuire's roughly $1 million.

AFTER THE ELECTION I filed another request to see the attorney general's records in December 2006. By then, I'd had an opportunity to interview most of the likely subjects who would have been contacted for questioning by the attorney general if there was an on-going investigation. Yet, I received the same response from Russ Willard. Open investigation. The file remained closed.

"I'm not buying it," I told Willard. "I can't find a single person who has been interviewed by your office."

I immediately phoned Deputy Attorney General Mike Hobbs and explained my request and Willard's response. Hobbs is a career bureaucrat and a straight-shooter who often gets the tough assignments. It wasn't surprising that the Deloitte & Touche audit ended up on his desk.

"I'll get back with you before the day is over," Hobbs promised. And he did. He said he couldn't tell me anything immediately but that in a few days I would get a letter that would explain everything.

On December 7, 2006, Russ Willard forwarded an e-mail with an attached letter signed by Attorney General Baker (but almost certainly written by Hobbs). The letter, dated December 5, 2006, was addressed to Regents Chairman Alan Vigil and Chancellor Erroll B. Davis Jr. (who by then had succeeded, respectively, Wooten and Meredith).

The seven-page letter, which completely escaped the media's attention, is remarkable for what it says—and what it doesn't say. (The complete text of the letter is in the appendix.)

Baker found several troubling things in the Deloitte & Touche report. He was particularly critical of Adams's secret side agreement to pay Coach Jim Donnan:

> While I cannot say definitively that Dr. Adams was without authority to agree to the $250,000 severance for Coach Donnan, if the findings of the Deloitte & Touche report are accurate the failure to notify the Association's governing body of a major decision concerning a large amount of money may constitute a violation of Dr. Adam's fiduciary obligation of forthrightness as president and as chairman of the Association.
>
> Frankly, I have never heard of any corporation, much less a non-profit such as the Athletic Association, entering into an oral contract which creates an obligation of a quarter million dollars. Not only would such thwart the legitimate interest of the citizens of this state in the manner in which this quasi-public body operates, but such is an indescribably bad business

practice. The Board of Regents should act to ensure that this kind of situation never occurs again.

It's curious that the attorney general's letter contained the phrase "*if the findings of the Deloitte & Touche report are accurate,*" since the facts surrounding this event were widely reported long before the Deloitte & Touche report and were undisputed.

Adams had acknowledged the secret verbal commitment to Donnan and admitted it was a mistake. The Athletic Association Board approved the payment retroactively to avoid a legal battle.

Baker called the Huckaby honorarium and Adams salary supplement from the UGA Foundation troubling. The payments were justified as additional compensation for exemplary work already performed. The attorney general said such payments "appear to violate the spirit of the Georgia Constitution."

Georgia's Constitution prohibits state government from granting gifts or gratuities or authorizing additional compensation after the service has been rendered. Baker wrote:

> The grant of additional private funds to a public official for performing his public duties in an exemplary manner raises serious conflict of interest issues that the constitutional provision was designed to preclude.

The letter doesn't mention one area that Attorney General Baker earlier had said was the most intriguing—the Wrigley-Witzleben telephone call.

And while Baker called some transactions cited by Deloitte & Touche possibly illegal or unconstitutional, he didn't address the attorney general's responsibility to attempt to recover any misappropriated state funds.

Baker said many of the problems experienced by the Board of Regents, the UGA Foundation, and the university stemmed from a failure to recognize that the Foundation is a separate entity. Foundations are established to benefit universities. However, foundations, by their very nature, "maintain a separate corporate existence and governance from the institutions they support," Baker wrote.

Indeed, UGA Foundation trustees felt that Adams acted as if he were the

CEO of the Foundation and tried to dictate to rather than work cooperatively with the Foundation.

Affiliated foundations were created largely because they are not limited to the budgetary and operational restrictions placed on government agencies. But the interests of the Foundations and the Regents and the institutions they serve are not always the same, Baker wrote. He said that the post-audit creation by the Regents of the Arch Foundation, operating under new procedures and guidelines, "has alleviated much of the public concern."

After receiving a copy of the attorney general's letter on December 7, I filed yet another request to see the "investigative file" that had taken three years to accumulate.

The file contained the following:

- A seven-page memorandum from King & Spalding to the Foundation Executive Committee outlining the fiduciary duties and liabilities of nonprofit directors.
- A five-page self-study on institutional control over athletics programs at the University of Georgia, conducted for the NCAA.
- Letters from Robert Miller requesting an attorney general's investigation into the Deloitte & Touche findings and responses from the attorney general's office,
- A handwritten note opening a case file and assigning it a "matter # 1040749." Also scribbled on the paper is a note to "review the Deloitte & Touche report"; "assign to MEH," an apparent reference to Deputy Attorney General Michael E. Hobbs; and "contact Robert W. Miller."
- A copy of the Deloitte & Touche report.
- UGA management's response to the Deloitte & Touche report.
- An attorney general's opinion to the chancellor regarding potential conflicts of interest of Regents who do business with the University System.
- The Board of Regents response to the Deloitte & Touche report.

In the Regents' response, they complained, as previously described, of having just three days to review the report before it was to be released to the public by the Foundation. A handwritten note, apparently made by the deputy attorney general reviewing the document, refers to this observation by the Regents as "2 [paragraphs] of whining."

Nothing in the attorney general's "investigative file" hints of a follow-up investigation as requested by Miller. No interviews. No telephone calls. No indications of an investigation of any kind.

And Miller said he never talked with anyone in the AG's office.

Did Baker's shop simply drop the ball on what might have been a meaningful criminal investigation? Or was there some more sinister reason for not following up on obvious leads?

Baker denied my request for an interview. "We're not going to comment on what took place in our investigation," spokesperson Russ Willard told me. "We're going to let the letter speak for itself."

Why did it take three and one-half years to write a letter?

"We're not going to comment on what took place in our investigation," Willard repeated. "We're going to let the letter speak for itself."

It does, and volumes.

"Our office took an extensive review of the various issues that have been raised in regard to the Board of Regents, member institutions and their supporting Foundations. We identified various issues that we felt needed to be addressed in the correspondence the attorney general sent to the chancellor. As far as our office is concerned this concludes the matter," said Willard.

It smacks of a cover up.

James Ponsoldt, the UGA law professor who urged the Board of Regents to seek a formal attorney general's investigation, thinks several potentially criminal issues needed investigation. He questioned whether the so-called "Rooker resolution" giving Adams a huge pay increase without Foundation board approval constitutes fraud. The Wrigley telephone call to Witzleben could constitute wire fraud. He said Adams might even be prosecuted under the federal "honest services" law, which the Feds often use to prosecute corrupt government officials based on the notion that the public is entitled to honest service from their public officials.

"Attorney General Baker represents the Foundation and the University.

He's also the chief law enforcement officer. What he chose to do in this case was to bury evidence of wrongdoing," said Ponsoldt.

Oliver Halle, the former FBI Special Agent and expert on white collar crime, who is familiar with forensic audits, read the Deloitte & Touche report and Adams's response. He said the report cried out for further investigation.

Griffin Bell agreed. The former U.S. attorney general said the audit report was simply a road map for further investigation by the Georgia attorney general or some other law enforcement agency. Bell said he did not recommend that the Foundation trustees turn over the audit to the attorney general themselves because he felt the Regents would see such a move as an effort to go around them. And he felt sure several of his friends on the Board of Regents would find the audit report alarming and would refer it to Baker's office.

At the time of these interviews, Griffin Bell, former federal judge, former U.S. attorney general, former special ambassador to the Helsinki Convention, former chief judge of the United States Court of Military Commission Review, and present senior counsel of one of the South's if not the nation's most powerful law firms, was in frail health and has since died. But he was perhaps the most credentialed and most respected legal figure in Georgia.

He said, "I also felt certain the Regents would be interested in this. I think it had to be given to the Regents—them and the attorney general. Under Georgia law only the attorney general has the authority to do anything and he never got into this. It's still the law that the attorney general is in charge of foundations. And I thought he would come in and say to the University of Georgia, 'This is what you've got to do. I'm looking at this and you've done something wrong or you haven't.' But just to leave it bobtailed like this didn't help anybody. Dr. Adams deserved to have it finished in a regular way."

13

Maybe Not Such
Strange Bedfellows

When Sonny Perdue won the office in 2002, he became Georgia's first Republican governor since Reconstruction. Few political observers would have looked ahead at that point and predicted that Don Leebern would retain his seat on the University System Board of Regents when his term ended in 2005. After all, Leebern had planted himself firmly in the Democrats' garden, fertilizing it with campaign contributions and reaping the rewards. Then-Democrat Zell Miller had appointed Leebern to consecutive seven-year terms on the Board of Regents and the wealthy liquor distributor had wasted little time in cozying up to Miller's successor, Roy Barnes. In June 2002, as the election approached, Leebern proclaimed a decade-long friendship with Barnes and his wife. "I admire him politically and all the things he stands for," Leebern told the *Atlanta Journal-Constitution*. When it was all over, Leebern family members had contributed $46,000 to Barnes's losing 2002 campaign, and it suddenly seemed that Leebern had positioned himself on the outside looking in.

Further, the incoming Perdue had promised "a new Georgia" to restore public trust in state government. Nothing short of a cultural sea change would reestablish a "principle-centered" government, Perdue said. At a national level, Perdue's political party and its preachers and talk show hosts were still taking Bill Clinton to the woodshed over his past extramarital dalliances. Meanwhile, practically in the shadow of the Georgia Arch, a prominent married member of the Board of Regents was openly shacked up with the university's gymnastics coach.

It seemed almost inconceivable that the church-going, moralistic Perdue, from small-town Bonaire, would reappoint such a man to anything, much less a coveted seat on the Regents board.

And that wasn't even all.

IN MAY 2004 LEEBERN'S paramour, Coach Suzanne Yoculan, rewarded six of her gymnasts with a two-night visit to New York City to celebrate winning an NCAA national championship. The delegation flew to New York on Regent Leebern's private jet and stayed at the posh Plaza Hotel. They attended a Broadway play, went shopping, and toured the Big Apple. In a small-world coincidence, the group ran into UGA Foundation Trustee Billy Espy, who was in New York on business. Later after he was back in Georgia, Espy mentioned the encounter to his friend Vince Dooley.

Dooley was still athletic director at the time and was obligated to notify Amy Chisholm, the university's NCAA compliance director. Chisholm verified that the outing in fact was a violation of NCAA bylaws that bar extra benefits for prospective, current, or former student-athletes. Athletic Director Damon Evans, who succeeded Dooley, then sent Yoculan a stern letter of reprimand. "I realize you thought this was permissible but, after twenty years of coaching, you should have asked," Evans wrote.

Because of the 2003 NCAA violations involving Georgia's men's basketball program, SEC Commissioner Mike Slive treated the New York incident as a major violation. Slive, whose growing impatience with rogue SEC athletics programs is well-known, stung Yoculan with the loss of a scholarship, banned her from off-campus recruiting in August 2005, and ordered her to attend an NCAA compliance rules seminar. The student athletes were each ordered to pay $730 (the conservatively estimated cost of the trip) to a charity of their choice.

(Neither the sanction nor the embarrassment has hindered the gymnastics team: in 2008 Georgia won its fourth straight gymnastics national championship.)

THE NEXT LEEBERN INCIDENT to leave university officials red-faced occurred in 2005 on the heels of the NCAA sanctions. Unbeknownst to the other Regents, Leebern's Georgia Crown distributing company had begun marketing wine emblazoned with the university's trademark arch. This was a direct violation of the Regents' own policy. The company agreed to stop marketing the California chardonnay and Cabernet Sauvignon only after the attorney general's office sent a letter to the Board of Regents recommending they tell Georgia Crown to cease and desist from using the university's trademark.

Deputy attorney general Daniel Formby said the labels were a serious misuse of university trademarks. "The Board of Regents is obligated to enforce vigorously its rights in and to the trademarks," Formby wrote. Two weeks later, Georgia Crown agreed to quit marketing the wine.

Plans to market the wine had been initiated by the Alumni staff as a way to make money for the university. Ironically, UGA officials were told repeatedly that they weren't authorized to market wine with the UGA trademark long before it hit grocery shelves.

In correspondence dated more than six months before Regents Chair Joel Wooten claimed the board learned of the wine endeavor, UGA Foundation attorney Floyd Newton warned them not to go forward.

"This is precisely the type of transaction the guidelines were intended to prohibit," Newton wrote. "Consequently I would not advise proceeding down the road on such a program unless the Board of Regents adopts a resolution or amendment to its existing policy."

UGA Foundation Director Cindy Coyle, whose office oversees use of University of Georgia trademarks, also told alumni staff to wait until she had gotten written approval from UGA senior administrators or the Regents. Instead the alumni office continued to move forward and the first bottles of wine arrived on shelves in June.

University officials pleaded ineptitude.

Wooten told former *AJC* reporter Kelly Simmons that they "probably should have asked Georgia Crown to stop shipping" when the office first heard of the wine being sold. But the Regents were busy with more important things at the time and were planning to review the policy that prevented using the trademark logo on alcoholic beverages.

"The rationale was that it was an old policy and we were in the process of reviewing the policy," Wooten said. Steve Wrigley, UGA senior vice president for external affairs, also told Simmons, "Internally we knew we couldn't put

a logo on the product and we knew we couldn't get a licensing agreement."
But, Wrigley said, the wine "got out there in the market before we were ready
for it to be in the market."

Georgia Crown sent the UGA Foundation a $9,000 check, designating
the ill-gotten money for President Michael Adams's supplemental expense
fund. The earmarking of the money was ironic because Adams had led a campaign against alcohol on campus, even urging TV networks to stop referring
to the annual Georgia-Florida football game in Jacksonville as "the world's
largest cocktail party." In any case, in the absence of a marketing agreement,
foundation officials subsequently returned the money.

On January 27, 2005, five days after Simmons's story about the logo
infringement appeared in the *Atlanta Journal-Constitution*, Leebern wrote a
letter to the newspaper defending his record as a Regent, his role in naming
Adams as president of UGA, and himself against detractors, including the
newspaper.

> Anyone who has held a position of public trust naturally makes political
> friends as well as enemies. And one's political enemies can always use the
> media to plant damaging story ideas. I'm experiencing that now, although
> I'm very proud of my fourteen-year service, spanning three governors, on
> the Board of Regents.
>
> It is up to the governor to reappoint me. That's his decision. But I'm
> willing to serve another term—and, yes, I support the general education
> agenda of Governor Sonny Perdue.
>
> I make no apology for heading the search committee that selected
> Michael Adams as president of the University of Georgia—even though
> some noisy diehards hold that against me. I make no apology for taking a
> stand with other regents to back Adams in his decision not to renew Vince
> Dooley's contract as UGA athletics director. And I'm proud of my regents
> record as a fiscal watchdog.
>
> Some journalists have blown out of proportion the good-faith decision
> of my company to distribute wine bearing the UGA arch at the request of
> the Alumni Association. It is a great fundraising tool, dozens of universities
> do it and the Alumni Association was its cheerleader. The regents had an

old rule barring such a policy, but it was to be rewritten.

This was discussed in an open regents meeting, yet there were no media stories—that is, until now. Georgia Crown sent a royalty check to a designated fund Adams could use for the Alumni Association. But it was properly returned when it was discovered the rule hadn't been revised.

I, along with other UGA boosters, sometimes provide a plane for administrators and coaches. I provided one for the Gym Dogs coach and a group of her close-knit former student-athletes for a goodbye trip. The coach took this trip openly, yet Dooley thought it was a violation. There was a claim that it was a secondary violation of NCAA Rule 16.02.3. Has anyone ever read that rule? It applies to current student-athletes, not former ones. In any event, in connection with this trip, tabloid gossip has been spread about my private life. No wonder polls consistently show Americans don't trust media "reporting."

It is a badge of honor that the *Atlanta Journal-Constitution* doesn't want me reappointed. I don't share its warped liberal agenda—and I make no apology for that.

The next day, Perdue reappointed Leebern to the Board of Regents. Leebern undoubtedly knew Perdue was going to reappoint him when he wrote the letter. The tone and tenor of the missive suggested to some that Perdue's office might have even helped craft it. The governor has expressed similar opinions about the newspaper.

ONE EXPLANATION FOR LEEBERN'S reappointment is that the political landscape in Georgia had changed. One can call Leebern many things, but slow and stupid are not among them. By 2005, Democrat election losses and defections had put the Republicans in control of the state senate and house and Perdue was up for reelection. Outspent nearly 10 to 1 in his 2002 race against Barnes, Perdue was building a war chest for the 2006 campaign. Leebern, the formerly loyal Democratic Party patron, kicked in $200,000 to the Georgia Republican Party.

Maybe that was all it took for Perdue, the champion of morality and "principle-centered" government, to discover that Don Leebern, beneath the bellicosity and the taste for high living and the open adultery, was an acceptable member of the governing board of the state's flagship university after all.

Ironically, it wouldn't have washed with former Governor Barnes. He counts himself a friend of Leebern, but he said he wouldn't have reappointed him.

"I'm loyal to my friends. [But] I'd have dropkicked Don," Barnes said. "I'd have brought him in and said, 'Don, you're a friend but you're radioactive.'"

14

CONCLUSION

It has been more than three years now since the Board of Regents cut loose the University of Georgia Foundation over its dispute with UGA President Michael Adams, and more than five years since Adams stunned Bulldog partisans by shoving Athletic Director Vince Dooley out the door. The unprecedented action of the Regents and the dismissal of Dooley shook the university to its core and shattered long-time relationships among prominent alumni.

Many observers predicted that Adams wouldn't weather the uproar over the Dooley firing and a subsequent damning forensic audit that accused him of mismanagement and laid out a solid case for a criminal investigation. For a college president to survive such a mess seems remarkable in an era when a politically insensitive comment can bring down a president of Harvard University. But Adams masterfully negotiated the minefields laid by his adversaries and emerged bloodied but still standing. Even his harshest critics had to be grudgingly impressed. Now in his eleventh year, Adams has served longer than all but seven of the university's twenty-one presidents.

This study of the controversies of the Adams era at the University of Georgia began in bemusement over a couple of simple questions: What was all the fuss really about? And how did Adams keep his job?

One thing that soon became clear in the research for the book was that the general public never understood the power struggle that had gone on in Athens and Atlanta. Nor could they have, because the particulars of the disputes were poorly reported and often mischaracterized by the state's mainstream media.

Early in the conflict, Adams managed to position the whole affair as a battle of control between the athletic support group versus the academic side of the house. In retrospect, this was never true. There were actually several conflicts involved—between Adams and the UGA Foundation, between the Foundation and the Board of Regents, between Adams and Vince Dooley, between Adams and the faculty, and broadly between the university interests and the political interests. You needed a scorecard just to keep up with the competing players, but over the course of numerous interviews, freedom-of-information filings, and a review of hundreds of pages of documents, a number of fundamental themes emerged. Throughout the research for this book, as we have seen in the preceding chapters, I was essentially exploring these key questions:

What should be expected of a major college president in terms of leadership, character, and judgment?

What is the role of affiliated fundraising foundations in an age of rising educational costs and declining state support?

What are the responsibilities of the board of trustees to maintain the separation of politics and academic governance, as well as to set a good example?

What should the public expect of a state's chief law enforcement officer when serious allegations are made concerning one of the state's most significant institutions?

The Tenure of Michael Adams

When he took over as president in 1997, Adams promised to take UGA "to the next level . . . The people of the state of Georgia deserve a flagship institution every bit as good as the citizens of Virginia or Michigan or California or North Carolina. I am committed to making the University of Georgia that kind of institution." His efforts to accomplish that goal can be evaluated in terms of financial stewardship, academic standing, university relationships, and his personal behavior.

FINANCIAL STEWARDSHIP. First among Adams's tasks was to improve the University's financial base, primarily by increasing private fundraising. This was expected to be his strength. More experienced and at home in politics than in academics, and packing a Rolodex fat with connections deep into the ascending Republican majorities in the state, Adams's ability to raise money (and with it the university's profile) was apparently one of his chief selling points to the presidential search committee that brought him from Centre College to Athens.

In light of those expectations, Adams has underperformed. This doesn't mean that he has had no success in fundraising. As his public relations staff points out, UGA's endowment has grown by $376.6 million over the past decade. Nonetheless, UGA lost ground to other schools in raising money from private sources, according to the New York-based Council on Aid to Education. UGA's endowment is smaller today than five of the twelve schools in the Southeastern Conference, but when Adams arrived in Athens, UGA's endowment was exceeded only by those of Vanderbilt and Florida. Since then Georgia has fallen below Kentucky, Tennessee, and Arkansas and remains well below Florida and Vandy.

During the same period Tennessee's endowment jumped by $427 million, Kentucky's by $585 million, and Florida's by $688 million. The disparity is even greater when UGA's numbers are compared with its fifteen "peer institutions" (as defined by the Board of Regents, national schools of similar size and with similar programs). Eight of the fifteen peer schools' total endowments exceed Georgia's $550 million, topped by the University of Michigan's $5.6 billion. It isn't that Georgia has been standing still. It's just that everybody has had to get into the game and others have been more successful than Georgia. According to the New York-based Council on Aid to Education, UGA raised $88.4 million in private donations during 2007, while the University of Virginia collected $282 million and the University of North Carolina $247 million.

In some other areas, Adams has been criticized as financially short-sighted. One example is the situation that now exists between the university and the UGA Foundation, in which one long-standing and effective fundraising group has basically been benched while a new foundation has been created, to the confusion of the public and of donors. The result is ineffectiveness. While the Regents implemented the rift, Adams instigated it. Another example is the drug patent case discussed in Chapter 12 in which former UGA researcher Renee Kaswan contends that Adams naively made a deal that shorted the university of $230 million or more. The Kaswan episode is telling. Its particulars reveal a penchant for secrecy and back-channel deals, a disregard for faculty, and a willingness to sacrifice long-term interests for immediate gain and acclaim. Interestingly, the terms worked out with the drug company over Kaswan's patent were hastily agreed to at a moment when Adams was under intense criticism. Some Adams critics have asked whether he was willing to settle for an upfront payment of $23 million, versus potentially hundreds of millions down the road, because he desperately needed to be able to say to the Regents that he had just brought a significant sum to the university. Only Adams knows the answer, but it is a fair question.

Lastly, Adams has presided over a number of questionable financial arrangements, as previously discussed, that have cost the university hundreds of thousands of dollars. The under-the-table commitment to former coach Donnan was one. The Adams-inspired purchase of a townhouse in Atlanta was another. The purchase of property in Costa Rica was another. And the redundant architectural expense for the still-unrealized Alumni Center is another.

However, Adams has certainly lived up to his reputation as a builder. He has championed projects that beautified the campus, turning parking lots into green space. Other projects include the $40 million Paul D. Coverdell Center for Biomedical and Health Research, a $43 million Student Learning Center, and a $79 million East Campus Village. The legislature has approved funding for the $45 million Special Collections Libraries. Multi-million dollar renovations and upgrades of a half-dozen other structures have been completed. And plans are well underway to establish a new Medical School in Athens. The school will be run by the Augusta-based Medical College of Georgia but will integrate services with UGA's biological sciences programs. The total value of construction during Adams's presidency is approaching $1 billion, according to university officials.

FINANCIAL SELF-INTEREST. On the other hand, Adams has done quite well for himself. The president's total compensation doubled in his first seven years at Georgia, from $281,498 in 1998 to $575,087 in 2004. The UGA Foundation had supplemented Adams's state salary until the Regents ended the Foundation's relationship with the University. Since then, the Regents have picked up Adams's salary supplement to keep his pay at roughly the same level. A 2005 survey by the American Association of University Professors put the median compensation for leaders of public research universities and public-college systems at $360,000. Adams earned $564,033 in 2005.

In the last three years his salary has leveled off. His total compensation package for 2007 was $575,731. That includes a base pay of $237,988, salary supplement of $116,614, longevity pay of $40,000, $150,000 deferred compensation, and $13,828 contribution to a executive retirement plan. Adams also receives a $15,500 housing allowance and a $1,800 life insurance allowance. Mary Adams, whose $48,000 a year payment essentially for being the wife of the president was an early issue of contention with the UGA Foundation, is no longer on the payroll.

Meanwhile, UGA faculty and staff went without a pay hike in 2003 and got what amounted to a 1 percent bump in the next two fiscal years. In testimony before a legislative subcommittee in 2006, Adams acknowledged that UGA has lost ground on faculty salaries. Between 2000 and 2005 national salaries increased by 19.2 percent while UGA's increased by 14.7 percent. During the same period UGA's average faculty pay dropped from sixth to twelfth among Georgia's fifteen peer institutions. Among SEC schools UGA dropped from second to third behind Florida and Vanderbilt. Adams acknowledged in 2008 that salaries at UGA under his tenure haven't kept up with other Southern research universities. In fact, Georgia ranks thirteenth out of the sixteen Southern states in the percentage of growth in salaries at top-tier universities during the last decade, according to the Southern Regional Education Board. And in the current economic climate, salaries aren't likely to improve. In December 2008, the Board of Regents ordered 6 percent cuts in budgets at all thirty-five state institutions of higher education.

ACADEMIC STANDING. Faculty compensation issues are especially worrisome in light of a 2005 survey on the Athens campus which showed that UGA freshmen studied an average of 12.7 hours a week—half of the time deemed necessary for academic success. Subsequently, a task force came up with recommendation for improving the school academically. One finding was that too many courses are taught by non-tenure track instructors and graduate assistants, a point that had been made by the faculty senate survey a year earlier. The new report suggested more competitive pay packages and sabbaticals to lure top-notch faculty. The task force also recommended scheduling more Friday classes to cut down on three-day partying.

Yet in 2007, for the first time in six years, UGA dropped out of the top twenty in the U.S. News & World Report's ranking of America's Best Colleges. The 2007 report also ranked UGA near the bottom of the nation's flagship institutions at offering access to minority and low-income students. A similar knock was received from the nonprofit Education Trust, which placed UGA near the bottom of its ranking of flagship institutions in offering access to minority and low-income students. For those minority students who did enter Georgia, however, the Education Trust gave an "A" for high graduation rates. Nonetheless, the 1961 desegregation of the University of Georgia was a defining moment in its history. While the administration has championed efforts to recruit more African American students to UGA, minorities still represent a small percentage of the total student body. And some black students have said they don't feel welcome.

UGA took a hit from the not-for-profit American Council of Trustees and Alumni (ACTA) in March 2008. The council placed UGA last among Georgia's largest four-year universities in the breadth of course requirements. UGA was the only school among the seven public universities surveyed that does not require students' exposure to government or history, according to the survey. The Washington-based nonprofit gave the entire university passing marks in composition, history, math, and science but an "F" for literature, foreign language, and economics. UGA also shared in a big fat "F" given to the entire University System of Georgia for intellectual diversity, a core value that ACTA says "lies at the very heart of educational enterprise." ACTA defines intellectual diversity as the free exchange of ideas. The council commissioned a national polling firm to conduct a survey of students at UGA and Georgia Tech to measure the level of freedom on campuses. "Far from indicating a healthy environment, the student responses underscore a significant perception that many Georgia university classrooms are hostile to a diversity of viewpoints," ACTA found. The council also gave the University System an "F" for cost-effectiveness, saying schools spend too much on administration and too little for instruction.

Adams has sought throughout his tenure at Georgia to publicly emphasize academics over athletics. But his meddling in athletics has tarnished the university's image, as in the scandal over the ridiculously easy exam questions administered to basketball players to help them maintain a high-enough GPA to stay on the team; the offending coach came to UGA as a result of Adams's intervention in the athletics hiring process. Adams has also continued the practice of giving presidential exemptions to talented athletes who wouldn't otherwise qualify to attend Georgia. Asked by a reporter about his policy of admitting marginal students, Adams replied, "We still have to compete in the [Southeastern Conference]." In fact, a 2006 NCAA report revealed that only 9 percent of UGA men's basketball players and 41 percent of football players who were accepted from 1996–99 graduated within six years. The graduation rate of basketball players was the second-worst among the 319 Division I institutions. Both rates were the worst among the twelve Southeastern Conference teams.

Further, figuring into the controversy Adams triggered by dismissing Vince Dooley was a general shift from previous presidents in how they dealt with the office of the athletic director. Obviously, Dooley was not simply another SEC athletic director. He was a Georgia institution. Even so, Adams overstepped the traditional role UGA presidents had taken toward the AD's office. He would later respond to the Deloitte & Touche audit by saying he was the target of a group of critics who were simply Dooley loyalists and who cared only about athletics. Yet, more than his predecessors in the president's office, Adams directly involved himself in decisions that were properly handled by the athletic director. Notable examples include the secret pay agreement and subsequent firing of football coach Jim Donnan and the personal intervention in the hiring of basketball coach Jim Harrick. Astoundingly, Adams even made disparaging public comments about the performance of Bulldog teams when they were not winning every game they played.

UNIVERSITY RELATIONSHIPS. Adams's perceived hypocrisy on the academics/athletics issue is no doubt only one factor in his uneasy relations with UGA faculty, culminating in a February 2004 vote of "no confidence" by 70 percent of the professors in Franklin College, the liberal arts program that is the university's largest college. Many faculty members had looked askance at Adams's thin academic credentials to begin with, while Adams's predecessor, the scholarly Charles Knapp, had been a campus favorite with professors and students alike. Modest by nature, Knapp governed by consensus and stressed academic excellence while leaving athletic decisions to Vince Dooley and others. By contrast, Adams behaved more like a corporate CEO, demanding a bigger office, more compensation, and spending the university's money like it was his own even as faculty salaries were stagnating.

In addition to surrounding himself with senior administrators whose loyalty seems to be first to him and secondly to the university, Adams also replaced every academic dean. Most went quietly. John Soloski, former dean of the Grady College of Journalism and Mass Communications did not. Accused of sexual harassment in 2005, Soloski was forced to resign. He subsequently sued, saying he hadn't been allowed to defend himself in the internal investigation and alleging that Adams had used the sexual harassment allegation to punish Soloski for refusing in 2003 to write a letter calling for an end to the controversy between Adams and the UGA Foundation. Soloski's lawsuit claims the intent of the letter "was to rebuild Adams's ailing credibility in the eyes of the public and university community."

U.S. Magistrate Judge Christopher Hagy issued a written opinion in December 2008 calling the university's finding of sexual harassment "a gross abuse of discretion." UGA spectacularly failed to meet legal standards necessary to prove harassment, Hagy wrote. He recommended that the university clear Soloski's name. Hagy laid out his conclusion in a report to U.S. District Judge Marvin Shoob, who had not made a final ruling at this writing.

Adams's critics will no doubt point to the Soloski case as being typical of his administration's pettiness. If criticism bothers him, Adams doesn't show it. In his April 2008 State of the University message Adams opined that the previous year had been the "best year ever" for UGA, citing an average SAT score of 1242 for incoming freshman and two Rhodes Scholars. UGA was the only public university with two Rhodes Scholars in 2007. Adams ticked off a list of research projects, new buildings, and accomplishments in athletics but called the new medical facility the most significant. "The development of such a campus on the Navy School property is perhaps the signature public service project of the early decades of the twenty-first century for this university," he said.

A man of considerable political skills, Adams has left no important politician's back un-slapped. In 2008, three former Georgia governors got their names on campus buildings. Former Governor Zell B. Miller, who supported Adams in his darkest hours, was honored for his public service. The building formerly known as the Student Learning Center is now the Zell B. Miller Student Learning Center. Former governors Ernest Vandiver and Joe Frank Harris also had campus structures named in their honor; Harris was another who stood by Adams during his fight with the UGA Foundation.

CHARACTER AND LEADERSHIP. Of all the areas in which a college president can be evaluated, this is the most subjective. However, a beginning point is that he must be like Caesar's wife: above suspicion. He not only is a highly placed, highly paid public official, but also the figurehead for an institution charged with the education and nurturing of young people. Tradition and culture are entrusted to his care.

It says something when a college president's detractors are the Griffin Bells and Vince Dooleys while his defenders are the Don Leeberns and the Sonny Perdues. And it says something when under-the-table contracts are kept secret, when petty financial manipulation and habitual obfuscation become routine, and when loyalty to an individual is demanded above loyalty to the institution. It says something when a university researcher's work results in a patent that had the potential of bringing in the single biggest financial contribution in the history of the school and, during negotiations, the president orders that the process be kept a secret from the researcher herself.

It also says something when at the 2008 Sugar Bowl the presidents of the participating schools, Georgia and Hawaii, were introduced to the fans and Hawaii's president was cheered while Georgia's was booed lustily. This, by the way, was the Sugar Bowl at which Adams, who moralizes about partying and drinking at campus football games, spent $138,000 on himself and a few dozen friends to whoop it up in New Orleans. The sum included $28,000 expenditure for a soiree at Pat O'Brien's on Bourbon Street hosted by the president and $9,000 for a food and beverage room at the Hilton. Adams saw no problem telling a reporter, "My sense is we probably do more than anybody else does, and no less. And of course," Adams added, "it's all paid for by athletic association monies, which is part of the revenue created by the bowl. So it's all part of the bowl culture . . ."

In short, Adams remains a polarizing figure. Some Georgians no doubt feel similar to Uga mascot owner Sonny Seiler, who says that while he doesn't agree with every decision Adams has made, he believes that Adams has basically done a good job at UGA, including spearheading the massive building effort that has transformed the campus. Adams still has the solid backing of Governor Sonny Perdue and a majority on the Board of Regents and apparently the new Arch Foundation.

Many others long to see his departure.

Vince Dooley's supporters still resent Adams's ham-handed handling of the iconic athletic director. Hackles were even raised in 2008 when UGA announced plans to immortalize Dooley by attaching his name to an athletics complex and by unveiling a fourteen-foot statue of him in a $2 million garden. The statue depicts Dooley being carried on the shoulders of offensive linemen Jeff Harper and Tim Morrison, members of his 1980 national championship team.

The gesture pleased Dooley but fans and former players remembered that Adams had consistently resisted their efforts to attach Dooley's name to UGA's football stadium.

They wanted Sanford Stadium to become Sanford-Dooley Stadium but Adams remarked that he "doesn't like hyphenated names," wrote *AJC* sports reporter Chip Towers.

"Every once in a while you think the fervor over Adams's treatment of Dooley a few years back has died down and then something like this comes around and you find out it hasn't. It's kind of like a volcano where the magma just goes dormant for a while before heating back up and resurfacing later," Towers wrote.

Atlanta public relations executive Bob Hope told Towers that, "If there ever is a Heisman Trophy for pettiness, Michael Adams will win it and there won't be a second place."

And Jeff Harper, depicted in the Dooley statue, wondered why Governor Perdue and other state officials haven't stepped forward in Dooley's behalf. "I don't know why the Regents haven't stepped up for Coach Dooley," he told Towers. "What about the governor? I'll tell you this. I'm giving no money to the University of Georgia until Michael Adams is gone. All Coach Dooley asked for was one more year and he wouldn't give it to him. Fire Adams and I'll resume my support."

Dooley, as always, was gracious after the December 1, 2008, ceremony at which Adams, Perdue and Senator Johnny Isakson spoke. "It's not about the 201 wins," Isakson said. "It's about the thousands of lives Coach Dooley touched."

After the ceremony, Dooley strolled to the $2 million garden built in his honor. "It's great that it's on the south part of campus where most of our sports are played. It's very beautiful and very fitting. These are the things that are most important to me," he said.

The Dooley athletic complex on the southwest end of campus includes Butts-Mehre Heritage Hall, Spec Towns Track, the Woodruff Practice Fields, Stegeman Coliseum, the Coliseum Training Facility, the Rankin M. Smith Sr. Student-Athlete Academic Center, Foley Baseball Field, the Dan Magill Tennis Complex including the Henry Feild Tennis Stadium and the Lindsey Hopkins Indoor Tennis Courts.

Dooley no doubt appreciated the honor. But accolades can't wash away the unease he feels for the man who heads his beloved Georgia. Dooley mostly kept his feelings to himself over the past five years, but in an interview in 2008, he spoke plainly.

"Adams is aggressive, outspoken and possesses good communication skills. Consequently he has developed some leadership techniques which has put him in key leadership positions. He is eloquent and sounds good but I believe that he is lacking in some of the most vital leadership principles . . . more so than any person I have been around in a responsible position. He is not trustworthy. Trust is the most precious and intangible leadership quality and Adams falls short in this vital principle," said Dooley. Adams, he said, has developed an ability to step out front and take credit when things are going well and push others forward if they go bad.

The Role of the UGA Foundation

Almost immediately after being named president, Adams began to have problems with some of the very people who most wanted to help him raise money, namely the members of the UGA Foundation. As the subsequent

Deloitte & Touche audit pointed out, there were problems with the Foundation's governance, yet no one can deny that the Foundation trustees were UGA loyalists, had money and access to money, and had a long track record of enabling growth in every facet of UGA affairs, both academic and athletic. These trustees were insiders and they were actively involved. To put it bluntly, Adams lost the confidence of key Foundation members because some of the trustees who dealt most directly with him came to see him as dishonest and money-grubbing.

Unbeknownst to the Foundation, even before arriving on campus on September 1, 1997, Adams had negotiated four years' paid tuition for his son Taylor to attend Emory University.

It was six years before the public found out that Regent Don Leebern, who headed the search committee that hired Adams, and then-Foundation President Dan Amos picked up the $89,000 tuition with tax-free donations to the UGA Foundation. Leebern's and Adams's relationship was further solidified when Leebern began paying Mary Adams $48,000 per year, also passed through the Foundation.

Once on campus, Adams wasted little time in finding soft spots in the UGA Foundation's financial rules and regulations. He took advantage of vague financial constraints to take questionable trips, buy expensive meals for himself and his senior staff, and even throw an invitation-only party for his son's law school graduation.

Foundation members were nonplussed by this behavior, which they had never experienced from previous presidents and had not anticipated from Adams. Representatives met with Adams to discusss the problems, tried to institute internal safeguards against spending abuses, and ultimately took away his Foundation-issued credit card. Finally, they instituted the Deloitte & Touche audit.

Foundation members go to great pains to stress that Adams's alleged financial improprieties, and his reactions to their efforts to rectify them, left them with few options in exercising their fiduciary responsibility. Many feel that Adams essentially was trying to gain complete personal control over the entire Foundation assets. At the same time, they concede that the controversy revealed shortcomings in Foundation governance and conflicts between the respective roles and responsibilities of the Foundation and the Board of Regents.

Many UGA Foundation trustees still despise Adams and see him as a charlatan or worse though they don't talk about it publicly. It doesn't help that he has beaten them politically at every turn.

Despite its sour relationship with Adams, the UGA Foundation continues to be the major financial supporter for the university and a more powerful force for fundraising than the new Arch Foundation. The UGAF endowment was about $550 million at the end of June 2008; the upstart Arch Foundation listed total assets of about $80 million.

So the University of Georgia will stumble along with two foundations competing for the loyalty of the alumni, and perhaps fall further and further behind other SEC universities in growing its endowment.

"It has been my experience that good leaders unite people," said Vince Dooley. "And in my forty-four years at Georgia I have not seen so much divisiveness among Georgia people who love their university. Because of the greater good of the university, most of this divisiveness which has been played out in public many times is now quiet and underground. Love for the university has taken top priority. Nevertheless, the best outward sign of this division is reflected in the university having two foundations which is unprecedented, counterproductive and vastly reduces the effectiveness of the university to maximize its great potential. One day we will again see one foundation united serving the university but only after we have a change of leadership."

It's impossible to accurately assess what impact the breakup has had on Georgia, especially on fundraising. The Archway to Excellence fundraising campaign supposedly exceeded its goal a year early with over $653 million in pledges. But to reach its goal, the university claims $152 million for priority ticket seating at athletic events, mainly football tickets, a category of revenue which had been explicitly excluded from the projected accounting during the planning of the campaign in 2000–02 by the UGA Foundation. However, the football priority seating revenues were added back in after the campaign was taken over by the new Arch Foundation. Without the seating revenues, the actual receipts as of June 30, 2008, would have been $458 million, well short of the campaign goal, according to the official campaign report. Meanwhile, the University of North Carolina, to which Adams likes to compare UGA, raised $2.38 billion in its fund-raising campaign which ended December, 31, 2007.

In spite of the current ill feelings, many Georgians believe that it's only a matter of time before the UGA and Arch Foundations join together. "Common sense will tell you that you can't have two foundations," says former Governor Roy Barnes. "I think it sends a signal that if nothing else that we have trouble running our own affairs. It's difficult to convince folks that we're world class but we can't control our own affairs."

The Role of the Board of Regents

In the 1940s, Governor Ellis Arnall tried to remove Georgia's academic institutions from the whims of the state's politicians. Sixty years later, it's apparent that whatever effort was made to separate politics from the University System Board of Regents has broken down completely.

The Regents laid the framework for its eventual conflict with the University of Georgia Foundation by using the foundation as a way to conceal the true salary of UGA's president. The policy of supplementing university presidents' salaries with private foundation funds began long before Adams arrival at UGA, and was being done at other state universities. The practice was seen as necessary by the Regents in order to be competitive with other institutions in attracting presidential candidates. But the salary supplements were an irritant to some UGA Foundation trustees who saw their role as support for students and professors. Gradually, the Chancellor and Board of Regents began to demand more and more for salary supplements. By 2004, the UGA Foundation was paying more than half of Adams's salary. The chain of command had become blurred and Foundation trustees felt they should have fiduciary responsibility over how their money was being spent and by whom. In demanding the salary supplements, the Regents had created that inherent conflict of interest. In 2004, in the wake of the dispute with the UGA Foundation, the Regents recognized the conflict and began paying presidents' full salaries with state funds. By then, however, the damage was done.

The Regents' next mistake was in allowing its oversight responsibility to be taken over through the political machinations of Leebern and Governor Perdue. In retrospect, it seems almost inconceivable that a university governing board—some members of which later admitted they had not even read the document—would have simply rejected out of hand the serious allegations contained within a forensic audit by a nationally recognized firm such as Deloitte & Touche, which had been commissioned for the investigation by a legal team headed by the senior partner of one of the nation's leading law firms, i.e., Griffin Bell of King & Spalding. And yet that is what happened in the Regents' rush to shoot the messenger.

Perdue, it now appears, was at least aware of and had given tacit approval of every act by the Board of Regents, which is, by the Constitution, supposed to be completely independent. As one former regent expressed it, "everything changed after Perdue came into office. Everything became political."

One of Perdue's closest allies explained it this way:

> When Perdue took office the Republicans felt Roy Barnes had so stacked the board with what he described as "political hacks" they were unable to get anything done. Perdue felt he needed to have input on the board and in Leebern, he found a vessel to deliver the governor's message. Perdue saw the need for strong leadership and he reappointed Leebern to a third term despite his considerable baggage.

In sticking with men like Leebern and Adams, the governor also sent a clear message to the people of Georgia that morals and ethical behavior matter on Sunday morning but have no place in the nether world of politics.

Regent Don Leebern still lives in Athens with Suzanne Yoculan while his wife, Betsy, resides in Columbus. In March 2006 he and Yoculan were walking their dogs near their home when a neighbor confronted them over their barking dogs. The then sixty-eight-year-old Leebern wound up in a fistfight with the neighbor, forty-nine-year-old Mason Lewis Bentley. Bentley ended up in the hospital with a collapsed lung, a broken nose, and facial cuts. Bentley told police Leebern challenged him to come to the street. Leebern said he was only defending himself after Bentley threw the first punch. No charges were filed.

Leebern apologized to his fellow Regents for the incident. University officials and fellow Regent Richard Tucker defended Leebern, as did President Adams.

"It has no bearing on his service," Tucker said at the time and Adams agreed. "He gets the big issues about as well as anybody I've ever worked with on a board," Adams said. "The service he has rendered to the university is exemplary."

In 2008, the Georgia Ethics Commission hit Leebern with a $37,750 civil penalty for failing to disclose to the state his personal finances for the years 2005 and 2006. Leebern dismissed the oversight as a minor annoyance.

The tragedy of Perdue's decision, perhaps not yet manifested, is the impact on future generations of Georgia leaders who will pass through the famous UGA arches. If such behavior is accepted and even rewarded by the state's top public official, what message does it send? To many Georgians it is simply unacceptable.

The Role of the Attorney General

The failures of Georgia's officials don't stop with the Governor and the Board of Regents. Georgia's attorney general, Thurbert E. Baker, whose responsibility it was to investigate this sordid mess, apparently decided instead to rope-a-dope with the media and public, pretending to investigate until everyone was weary of the issue. Even the attorney general's letter described in Chapter 13, which was pried out of his office through persistent open records requests, begs for explanation.

Why, for example, if bonuses paid to Dr. Adams and senior vice President Hank Huckaby "appear to violate the spirit of the Georgia Constitution," was this not actionable?

As Attorney General Baker's letter eloquently states, the Georgia Constitution speaks not only to the prohibition against such gifts "but also to the evil that may arise from providing additional compensation to public officials, no matter what the source of the funds. The grant of additional private funds to a public official for performing his public duties in an exemplary manner raises serious conflict of interest issues that the constitutional provision was designed to preclude."

In August 2004, the Regents developed new rules for dealing with co-operating organizations such as the Foundation. Under the new rules, no employee of the institution or his immediate family may receive gifts or payments from the cooperating agency without approval of the president, or in the case of the president's family, the chancellor, or in case of the chancellor or chancellor's family, the Board of Regents.

Thus, the Regents have institutionalized the authorization of compensation that, "if applied to gifts for services or compensation for work already performed, is clearly prohibited by the Georgia Constitution."

Conspicuously absent from Baker's letter was any mention of the phone call from Wrigley to Witzleben in which Wrigley allegedly asked Witzleben to arrange what amounted to hush money for Costello. If this allegation is true, it sounds as if a crime was committed. If Baker had mentioned this in his letter, he presumably would have been obligated to investigate it. By not mentioning it, he dodged the issue.

Basically, he also dodged his responsibilities in all the matters that he should have investigated and which were pointedly and repeatedly brought to his attention by, among others, attorney Robert Miller.

Ducking and weaving are admirable traits in a boxing ring, less so in the office of a state's chief law enforcement officer.

* * *

IN THE END, THE issues, as they often do where politics is concerned, come down to leadership, governance, and public trust, in this case involving the overall direction of a significant state institution. Not just any institution, but one entrusted with educating and instilling a framework of judgment and morality within a state's young people. That mission has never been more important or more challenging than today, as the costs of getting a college education are higher than ever and the costs of not having one are even higher. One can't help feeling that the citizens of the state of Georgia have been ill-served over the past decade by a series of actions and inactions at their flagship university. One has the sense that the system of governance put in place to protect higher education from the corrupting influence of politics has been corrupted. One has the sense that if Abraham Baldwin could stride beneath that fabled Arch on the campus he began building two centuries ago, he might have a few questions to ask about what happened to the "forming hand of Society" under which his students were to be "moulded to the love of Virtue and good Order." One has the sense he might feel like ripping up some hedges and replanting.

~

Appendix

Appendix A: The Deloitte & Touche Audit

Following is the text of the Deloitte & Touche audit commissioned by the UGA Foundation and released to the Board of Regents and Chancellor on October 27, 2003:

Introduction

Retention of D&T

The special practice unit of Deloitte & Touche ("D&T") for conducting fraud and forensic investigations was engaged by King & Spalding ("Counsel") and its client, the University of Georgia Foundation ("Foundation") to conduct a special review of certain transactions, events and issues identified by the Foundation Trustees. Due to the nature of this special review and the possibility for bias, Counsel and the Foundation did not wish to utilize either its internal auditor or the external audit professionals normally charged with conducting the Foundation's annual audit. We understand the trustees' desire was to engage a group of professionals that are experienced in analyzing both financial and non-financial information, conducting interviews and making an assessment of events that transpired.

The D&T professionals that performed this special review had no prior direct relationships with The University of Georgia ("UGA"), the Foundation, Dr. Michael Adams, President of UGA, or any of the trustees or individuals that we interviewed. This is important to note, given the atmosphere that has surrounded many of the issues we were asked to review and the individuals D&T interviewed.

A final, important point is critical to keep in mind before detailing the facts and findings we uncovered. D&T's assessment of how the Foundation trustees, Dr. Adams or any other individual acted relative to any specific transaction is based to some extent on our assessment of how these same parties were involved in all the transactions and issues that we reviewed. This speaks to the natural inclination the reader might have to reach an opinion on any given topic without first considering all of the facts mentioned in this report. We make this point at this juncture to suggest that this report must be read in its entirety to provide context and better understanding of any particular topic and the subsequent information offered.

Scope of Work

D&T was charged with examining at least six specific issues and reporting our findings surrounding the facts and circumstances of these matters. These issues are as follows:

- Dr. Michael Adams' Expenses
- Dr. Michael Adams' Compensation
- Mary Adams's stipend
- Hank Huckaby's $30,000 Honorarium
- Coach Jim Donnan's $250,000 Side Agreement
- Costa Rica Ecolodge Purchase
- Alumni Center Project

Additionally, D&T was asked to report any other findings that came to our attention in the process of performing our work. A number of such issues were identified and our findings on some of these issues are included in this report. Other issues were reviewed to a limited extent and were not pursued in greater detail for a variety of reasons, including:

- The topic was not sufficiently related to the topics with which we were charged and did not appear to provide other corroborative indicators of how the Foundation or Dr. Adams have acted elsewhere
- The inability to obtain a reasonable amount of credible evidence substantiating the allegations made
- The fact that some individuals were unwilling to risk information becoming public but were willing to share certain things with D&T under a promise of confidentiality

For each item reviewed, D&T provided herein information that answers the following questions:

1. Were Foundation funds used?
2. Were proper procedures and policies followed by all parties connected to this transaction or were there improprieties?
3. What approval was obtained?

D&T began its work by making an extensive request for the production of Foundation documents from the office of Ms. Cindy Coyle, Chief Financial Officer of the Foundation. D&T then conducted initial interviews with Ms. Coyle and Mr. Tom Landrum, the former Executive Director of the Foundation and Chief of Staff to Dr. Adams, in order to obtain an overall understanding of the Foundation's operating and financial history as well as an understanding of how UGA operated and interacted with the Foundation. Subsequently, D&T interviewed all the current trustees of the Foundation Executive Committee ("FEC") along with certain former Foundation trustees. Based on the information gleaned from these interviews, D&T selectively expanded the number of individuals interviewed. Ultimately, almost all the individuals that were suggested by FEC members to be interviewed were interviewed by D&T. Dr. Adams also voluntarily made himself available for interview and was interviewed by D&T. Exhibit A includes a list of all the individuals that D&T interviewed and which supplied information that was evaluated and noted in this report.

In addition to these interviews and the production of documents from the Foundation CFO's office, D&T has also reviewed information obtained from the President's office, UGA employees, Foundation trustees and certain other individuals possessing relevant information. Where appropriate, D&T conducted its own research in order to corroborate specific information or to obtain additional facts not available from the sources previously mentioned. Finally, D&T had several discussions with counsel that encompassed virtually all aspects of our review. D&T has relied on the advice of counsel throughout this report in making a determination of the propriety of any action or inaction by all involved parties, particularly where the Bylaws of the Foundation are concerned.

BACKGROUND

In order to provide context for our findings and answering the above questions, two items must be understood. First, some Foundation history is relevant. Second, there are broader issues surrounding Foundation Bylaws, policies and procedures, etc., that must be addressed in order to understand whether there were any improprieties or whether policies and procedures were correctly followed. Each of these items is discussed herein.

Foundation History

The Foundation is a private entity established in 1937 whose current mission is to "provide volunteer leadership to University of Georgia development and fund-raising programs, to administer the assets of the Foundation, and to provide advice, consultation, and support to the President of the University of Georgia."[1] Judged by current activity, the Foundation was largely a dormant entity until the mid-1980s. At such time it became apparent to administrators, faculty and friends of UGA that it was critical for UGA to strengthen and grow the Foundation's assets in order to supplement dwindling government funding to students and faculty alike. Also important was the desire by all interested parties that UGA have the resources necessary to move into the highest echelon of U.S. public universities as an academic institution.

The Foundation's board of trustees plays a critical role in fundraising efforts since it is this governing body that has the capacity in terms of leadership and resources to effect change. D&T interviewed all the current and some former members of the

FEC to better understand how the Foundation has operated in the past and to obtain a better understanding of the role of the FEC and the board of trustees in the matters we reviewed. (See Exhibit A) Many of these interviewed by D&T indicated the board of trustees has historically operated more like an "alumni club" than a board of trustees administering a foundation. As a result, power has been concentrated largely in the hands of the Foundation's officers. The decisions of these officers, primarily the Chairman of the Foundation and the Chairman of the Foundation's Finance Committee, have been largely accepted and approved by the board of trustees without debate as being in the best interests of the Foundation and UGA.

As a result of this operating style, the board of trustees for the Foundation has operated with less regard for the Foundation Bylaws or policies and procedures than appropriate. Decisions have historically been made with the simple principle of doing what is best for UGA. In the same vein, it has generally been believed by the board of trustees that the President of the University ("President"), who currently is an Ex-Officio member of the board of trustees and the FEC, was also acting in the best interests of the Foundation and UGA. Therefore, the Foundation's board of trustees has exuded a desire and willingness to grant the President special consideration in his requests for funding or in other initiatives. The net result has been a focus by the Foundation board and by the President of UGA on achieving results with less regard for the Foundation's Bylaws and policies and procedures.

The number of members of the Foundation's board of trustees has also fluctuated over time. During Dr. Knapp's Presidency at UGA, it was decided that the Foundation board of trustees was too large and unwieldy for functioning effectively. As a result, the size of the Foundation board was reduced.[2] Later, when Dr. Adams was hired as the UGA President, there was a renewed focus on fundraising in order to expand the Foundation's endowment. In fact, it is common knowledge that one of Dr. Adams' primary charges was to increase giving to UGA via the Foundation. With this goal in mind, Dr. Adams was a strong proponent of increasing the size of the Foundation's board of trustees in order to expand the potential circle of influence this body would have on UGA alumni.[3]

With this fundraising mindset, the Foundation board was subsequently expanded from 32 managing trustees to 36 managing trustees. Additionally, another 12 advisory trustees were added to the present four advisory trustees—all of whom are appointed by the Chair of the Foundation.[4] Even more recently, it was recommended that the board of trustees add an additional 8 members, bringing the total membership to 60 trustees.[5] At the same time, however, Dr. Adams believed, as did others on the Foundation board of trustees, that much of the decision-making could be administered by the FEC. This would allow the board of trustees to remain effective. D&T's review indicates that the FEC has, in fact, acted as the real decision making body for the Foundation board of trustees. These issues are dealt with in a separate report by King & Spalding to the Foundation board of trustees.

Mission of the Foundation

In performing our review, it was important to understand the mission of the Foundation and in turn, how the Foundation derives its authority and ability to operate as an entity within the State of Georgia as a part of the University System and as an integral part of the University of Georgia. Further, it is important to understand the authority structure that governs the Foundation internally and externally.

The bylaws of the Foundation, past and current, have stated the following in paragraph 1:

> "It is the mission of The University of Georgia Foundation to administer with fiduciary care the assets of the Foundation for the long-term enhancement of The University of Georgia to provide volunteer leadership and assistance to the University in its development and fund-raising activities; and to provide broad advice, consultation and support to the President of the University."

Based on discussions with Counsel, this mission statement provides that the Foundation serves the University of Georgia and also serves in an advisory and support role to the President of the University. This mission statement reflects a collaborative role between the Foundation and the President, with neither being subservient to the other.

Executive Committee

The Bylaws of the Foundation, past and current, have stated the following in paragraph 33:

> "Subject to such limitations that may be imposed from time to time by the Board of Trustees, the Executive Committee shall be authorized to conduct the business of the Foundation and to exercise any and all powers and responsibilities of the Board of Trustees in the interim between meetings of the Board; provided however, that no committee of the Board of Trustees may: (1) authorize distributions; . . ."

The Bylaws of the Foundation further states within the same paragraph 33 that:

> "At each meeting of the Board of Trustees of the Foundation, the Executive Committee will report on actions taken by the Executive Committee since the last meeting of the Board of Trustees."

The Policies and Procedures manual, Section I.C. of the Foundation states that:

"The Executive Committee is also authorized to act, when necessary, on behalf of the full Board of Trustees. Finally, the Executive Committee supports and gives advice and counsel to the Executive Director of the Foundation and the President of the University of Georgia."

President of the University of Georgia

The Policy and Procedures manual for the Foundation states under Section VIII.A. that, "All University of Georgia employees are employed by the University System of Georgia and are therefore subject to University System rules with respect to expense reimbursement and other financial support." The President of the University of Georgia is a University of Georgia employee and thus is employed by the University System of Georgia. As such, it appears the President is subject to University System rules.

The Bylaws of the Foundation, in paragraph 6, state that the President is a Managing Trustee of the Foundation and serves as an ex-officio member of the Managing Trustees during their term in office. In this capacity, the President is part of a group of Trustees that "shall manage the business and affairs of the Foundation and may exercise all powers of the Foundation, subject to any restrictions imposed by law, by the Articles of Incorporation or by these Bylaws."

The Bylaws of the Foundation, in paragraph 32, state that the President serves as an ex-officio member of the Executive Committee.

The Policies and Procedures manual of the Foundation, Section I.C., states that, "Subject to the discretion of the Chair, the President of the University . . . will be invited to attend all meetings of the Executive Committee."

Using and Requesting Unrestricted Funds

The Policies and Procedures manual of the Foundation, Section XI.A., states that:

> "All UGAF unrestricted funding must be approved by the Finance Committee and by the full Board of Trustees. Unrestricted gift funds that are contributed to the UGAF may be used for the benefit of the University of Georgia in the following ways, listed in order of priority:
> 1. To be made available to the President of the University of Georgia to use at his discretion to meet extraordinary needs or targets of unusual opportunity of special benefit to UGA.
> 2. . . ."

The Policies and Procedures manual of the Foundation goes on to state in Section XI.A. that the following process is required to request funding:

- The CFO of UGAF is responsible for preparing requests for funding approval of the Finance Committee. Annually, the CFO of the Foundation shall report to the Board of Trustees on the use of funds.

- Any planned uses of the funds shall be approved by the Finance Committee as part of the regular budgeting process.
- Any discretionary use of the funds in excess of $25,000 requires prior approval of the Finance Committee
- Any discretionary use of the funds shall be reported annually to the Finance Committee and the Board of Trustees.

The role of the President of the University in determining how one-time funding requests are utilized is important to note. Section XI.B. of the Foundation's Policies and Procedures manual delineates the process and the role the President plays in this effort. Typically a Director, Dean, Provost or other college and University official makes a request for funding and submits this request for approval from a higher-ranking official. If it is deemed that Foundation funds are best suited to fund the request, "the request will be forwarded to the President for consideration."

Policy XI.B. further states "The President will determine the funding priority of the requests for the University as a whole." The President then should submit the proposed requests in order of priority to the UGA Foundation Finance Committee at least three months in advance to allow for the review process before consideration at the Foundation's Finance Committee meetings. Approved requests for one-time funding by the Foundation's Finance Committee are then presented to the Board of Trustees for approval.

Detailed Findings

The remainder of this report provides details of the primary issues we were asked to review and also detail some of the other matters that came to our attention in the course of our review. For each item we will provide an initial summary of findings, which answers the three primary questions posed to D&T on each transaction. We will also provide details relating to the facts of each transaction and our findings.

DR. MICHAEL ADAMS' EXPENSES

Summary

1. Were Foundation funds used?

   - Yes. The Foundation pays for many of Dr. Adams' expenses, either from restricted funds designated for his discretionary use or from appropriate Foundation funds for Dr. Adams' expenses that have first been submitted for payment to UGA but exceed state allowed amounts.

2. Were proper procedures and policies followed by all parties connected to this transaction or were there improprieties?

- The answer to this question is mixed. Unquestionably, over the course of the six years that Dr. Adams has been the President of UGA, the majority of expenses have complied with all policies and procedures. However, in some instances this has not been the case, often due to human error and mistakes. In some instances it appears that Foundation funds may have been misappropriated.

3. What approval was obtained?

- Currently Dr. Adams' own office reviews his expenditures prior to sending them to the Foundation's accounting office for further review. Also, the Chairperson of the Foundation and the Chairperson of the Foundation's Finance Committee review Dr. Adams' expenditures on a quarterly basis for final approval. Finally, the Foundation's internal auditor reviews Dr. Adams' expenses

Background and Timeline

D&T understands one of the first actions taken by Dr. Adams when he became President of UGA was to stop the mandatory audit of the Foundation accounts over which he had control.[6] Dr. Adams requested and was granted approval from the Foundation Finance Committee to discontinue the mandatory audit of these accounts, which included the following:

- President's Fund Discretionary
- President's Venture Fund
- Knapp Fund for Academic Excellence
- President's Special Programs
- President's House Support

Apparently, Dr. Adams believed that since these were accounts over which he had authority and were Presidential discretionary accounts, along with the possibility these accounts could still potentially be audited under normal sampling procedures, there was no need for them to be audited on a mandatory basis.[7] These accounts had been audited on a mandatory basis under the previous President of UGA, Dr. Knapp.[8] In May 2001, the mandatory auditing of these Presidential accounts was recommended after the Foundation took issue with the manner in which Dr. Adams utilized some credit cards and the negative publicity received as a result of Dr. Adams' office chartering a plane for certain staff members to attend President George Bush's inauguration in Washington, D.C., in 2001.[9]

D&T believes that both Dr. Adams and the Foundation erred in the initial decision not to continue the mandatory audit of the President's accounts. The Foundation has acknowledged this mistake by reinstating the audit of these accounts. As a very public official, Dr. Adams has, and will continue to receive extra scrutiny. A number of FEC trustees informed D&T they spoke with Dr. Adams at various points in time about Presidential expenditures, warning him about the scrutiny he could expect.[10]

Certain of Dr. Adams expenditures have already received a great deal of attention in the past several years, both by the Foundation and in the media. However, it should be pointed out that over the course of the six years Dr. Adams has been the President of UGA, the majority of Dr. Adams' Presidential expenses have complied with all policies and procedures of UGA and the Foundation. The inherent difficulty of Dr. Adams' role as the President of a public institution, and one where he has been charged with raising funds for the Foundation, is that a substantial portion of his private life is intertwined with and in many instances indistinguishable from his duties as President of UGA. As a result, evaluating Dr. Adams' expenditures on the basis of business intent and benefit to the Foundation can occasionally be difficult and involves a good deal of subjective judgment by those charged with this task.

Expense Review Process

In light of the difficulty in assessing and justifying expenditures, it is important to understand the review process undertaken regarding Dr. Adams' expenses before final approval is given to the expenses submitted.

Generally, there are two types of expenditures: (1) normal, recurring expenditures for travel and business that the President conducts and (2) expenses for events and functions, which must receive approval prior to being incurred.[11]

After Dr. Adams has incurred an expense, he submits his expense receipts to his staff to sort and input into the proper expense reimbursement summary forms. This task is done by one of his assistants. Part of the assistant's task is to also identify and separate out any expenses that may be of a personal nature. Dr. Adams' assistant also decides if all or part of any expense should be submitted to UGA or to the Foundation for reimbursement. As a state employee, Dr. Adams is generally required to first obtain reimbursement for his expenses from UGA. Naturally, UGA has its own policies and procedures that limit the nature and the amount of the expense. Those expenses incurred that are deemed to benefit UGA are first submitted to UGA for reimbursement. Any approved amount that UGA does not pay is then submitted for approval from the Foundation.[12]

Another factor complicating the expense reimbursement process is that Dr. Adams is frequently invited to speak or attend other functions in the State and in the nation. Often, the expenses that he incurs on these trips are then paid for by these organizations. These expenses must then to be coded and sent for reimbursement from these organizations or be pro-rated based on how Dr. Adams traveled and the nature of the expense incurred. Until August 2003, a final review of Dr. Adams' expenses was performed by Mr. Landrum before submitting them to the appropriate entity.[13]

After Mr. Landrum's review, the Foundation accounting department received the expenditures for which it was the designated payor. The Foundation then performed its own review. Until August 2003, if there were any questions, they were noted and discussed with Mr. Landrum. Mr. Landrum then made the final decision on any disputed items. After Mr. Landrum reached a final decision, the Foundation processed the expenses for payment.[14] (It should be noted that for the last few years, the Chief Financial Officer of the Foundation has reported to the Executive Director of the Foundation. Since October 1998, those persons have been Mr. Landrum, and his predecessor, Ms. Costello. Both of these individuals were also UGA employees who reported directly to Dr. Adams. This arrangement was stopped by the Foundation in August 2003 due to some of the inherent conflicts that it presented).

New procedures put in place in 2001 required the Foundation Chairperson and the Foundation Finance Chairperson to also perform a subsequent review of Dr. Adams expenditures.[15] D&T understands that on a quarterly basis, both of these Chairpersons would review a descriptive schedule of all the expenses incurred by Dr. Adams on behalf of the Foundation and grant signature approval.[16] D&T understands that since the new procedures were implemented in 2001, no expenses submitted by Dr. Adams have been rejected by the Foundation Chairpersons.[17]

An additional control was implemented by the Foundation in November 1999 when a retired D&T partner, Mr. Gerald McCarley, became the Foundation's internal auditor. Mr. McCarley also reviews various aspects of the Foundation's accounting and reports his findings to the Foundation board of trustees on a regular basis.[18]

As mentioned earlier, in the case of special events, one additional step must occur. Namely, Dr. Adams must receive pre-approval of the expenditure from the UGA administration. For this, Mr. Landrum typically grants the approval. After the event, if Foundation funds were expended, the approval process flows as discussed in the above paragraphs.[19]

D&T makes note of this process for several reasons. Understandably, this process is not very straightforward, and as such, makes it susceptible to human error. In conjunction with this, Dr. Adams has a very heavy travel schedule and is constantly engaged in various meetings and activities relative to his office. This results in a fairly significant volume of expenses that must be coded and billed to the proper entities. To some degree mistakes are almost inevitable and perhaps understandable. Based on our review, D&T believes that Dr. Adams and his office, and the Foundation's trustees appear to have implemented reasonable safeguards to ensure that this process captures and records the majority of Dr. Adams' activity properly and that Foundation funds are properly utilized.

Notwithstanding the above, a limited number of transactions have raised questions in the past over the benefit or business nature of the expenditures for which Foundation funds were expended or how the Foundation reported these expenditures for income tax purposes. This list of questionable expenses includes the following:

- Charter plane to President George Bush's Inauguration in Washington, D.C., in 2001
- Slow credit card payments while awaiting Dr. Adams' expense explanations
- Scotland golf trip where personal expenses were charged to the Foundation and later reimbursed
- Questionable spending on the President's house and the Administration offices

These transactions were discussed by the Foundation trustees and it was realized that to some extent, there was a lack of sufficient guidance for Presidential expenditures. Therefore, as mentioned earlier in this report, the Foundation trustees implemented additional policies and procedures for the President's office.[20] Based on our interview with the Foundation CFO, Ms. Cindy Coyle, since these new policies and procedures were implemented in 2001, there has been an improvement in both the quality of documentation provided and the nature of the expenditures incurred by Dr. Adams. Given the controls that are in place, the D&T team charged with this special review, did not attempt to audit or analyze Dr. Adams' historical expenditures, in detail, as part of this engagement. However, several transactions did come to our attention as we interviewed various individuals and also reviewed the expense documentation submitted by Dr. Adams.

D&T Findings

As of October 7, 2003, D&T has not further analyzed some of the historical expenditures for which the Foundation has reached an apparent resolution. A handful of other Presidential expenditures came to D&T's attention. These include:

2002 Law School Reception

A September 7, 2003, news article by the *Athens Banner-Herald*, titled "Foundation supports Adams by footing the bills," listed a number of event expenditures incurred by UGA's President's office.[21] Each of these expenditures listed by the *Athens Banner-Herald* was considered a legitimate expense by the Foundation, since the Chairman of the Foundation and the Chairman of the Finance Committee reviewed and approved these expenditures by the President's office. One of the items mentioned was "$9,042.48 for food and beverages for the 2002 law school commencement luncheon."

Upon initial review, this expense appears to be an appropriate activity for the President to have hosted. As mentioned, the Foundation did review and approve this expense and the attendant description. However, additional facts have become apparent that were not recognized by the Foundation at the time.

This particular luncheon, which was hosted by Dr. Adams at the President's house, was for the UGA law school class that graduated in 2002. Apparently, many law students, parents and faculty where present. What makes this luncheon noteworthy is the UGA law school graduating class for 2002 included Dr. Adams' son, David Adams.[22] D&T received confirmation from the former Dean of the UGA Law School that this was a "by invitation only party," and that he was confident not all the faculty were invited to this luncheon.[23] This assertion was further supported by another eight faculty members from the UGA law school in a recent interview with the *Athens Banner-Herald*. In the issue dated October 3, 2003, eight law school faculty members stated among other things that this luncheon was an invitation only luncheon.[24] D&T received further confirmation from the Foundation accounting files that such a luncheon was never held by the President for the law school prior to that time nor has any such event been hosted since.

It is a fairly common practice for each of the UGA colleges and schools to hold graduation receptions. However, upon request from D&T, the Foundation researched and failed to find any other instances where Dr. Adams hosted a luncheon for a particular college or school at UGA over the past six years. D&T was told that luncheons have been hosted by Dr. Adams and others where commencement speakers and the like have been guests to the President and a small select group of individuals. Historically, however, a luncheon of this scale and expense had not previously occurred.

On October 4, 2003, the *Athens Banner-Herald* published another article that indicated Dr. Adams had reimbursed the Foundation for $10,000. This reimbursement apparently covered the cost of the event and an additional $468.85 for floral arrangements that were a part of the luncheon festivities.[25] The Foundation has in fact received this $10,000 reimbursement.[26] It also appears the reason that the Foundation paid for this reception is due to the fact that Dr. Adams' office did not fill out the proper reimbursement request form that is to be utilized for events that are special invite and selected guests only. We understand if an entire school is invited, this particular form is not required.[27] Given the fact such a form was not utilized by the President's office and being provided no other facts, the Foundation CFO, Foundation Chairperson and Foundation Finance Committee Chairperson saw no reason not to approve these expenses.

It is possible an argument can be made (and, in fact, already has been made by Dr. Adams) that this luncheon was beneficial to UGA and the Foundation since it potentially could serve to cultivate future donor relationships with students and parents alike. However, the timing and circumstances for having this particular event do not appear to be justified.

Charter Airplane to Funeral of Former Centre President

Another expense that came to D&T's attention was the charge of $2,255 in Foundation funds for Dr. Adams to utilize a chartered airplane to Winter Haven, Florida on September 4, 1998 to attend the funeral of Mr. Bob McLeod, the former President of Centre College, in Kentucky. Mr. Tom Landrum approved this request for reimbursement from the Foundation.[28] It is not clear to D&T how UGA benefited from this particular expense. It appears that this expense was personal in nature to Dr. Adams and Foundation funds should not have been utilized to pay for this expense.

Additional Expense Issues Identified

D&T also examined several other more recent expenses that came to our attention in the process of reviewing Foundation records and conducting interviews. One issue dealt with Dr. Adams' use of a Foundation vehicle as well as his use of a State-provided vehicle. D&T's limited review of this issue indicates no impropriety in how these vehicles were utilized. An additional issue that came to our attention was a $58.50 charge paid with Foundation funds when Dr. Adams had overnight guests that resulted in Dr. Adams' son staying in a hotel.[29] This was in an effort to allow the guests to occupy the President's house. Dr. Adams' has recently repaid the Foundation for this charge.[30] Finally, as referenced under the Compensation section of this report, Dr. Adams' office apparently stipulated that his deferred compensation accounts not be assessed the standard Foundation management fee.[31] After D&T inquired into this issue, Dr. Adams had the Foundation management fee reinstated.[32]

Presidential Funds

Another aspect of Presidential expenditures that required review involves a discussion of those Presidential funds (listed earlier) for which Dr. Adams has discretionary authority. Based on our interviews, it appears there is a mistaken belief among some members of the Foundation Board of Trustees, Dr. Adams and his staff, that certain funds, which were endowed and restricted for Dr. Adams' discretionary use, are simply Dr. Adams funds to do with as he pleases. This is not an entirely accurate understanding of these discretionary funds.

Based on advice from counsel, the expenditures that occur in these accounts are subject to governmental regulations, Foundation bylaws and Foundation policies and procedures as much as any other fund within the Foundation. The overarching mandate being that all expenditures must not inure to the benefit of any particular individual and that all expenditures demonstrably benefit the Foundation or serve its corporate purposes. The only difference for these Presidential Discretionary funds versus any other funds of the Foundation is that the President was given sole discretion to determine how these funds were to be expended to further the Foundation's corporate purposes rather than giving this authority to the Foundation board of trustees.

Dr. Michael Adams' Compensation

Summary

1. Were Foundation funds used?

   • Yes. A substantial part of Dr. Adams' compensation is paid from Foundation funds.

2. Were proper procedures and policies followed by all parties connected to this transaction or were there improprieties?

   • The FEC has not engaged the Foundation's full board of trustees to discuss and vote on Dr. Adams' compensation. This is not a violation of the Foundation's policies and procedures, however, it may not be in the best interests of the Foundation to do so.
   • Foundation Chairman, Mr. Jack Rooker, has provided inadequate communication to both the FEC and the full board of trustees about Dr. Adams' compensation. The most recent compensation resolution dated February 14, 2003 appears to indicate that the FEC authorized this resolution, when in fact it has not. This resolution was signed by Mr. Rooker and Ms. Rachel Conway (FEC trustee), but it was never presented to nor approved by the FEC, much less the full board of the Foundation. This is improper.
   • Currently, Dr. Adams does not have a contract with the Foundation due to the fact that he has not signed the most recent contract proposal that is predicated on the February 14, 2003 resolution that was never authorized by the FEC. This appears to be a violation of Foundation policy.
   • The FEC appears to have allowed the Board of Regents to dictate the terms of Dr. Adams' compensation to a much greater extent than they should, in light of the fact that Dr. Adams receives the majority of his income from the Foundation (cumulative basis from 2001–2004). This presents some inherent conflicts for the Foundation.
   • The proposed incentive compensation appears to be in dispute among Foundation board members due to a misunderstanding by the committee of the Foundation considering his compensation. This misunderstanding around giving levels as a basis for incentive compensation was not corrected by Dr. Adams and/or his staff. This misunderstanding could cause Dr. Adams to be overpaid based on the fundraising element of his incentive clause.
   • Dr. Adams may have misled Mr. Rooker and others regarding the level of compensation allegedly offered by Ohio State University ("OSU") when Dr. Adams interviewed for the Presidency of OSU.

3. What approval was obtained?
   • The FEC typically has approved Dr. Adams' compensation. The most recent resolution, dated February 14, 2003, has not been presented to nor approved by the FEC or the full board of the Foundation.

Background and Timeline

For purposes of this discussion, a summary of Dr. Adams' pay from fiscal year 1998 to fiscal year 2004 is outlined below.

Table 1[33]

Fiscal Year	Compensation, Allowances & Club Memberships	Deferred Compensation & Taxable Fringe Benefits	Total Compensation
1998	$255,868	$25,630	$281,498
1999	$279,088	$26,221	$305,309
2000	$291,594	$32,943	$324,537
2001	$333,696	$224,861	$558,557
2002	$352,826	$91,279	$444,105
2003	$362,803	$40,701	$403,504
2004	$362,827	$212,260	$575,087

Dr. Adams took office as the President of UGA on September 1, 1997.[34] His total compensation for fiscal year 1998, before accounting for taxable fringe benefits or deferred compensation, was $255,868. A projection of Dr. Adams fiscal year 2004 total compensation, before accounting for taxable fringe benefits or deferred compensation, is $362,827. This is a 42% increase over the 1997 to 2004 time period. These pay increases, which were granted by the Foundation at the request of the Board of Regents were done in an attempt to keep Dr. Adams' compensation competitive with other large, public universities. In a further attempt to keep Dr. Adams pay competitive and to provide an incentive to Dr. Adams to stay at UGA long-term, additional deferred compensation has been granted to Dr. Adams the last few years.[35]

Generally, Dr. Adams base salary and supplemented compensation has risen over the years due to merit increases granted by the Board of Regents.[36] It was not until fiscal year 2001 that Dr. Adams received $200,000 in deferred compensation placed into an account that would only vest in full on October 1, 2007.[37] There is no partial vesting over time for this $200,000. Based on that contract agreement, if Dr. Adams is still the President of UGA as of that date, he receives the full sum. Otherwise, he receives nothing. During fiscal year 2002, Dr. Adams received another $78,673 as a one-time payment in stock which was also deferred in nature.[38]

In the summer of 2002, two events occurred which caused Dr. Adams' compensation to increase significantly. Both of these events occurred almost simultaneously. The Board of Regents desired to ensure that Dr. Adams pay was equivalent to the pay of Dr. Wayne Clough, President of Georgia Tech University.[39] The other significant event was an apparent offer made by OSU for Dr. Adams to become the President of OSU.[40] Dr. Adams informed D&T he had three significant opportunities presented to him during 2002. Dr. Adams stated all three of these opportunities would have paid him significantly more than the total compensation he was currently receiving at UGA. The most appealing of the three offers was the offer from OSU, Dr. Adams' alma mater. According to Dr. Adams, the OSU offer was for approximately $850,000.

Ultimately, Dr. Adams turned down the OSU job offer, by his account, largely due to personal reasons, most of which revolve around his family having established fairly strong roots in Georgia. The other reason given by Dr. Adams was the assurance provided by Mr. Rooker, the Chair of the Foundation, that the Foundation would supplement his Board of Regent's compensation to provide a total compensation package that would pay Dr. Adams approximately $600,000 annually.

The Foundation trustees involved in considering Dr. Adams' compensation believed that given the current environment where faculty and staff at UGA had received little to no pay increases, it was important they structure Dr. Adams' compensation in such a fashion that it would be largely incentive based.[41] The Resolution of the Trustees of The University of Georgia Foundation, dated February 14, 2003, is attached in its entirety.[42] This resolution was prepared by Mr. Rooker and was to encompass the latest additions proposed by the ad hoc compensation committee. D&T understands that this resolution, which is made to appear as if it was adopted by the FEC, actually was not even presented for approval to the FEC. The resolution was simply prepared by Mr. Rooker and signed by Ms. Conway, the Secretary for the FEC.[43] Despite its heading, it was never approved by the board of trustees. It should be noted that the full board of the Foundation also met on February 14, 2003.[44] It is unclear why Mr. Rooker did not present this resolution to the full board of the Foundation trustees. The minutes for the FEC in the surrounding period and the minutes for the Foundation do not reflect any discussion about Dr. Adams' compensation.

From 1998 to 2004, Dr. Adams' State-paid compensation has ranged from $190,000 to $239,103 (Table 2, page 208). In addition to his State salary, Dr. Adams' current compensation as proposed in the February 14, 2003 resolution would be comprised of two parts. The first is a supplemental portion that includes his supplemental compensation of 49 percent of the Board of Regents base pay, an annual $40,000 longevity supplement, payment of up to $1,800 for a premium for a life insurance policy of $500,000 and reimbursements of various expenses.[45]

The other component of Dr. Adams' proposed compensation arrangement is the Deferred Compensation Agreement. This part of Dr. Adams' compensation would provide for $60,000 in longevity credits for each year he is UGA's President and two incentive formulas, whereby Dr. Adams would be credited for the growth that occurs in total gifts to UGA and for the growth that occurs in the Foundation's Endowment. The longevity credit based upon total gifts given to UGA as a basis includes giving to Athletics. The apparent justification for including Athletic giving in this computation is that the President is charged with overseeing all aspects of UGA life, including Athletics.[46]

One of the components to Dr. Adams' deferred compensation calculation includes a minimum threshold of fundraising money that must be raised before Dr. Adams receives the benefit of that incentive. Originally, the ad hoc compensation committee believed $50 million would be a good threshold to establish.[47] At that point in time, the ad hoc compensation committee believed that this threshold should be based on non-Athletic giving.[48] However, Dr. Adams insisted that Athletics' fund raising should be included in the formula since Dr. Adams, as President of UGA, was also in charge of Athletics. Apparently, the ad hoc compensation committee performed only a cursory review of a fundraising datasheet that was provided to them by UGA. This fundraising data sheet appeared to indicate that Athletics accounted for $12 million in fund raising for the 2001–2002 year.[49] Whereupon, the ad hoc compensation committee decided that the threshold should then be increased by this $12 million to $62 million. Further discussion resulted in this figure being trimmed to $60 million.[50]

Once Dr. Adams' deferred compensation formula had been determined, it was forwarded to Dr. Adams' office. Later, more easily understandable data on fundraising was released that indicated that for the 2001–2002 year, the total Athletic Department fundraising was actually about $19.4 million and not $12 million as originally thought. The ad hoc compensation committee had inadvertently left off two line items for an additional $7.4 million in Athletic gift receipts and pledges.[51] The net effect of all of this would be to permanently understate the base in the incentive formula. This then became part of the formula by which Dr. Adams' incentive compensation would be calculated. This could result in Dr. Adams receiving more compensation than merited based on having a more readily attainable number to achieve.

The question that has been asked regarding this is how could Dr. Adams or those in his office not know that the original number for Athletics was $19.4 million instead of the $12 million that was put into the compensation formula. Why did someone not notify the ad hoc compensation committee of their error? Given the magnitude of this incentive amount and the personal nature of this to Dr. Adams, it appears improbable that this calculation would not have received a fair amount of scrutiny by Dr. Adams. At this time, D&T understands that Dr. Adams and the Foundation have not signed an agreement evidencing the arrangement outlined above.[52] D&T has not obtained a clear understanding of why that is. The first payment into a deferred compensation account to occur under this new contract was to be made September 1, 2003. Since the contract is not signed by Dr. Adams, the Foundation has not made this first payment.[53]

On December 13, 2002, the FEC did agree to reward Dr. Adams with a $40,000 bonus for the good work he had done as President of UGA.[54] Mr. Rooker stated to D&T that the FEC will reconsider paying Dr. Adams a bonus of similar size on an annual basis. This $40,000 was in fact paid to Dr. Adams in December 2002.[55]

D&T Findings

It is readily apparent to D&T that Mr. Rooker has not engaged the Foundation's full board of trustees to discuss and vote on Dr. Adams' compensation. Apparently there is some concern as to how the faculty and staff of UGA would react to Dr. Adams receiving significantly greater raises, bonuses, etc. than the faculty and staff of UGA have received. In some years, UGA faculty has received no pay increases.[56] While the FEC has largely felt justified in making these upward adjustments in Dr. Adams' compensation, the desire by certain trustees to minimize the potential publicity of having the full board review and approve Dr. Adams' pay is not in the best interests of the Foundation and therefore not justified.

It is also apparent to D&T that FEC Chairman, Jack Rooker, has provided inadequate communication to both the FEC and the full board of trustees about Dr. Adams' compensation. The most recent compensation resolution dated February 14, 2003 appears to indicate that the FEC authorized this resolution, when in fact the resolution itself was not presented to the FEC. This resolution was signed by Mr. Rooker and Ms. Rachel Conway (FEC trustee and Secretary of the Foundation), but there is no indication that this resolution was ever presented or approved by the FEC. Interviews with several FEC trustees have generated no recall of any discussion of this resolution. The minutes for the meetings of both the FEC and the full board of the Foundation in the surrounding time periods give no indication that this resolution was discussed and approved. If, in fact, a contract was presented to Dr. Adams for approval and the resolution was never properly approved by the Foundation, this would be a violation of the Foundation's policies and procedures.

Compensation Responsibilities

Regarding Dr. Adams' total compensation, D&T reviewed the amount of Dr. Adams' compensation that is State Salary (Board of Regents approved) versus non-state compensation. When Dr. Adams was first hired by UGA, the Board of Regents stipulated that the Foundation could provide "a salary supplement of ⅓ the annual state-provided salary."[58] On June 26, 2000, the Board of Regents allowed UGA to provide up to 49% of Dr. Adams annual state-provided salary in the form of a salary supplement.[59]

In an October 4, 2000 letter from Mr. Pittard, Chairman of the Foundation, to Dr. Stephen Portch, Chancellor of the University of Georgia System, Mr. Pittard acknowledged this 49% increase allowed by the Board of Regents. The Foundation's share of the salary supplement was limited to 49% of the Board of Regents' base pay for Dr. Adams.[60] However, in 2001, the Foundation paid the majority of Dr. Adam's total compensation, including memberships, deferred compensation and taxable fringe benefits.

Table 2[61]

Fiscal Year	State Compensation	Non-State Compensation (included Deferred Compensation)	Total Compensation	Percent of Compensation from Non-State Sources
1998	$190,500	$90,998	$281,498	32%
1999	$203,975	$101,334	$305,309	33%
2000	$213,087	$111,450	$324,537	34%
2001	$219,402	$339,155	$558,557	61%
2002	$232,341	$211,764	$444,105	48%
2003	$239,103	$164,401	$403,504	41%
2004	$239,103	$335,984	$575,087	58%

Interestingly, in the same October 4, 2000 letter, Mr. Pittard also acknowledged the fact that, "The President of the University of Georgia is employed by the Board of Regents which has the responsibility for evaluating the President and for setting his compensation on an annual basis." This statement encapsulates the problem with which the Foundation is faced ever since fiscal year 2001. The Foundation is in a position of having the Board of Regents expect the Foundation to pay a significant portion of the President's salary, however, the Foundation has no authority to evaluate, much less hire or fire, the President.[62]

D&T interviewed Board of Regents trustee, Mr. Donald M. Leeburn, Jr. During our interview, D&T asked Mr. Leeburn why the Board of Regents did not simply pay 100% of the President's compensation. Mr. Leeburn responded that the Board of Regents could pay 100% of the President's compensation, however, there was no reason for the Board of Regents to do this since the Foundation was there to supplement state money. In fact, Mr. Leeburn indicated that he believed he would be derelict in his duties as a member of the Board of Regents if he pursued this course of action.

Fringe Benefits

An issue regarding taxable fringe benefits that came to D&T's attention relates to Dr. Adams' use of UGA football tickets. There have been allegations that Dr. Adams has not properly accounted for the number of tickets that are actually utilized by family and friends. More specifically, it is alleged that Dr. Adams has counted many of his family and friends as being either donors or potential donors, thus making the value of the tickets a legitimate tax deduction for the Foundation. The IRS considers the personal use of tickets as a taxable fringe benefit.

Based on our work, D&T has determined that Dr. Adams has, in fact, paid some taxes on an annual basis for tickets used by family and friends. D&T also understands that at times there are a number of tickets allocated to the President's box at the football stadium that go unused for any given game. However, in certain instances, D&T's analysis indicates Dr. Adams' office repeatedly classified friends and family as being business in nature. As noted by Mr. Landrum in a note to the files on November 30, 2001, Mr. Landrum indicated that relative to the attached Complimentary Ticket Usage forms, "a guest is either a donor prospect or a special invitee of the President for reasons of institutional interest."[63] The following individuals have been classified by Dr. Adams' office as being business in nature, some repeatedly being listed as being "MGP" (major gift prospects) at various UGA football games:[64]

- Jim Etheridge - Ms. Adams' brother (3 games)
- Julie Etheridge - Wife to Ms. Adams' brother (3 games)
- Jeff Kelley - Brother in law to Dr. Adams (3 games)
- Marsha Kelley - Sister to Dr. Adams (2 games listed as business, sometimes listed as personal)
- Grant Kelley - family of Jeff Kelley (2 games)
- Julie Kelley - family of Jeff Kelley (1 game)
- Adam Kelley - UGA student and family of Jeff Kelley (1 game)
- Beth Kelley - UGA student and family of Jeff Kelley (1 game)
- Hubert Adams - Father to Dr. Adams (1 game listed as business, other games listed as personal)
- Jean Adams - Mother to Dr. Adams (1 game listed as business, other games listed as personal)
- Jack and Mary Barker - Dr. Adams' high school teacher (4 games)
- Carrie Ferguson - UGA student and girlfriend to Taylor Adams (13 games listed as business, some games as personal)
- Mary Paige Tucker - UGA student and girlfriend to David Adams (6 games)
- Allen Tucker - family to Mary Paige Tucker (1 game)
- Al Tucker - family to Mary Paige Tucker (1 game)
- Honey Tucker - family to Mary Paige Tucker (1 game)

Several other couples that were friends of Dr. and Ms. Adams primarily from Nashville, Tennessee and also from California, were listed as being major gift prospects. Ms. Jackie Kohler, a former Executive Assistant in Dr. Adams' office both at Centre College, Kentucky and at UGA, confirmed to D&T that these individuals were personal friends to Dr. Adams prior to his Presidency at UGA. These individuals attended the UGA vs. Vanderbilt game in Nashville, Tennessee, receiving complimentary tickets from Dr. Adams. The dates for the games which almost all these couples attended, were October 17, 1998, October 14, 2000 and October 19, 2002.[65] The individuals are as follows:

- Mr./Mrs. Bill and Jane Connelly (3 games)
- Mr./Mrs. John and Carol Dawson (2 games)
- Mr./Mrs. Preston and Jane Kopf (3 games)
- Mr./Mrs. Jerry and Linda Rainey (2 games)
- Mr./Mrs. Lucien and Patricia Simpson (3 games)
- Mr./Mrs. James and Kanet Thomas (2 games)

D&T also noted that on several occasions, Mr. Steve Shewmaker, his wife Gail Spears and other Spear family members were listed as business and major gift prospects for UGA, attending several football games with Dr. Adams during 1998 and 1999.[66] This was the period prior to Mr. Shewmaker becoming an employee of UGA in January 2000 and providing legal counsel to Dr. Adams' office. D&T understands that Mr. Shewmaker was a close personal friend of Dr. Adams from his years as a judge in Kentucky while Dr. Adams was President at Centre College.[67]

Based on our review, D&T believes that Dr. Adams and his office have knowingly provided inaccurate and or incomplete documentation to the Foundation about the true nature of the relationship the aforementioned individuals have with UGA and Dr. Adams. It appears Dr. Adams should have received the value of the tickets for these individuals as taxable fringe benefits to himself and paid the resultant taxes associated with these benefits. Dr. Adams' actions are a violation of Foundation policies and procedures and may further violate IRS code regulations.

Administrative Fees

An item that falls loosely into the compensation category came to D&T's attention and is worth noting. All funds that are managed by the Foundation (of which there are well over 1,000 funds) have an administrative fee of .4% (4/10ths of one percent) assessed by the Foundation against those funds to cover expenses of the Foundation. In addition to this fee, all funds have an advisory fee assessed by the investment firm that is managing these funds.[68] As was mentioned in the section of our report that dealt with Dr. Adams' compensation, Dr. Adams has received over $270,000 in deferred compensation from two separate funds established for just this purpose. These funds were placed under the management of the Foundation in fiscal year 2001 and 2002.[69] In reviewing much of Dr. Adams' compensation information that was supplied by the Foundation, D&T uncovered a memo from the Foundation CFO, dated June 5, 2002, that instructed one of the Foundation accountants to exempt Dr. Adams' deferred compensation accounts from the Foundation's internal administrative fee.[70] Upon further review and questioning by D&T, it was determined that Dr. Adam's Chief of Staff, Mr. Landrum, had instructed the Foundation CFO to stop assessing this fee to Dr. Adams' deferred compensation accounts.

After D&T questioned Mr. Landrum about the reasoning for this instruction, Mr. Landrum apparently relayed this information to Dr. Adams. Dr. Adams then gave instructions that the Foundation resume assessing the administrative fee and assess the administrative fee retroactively for any months not assessed.[71] While it appears improper for the President's office to have requested the removal of the administrative fee, D&T believes that this recent corrective measure by Dr. Adams was appropriate. However, no adequate explanation was provided for the President's office initially requesting that Dr. Adams' accounts be treated differently.

Additional Compensation Issues

As part of our review regarding Dr. Adams' compensation, D&T also conversed with the Chairman of the Search Committee for Ohio State University, Mr. Jim Patterson. In 2002, OSU ultimately selected Dr. Adams' former VP and Provost, Ms. Karen Holbrook, to be their next President. Mr. Patterson verified a few of the details regarding the OSU job search provided by Dr. Adams to D&T, including the fact that Dr. Adams had indeed been one of the finalists for the position of OSU President. Due to confidentiality agreements Mr. Patterson had entered into, he would not reveal whether Dr. Adams actually received a job offer.

However, Mr. Patterson flatly refuted two claims made by Dr. Adams regarding his candidacy for the OSU Presidency. The first was concerning the amount of money that might have been offered to any candidate for this position. Dr. Adams stated twice in his interview with D&T the OSU offer was over $850,000 annually. The second time he referenced it in D&T's interview, Dr. Adams stated the compensation package offered him by OSU ranged from $850,000–$1 million.

Mr. Patterson told D&T that OSU did not make an offer to any candidate (if, in fact, anyone other than Ms. Holbrook received an offer) that came close to this amount. In fact, upon further questioning, Mr. Patterson responded that a total compensation package even reaching $600,000 was "out of the question." He further stated that a total compensation package that included a base salary, deferred compensation and a bonus might get to approximately $500,000.

A second representation of Dr. Adams refuted by Mr. Patterson dealt with Ms. Holbrook. In the interview with D&T, Dr. Adams concluded his discussion as to why he turned down the OSU job by saying it was he who "helped engineer Ms. Holbrook going to Ohio State." When D&T mentioned this to Mr. Patterson, he immediately responded that such a comment was absolutely false. Mr. Patterson stated that Ms. Holbrook's name came up before Dr. Adams name ever did and Ms. Holbrook interviewed with OSU before Dr. Adams did. Mr. Patterson added that two people had recommended Mr. Patterson contact Ms. Holbrook from the very beginning of their search for a President.

These facts could raise concern to the Foundation as to whether Dr. Adams provided false information to the Foundation with the intent of inflating his market value in order to obtain a better offer from UGA.

Mary Adams Stipend

Summary

1. Were Foundation funds used?

   • Yes. Foundation funds have been utilized to pay compensation to Ms. Adams for every year since fiscal year 2001. Ms. Adams' current annual compensation is $48,000.

2. Were proper procedures and policies followed by all parties connected to this transaction or were there improprieties?

   • Certain procedures were properly followed. However, proper procedures appear to have been violated by the then Chairperson of the Foundation, Mr. Pittard, by adding an additional $800 per month into a retirement account for Ms. Adams without the approval of the FEC.
   • The FEC attempted to conduct this transaction in a secretive manner.
   • No documentation of the FEC meeting approving Ms. Adams' compensation is available.

3. What approval was obtained?

   • The FEC appears to have granted approval for $3,200 per month of Ms. Adams compensation. Mr. Pittard appears to have granted the approval on the final $800 per month for funding Ms. Adams' retirement.

Background and Timeline

Dr. Adams began his Presidency at UGA in September of 1997. No one D&T spoke with had any recollection of conversations by Dr. Adams or his wife, Mary, that at the time of Dr. Adams' hiring, she desired to be compensated for her role and anticipated work at UGA. However, according to Mr. Jim Nalley, FEC Chairman from 1998 to 2000, Dr. Adams subsequently approached him and stated that he thought that due to Ms. Adams' hard work, she should have her own income. According to Mr. Nalley, Dr. Adams told him that Ms. Adams had a job and received a stipend from Centre College while he was President of Centre College.[72] Apparently, Ms. Adams was involved in some development work at Centre College.[73] Mr. Nalley advised Dr. Adams that while he agreed that Ms. Adams worked hard, he thought the issue would cause Dr. Adams a great deal of grief and, therefore, was not worth it. Mr. Nalley did, however, present this idea to the FEC who also agreed with Mr. Nalley that such an arrangement was not a wise idea.[74]

Sometime in 2000, Dr. Adams spoke with Mr. Pat Pittard at a dinner engagement with their wives about the fact the UGA Veterinary School wanted to hire

Ms. Adams to assist in development efforts. However, due to UGA's nepotism rule, she was prevented from doing so. Mr. Pittard apparently then developed the idea of paying a stipend to Ms. Adams as a way avoid the nepotism rule (Mr. Pittard is experienced in personnel matters, since he was the Chairman and CEO of Heidrick & Struggles, Inc., an Executive Search firm).[75] There was also some belief among various FEC members that Dr. Adams was underpaid relative to his peers. Therefore, insomuch as this was a way to pay additional compensation to Dr. Adams, paying Ms. Adams a stipend was appropriate. Further, it was generally acknowledged that Ms. Adams was very much involved in UGA affairs and would thus be deserving of this compensation.[76]

Mr. Pittard stated to D&T that he called every member of the FEC and of the Foundation Finance Committee to discuss this proposal. According to Mr. Pittard, only two members were neutral about the idea while everyone else approved it. Concurrently, the Foundation received a contribution from a donor that established a restricted fund allowing for discretionary expenditures by the President. This particular fund became the source for compensating Ms. Adams and providing for her expenses.[77]

According to files obtained from the Foundation, the FEC met and approved a stipend of $2,500 per month plus a car allowance of $700 per month. In addition, the FEC approved reimbursable expenses of $800 per month. Some time later, at the request of Mary and Mike Adams to Mr. Pittard, it was agreed that the $800 reimbursable expense money would be placed in a supplemental retirement account which Ms. Adams had previously opened with TIAA-CREF. The Foundation began making these monthly payments as of October 1, 2000.[78]

At the October 12–14, 2000 meeting of the Foundation board of trustees, the full board was notified that the FEC had approved the creation of a Stipend for the Spouse of the University President. The Foundation board minutes also stated that this action did not require full board approval.[79]

D&T Findings

D&T notes there are no FEC minutes that reflect any kind of action being taken on Ms. Adams compensation. That is not to say that it did not occur. Based on the response D&T received from FEC trustees who were present at that time, this issue was dealt with by the FEC. However, the lack of documentation of this approval has contributed in part to the misunderstanding and confusion surrounding the details of what was agreed upon by the FEC regarding Ms. Adams' stipend. Subsequent documentation that outlined the foregoing details had to be generated by Ms. Costello for Mr. Pittard's signature in order to confirm the actions of the FEC.[80] Almost every FEC trustee told D&T that they remembered either $30,000 or $40,000, or something in that range, as being the agreed upon amount. Several trustees still continue to be unsure as to how Ms. Adams' total annual compensation became $48,000 since the original vote on her stipend.

Based on Foundation records reviewed by D&T, combined with interviews of the individuals involved, it appears that the FEC did vote initially to approve a $2,500 per month stipend plus an additional $700 per month for a car allowance. This amounts to $38,400 annually, with $30,000 of this total being the stipend amount alone. Ms. Costello relayed this information to Ms. Coyle, CFO of the Foundation after the FEC meeting in October 2000. Approximately one week later, Ms. Costello called Ms. Coyle and stated that the compensation package included $800 for reimbursable expense money that would actually be placed into a supplemental retirement account. Ms. Coyle questioned Ms. Costello as to how this additional $800 was determined, when it apparently had not been voted on in the original FEC meeting. Ms. Costello brought this issue to the attention of the Foundation Chairperson, Mr. Pittard.[81]

On December 11, 2000, Ms. Coyle received a letter dated December 5, 2000 that was addressed to Mr. Patrick S. Pittard, from Kathryn R. Costello.[82] This letter was to obtain Mr. Pittard's confirmation of Ms. Adams' compensation. The letter reads in part:

"This letter is to confirm for our confidential UGA Foundation records, the actions of the Executive Committee *and subsequent modification of that action* regarding the stipend and expense money for Mary Adams.

The Executive Committee of the Board approved a stipend of $2,500 per month plus a car allowance of $700 per month. *In addition, the Committee approved expenses of $800 per month.* Subsequently, at the request of Mary and Mike Adams, you agreed that the $800 expense money could be placed in Mary's SRA." . . . [italics added by D&T]

It appears this letter acknowledges that a subsequent modification was made to Ms. Adams' compensation by the "Committee." The letter also appears to distinguish between the Executive Committee and the Committee. Ultimately, this letter appears to confirm information provided by Ms. Costello and Ms. Coyle. This may also explain why almost no one has a recollection of how Ms. Adams' compensation became $48,000. Based on this analysis, it appears that the FEC may not have authorized the $800 paid on a monthly basis into Ms. Adams retirement account.

Even if the Committee approved "expenses of $800 per month," the net effect of placing this money into Ms. Adam's retirement account, was to guarantee an additional $9,600 of annual income. Where previously, Ms. Adams could expense up to $800 a month, she now was guaranteed $800 a month and could continue to submit any additional expenses she incurred to the Foundation for reimbursement. Again, there is no indication that the FEC authorized this subsequent change in Ms. Adams compensation.

There have been questions regarding Ms. Adams' efforts on behalf of UGA and to whom she reports, if anyone. D&T learned the following additional information. Since Ms. Adams is paid by the Foundation, it was decided by the Foundation trustees that Ms. Adams would be responsible to the Chairman of the Foundation in executing her duties. Mr. Rooker told D&T that he had conducted a job review with Ms. Adams in the last year and further noted that Ms. Adams had made it her primary focus to enhance UGA's relationship with the community in the city of Athens, Georgia. As part of our review, D&T received a schedule of activities and events that Ms. Adams was involved in over the course of the last year. By all accounts, Ms. Adams' work in conjunction with Dr. Adams and on behalf of UGA have been much appreciated and well received.

Certain FEC trustees have also expressed the thought to D&T that a realization existed among the Foundation trustees that by paying Ms. Adams, the Foundation would be able to maintain Dr. Adams' compensation within the formula previously agreed upon with the Board of Regents. This formula dictated that the Foundation would pay Dr. Adams' compensation equivalent to 49% of the base compensation that he received from the Board of Regents. By paying his wife, the Foundation avoided literally violating the 49% rule. The other sensitivity expressed by these trustees was that paying Ms. Adams versus paying Dr. Adams directly effectively concealed this increase in compensation to Dr. Adams and lessened the possibility that UGA faculty might become upset with Dr. Adams receiving additional pay, since the faculty did not receive a pay raise during the same period.

Finally, D&T notes that Dr. Adams' recount of the facts to D&T reflect a variance from other sources. Dr. Adams made it clear to D&T that it was Mr. Pittard who initiated the idea of compensating Ms. Adams for her role at UGA. It is quite possible Dr. Adams simply forgot that he had actually approached Mr. Nalley earlier in time about the same issue and been advised by Mr. Nalley and the FEC that this was an ill-advised idea. At any rate, Mr. Rooker, Mr. Nalley and others all had specific recall about Mr. Nalley being first approached by Dr. Adams.

It is notwithstanding that several individuals mentioned to D&T that Dr. Adams was very focused on his compensation, along with Ms. Adams' compensation. Apparently so much so, the compensation issue outweighed any consideration for substantive discussions on other topics.

HANK HUCKABY HONORARIUM

Summary

1. Were Foundation funds used?

   • Yes. The honorarium of $30,000 was paid with Foundation funds.

2. Were proper procedures and policies followed by all parties connected to this transaction or were there improprieties?

   • The FEC did not follow proper procedure.

- According to Counsel, the FEC meeting held to approve the expenditure violated Foundation by-laws.
- While well intentioned by the FEC, the expenditure itself benefited Mr. Huckaby for performing state work, with little to no apparent benefit to UGA, thus violating Foundation Bylaws.
- The Foundation trustees should be more cognizant of the budgeting process in determining how any project or proposal will be paid.

3. What approval was obtained?

- The FEC granted approval for the honorarium.

Background and Timeline

Mr. Hank Huckaby is the Senior Vice President of Finance and Administration at UGA. Mr. Huckaby is also the Treasurer of the UGA REF.[83] When the current Governor, Mr. Sonny Perdue, was elected to office in 2002, the Governor called Dr. Adams to ask if he would loan Mr. Huckaby to the Governor's office to work on the State budget.[84] Specifically, Mr. Huckaby was asked to serve as Chief Fiscal Officer on the Governor's transition team during the first four months of the Governor's administration. In this capacity, Mr. Huckaby was tasked with reviewing the State's $16 billion plus budget. This he did while remaining in his position at UGA.[85]

Mr. Carl Swearingen, a FEC member who served as the Chairman of the Governor's transition team, was aware of the effort being expended by Mr. Huckaby over a six-month time frame in order to perform both jobs. Since Mr. Huckaby was not paid by the State for his services, Mr. Swearingen thought it would be a nice gesture for the Foundation to compensate Mr. Huckaby for "invaluable service far beyond the call of duty."[86] Mr. Swearingen approached Mr. Pat Pittard and, subsequently, Mr. Rooker with this idea.[87] Mr. Rooker discussed the idea with both the Chancellor of the Board of Regents and Dr. Adams.[88] Dr. Adams thought this would be a good proposal to bring before the FEC.[89]

Consequently, Mr. Rooker told D&T that he spoke with all the FEC trustees over a 12-week period of time about this idea and received approval from all the FEC trustees. The next Foundation board of trustees meeting occurred at The Cloisters, Sea Island, Georgia, from May 21 to 22, 2003.[90] In the middle of this multi-day event, Mr. Rooker convened the FEC at 7:30 A.M. of May 22, 2003 to consider two primary action items. One was a $40,000 bonus for Dr. Adams and the second was the $30,000 honorarium to Mr. Huckaby. All members of the FEC were present with the exception of Mr. Wyck Knox and Mr. Carl Swearingen.[91] Mr. Swearingen obviously was in favor of this proposal. Mr. Knox had been approached by Mr. Rooker the previous day about the fact that he intended to propose the honorarium the next day in a FEC meeting. Mr. Knox gave his approval to the idea and left for a wedding.[92] Both proposals received the unanimous approval of the FEC and the meeting was adjourned.

D&T Findings

The manner in which payment of this honorarium was approved appears to violate the Bylaws of the Foundation. Based on advice from counsel, the FEC is not authorized to act on behalf of the Foundation during a full board meeting of the Foundation trustees. Regardless of the interpretation of the Bylaws, it is unclear why this FEC meeting was held in this manner when the full board was available to take all appropriate actions.

Again, based on advice from counsel, an additional reason payment of this honorarium was inappropriate is because there is no evidence that payment of this honorarium was for services rendered to, or for the benefit of, the Foundation or UGA, as opposed to the State. Several individuals told D&T that Mr. Huckaby surely had to have created goodwill for UGA with the new Governor, due to his work. Certainly it could not have hurt. Others have pointed out, however, that Governor Perdue is a UGA graduate and was a UGA football player, creating doubt as to how Mr. Huckaby's actions would have made a significant impact in this regard. Perhaps more important than arguing over how the Foundation benefited is the fact that it appears the Foundation has made itself a willing party to expending funds in place of and on behalf of the State. The benefit to the Foundation or to UGA appears too indirect to support this use of Foundation funds no matter how laudable Mr. Huckaby's service to the State may have been. Others have also questioned why Mr. Huckaby was paid an honorarium while the UGA faculty and Deans of various schools received little to no increases in pay during the same period, much less bonuses of any type.

The final issue to discuss with regard to Mr. Huckaby's honorarium is the manner in which the Foundation board of trustees handles its budget. More specifically, the question arises as to whether the Foundation board of trustees and the FEC in particular pay sufficient attention to process and procedure in expending Foundation funds.

The day prior to the FEC meeting on May 22, 2003, the Foundation Finance committee met to discuss and finalize the budget for the year. Several of the same FEC members that approved Mr. Huckaby's honorarium the very next day were in attendance at this Finance Committee meeting. Throughout this meeting, no mention was made of any intent to pay a $30,000 honorarium to Mr. Huckaby. The Finance committee essentially finalized the budget for the year. The very next day, the FEC awarded Mr. Huckaby with an honorarium. No discussion occurred by the FEC as to where the funds for this honorarium would originate.[93]

Setting aside the merits, if any, of paying an honorarium to Mr. Huckaby, it appears the Foundation board of trustees and the FEC in particular should be more aware of the budgeting process and in determining how any project or proposal will be funded.

Finally, D&T will note that it understands Mr. Huckaby contacted Mr. Rooker and volunteered to return the honorarium to the Foundation. Mr. Rooker did not accept this offer.[94]

COACH JIM DONNAN SIDE AGREEMENT

Summary

1. Were Foundation funds used?

- No. The UGA Athletic Association paid approximately $250,000 plus some accrued interest to Coach Donnan to settle the side agreement.

2. Were proper procedures and policies followed by all parties connected to this transaction or were there improprieties?

- Dr. Adams did not follow proper procedures in authorizing the payment of this side agreement that was initially kept hidden from the knowledge of the Athletic Association Board. Further, it was improper of Dr. Adams to attempt to hide the payment of this side agreement without the knowledge of the Athletic Association's full board. The Foundation played no role in this matter, other than Mr. Jim Nalley (FEC trustee) acting as an intermediary for Dr. Adams and Mr. Donnan and Mr. Donnan's agent, Mr. Richard Howell.

3. What approval was obtained?

- Dr. Adams gave the final approval to the verbal side agreement that ultimately obligated the Athletic Association to pay this $250,000.

Background and Timeline

Mr. Donnan was the football coach for UGA prior to Dr. Adams' arrival as President. After having a successful season in 1997, Mr. Donnan began to receive inquiries about his willingness to coach elsewhere. Ultimately, the University of North Carolina decided to make Mr. Donnan an offer that was reputedly in the range of $1 million. Mr. Donnan, while very interested in the University of North Carolina opportunity, decided his preference was to stay with UGA if at all possible. To assist him, Mr. Donnan hired an agent, Mr. Richard Howell, to negotiate with UGA about amending his contract.[95]

In order to be responsive to the North Carolina offer and ensure that Mr. Donnan stayed at UGA, Dr. Adams and Vince Dooley, UGA's Athletic Director, held a telephone conversation with Mr. Donnan and agreed to the basic terms of a new contract. It was agreed among these parties that UGA would formalize Mr. Donnan's contract in writing as soon as possible. The basic terms of the contract were for Mr. Donnan to receive a six-year contract that paid him $650,000 annually. This phone call occurred in December 1997. Apparently, this phone conversation did address the fact that the UGA Athletic Association would guarantee some aspect of

Mr. Donnan's contract if it was terminated prior to a specified date, However, a set number of guaranteed years of income were not specified.[96]

Negotiations commenced to finalize the details of the contract. By July 1998, after months of negotiation, it became apparent the primary impediment to reaching a new agreement was the number of years Mr. Donnan would receive guaranteed income. The most that Mr. Dooley was in favor of offering was two and a half years guaranteed income. The minimum number of years that Mr. Donnan would agree to was three years of guaranteed income.[97]

At this point, some furor arose amongst players, coaches and some alumni over why Mr. Donnan's contract extension had not been completed. Mr. Nalley, who was a friend to Mr. Donnan, broached this topic with Dr. Adams while golfing with Dr. Adams. Mr. Nalley informed Dr. Adams of Mr. Donnan's request and communicated Mr. Donnan's concerns regarding the negotiations and what he felt were unfulfilled promises on the part of UGA. Mr. Donnan believed that his negotiations with Mr. Dooley were not making progress and felt that he needed to see if Dr. Adams would intervene on his behalf.[98]

After some discussion, Dr. Adams instructed Mr. Nalley to go ahead and "get the deal done," and if Mr. Donnan was fired (triggering the payment), they would "deal with it at that point." Dr. Adams told D&T that he believed Mr. Dooley had agreed verbally to three years of guaranteed income.[99] However, both Mr. Donnan and Mr. Howell have confirmed to D&T that this was never the case, and the most Mr. Dooley was willing to agree to was two and a half years of guaranteed income. Mr. Dooley personally confirmed this to D&T. Nevertheless, Dr. Adams concluded that since the whole deal was at a standstill over this one item, UGA should just "get the deal done." Dr. Adams viewed this decision as a $250,000 decision which equated to $50,000 per year under the proposed contract. Dr. Adams noted to D&T that UGA's budget is in excess of $1 billion and further, that he makes $50,000 decisions "all the time" at UGA. Therefore, in Dr. Adams opinion, this was not a big commitment.

D&T will not elaborate in this report on the details of how this amount is determined based on a six year, $650,000 annual compensation package. Suffice it to say that no party has debated the amount of the verbal side agreement and how the $250,000 was calculated. The amount is not at issue here.

Having agreed to the guarantee aforementioned, Dr. Adams stated that he instructed Mr. Nalley to communicate the same to Mr. Donnan. The only stipulation being that the $250,000 would not be a part of the written contract. The $250,000 would be a verbal agreement that should not be shared with anyone, other than those who presently were aware of it; namely, Dr. Adams, Mr. Nalley, Mr. Donnan and Mr. Richard Howell. According to Dr. Adams, he made that decision fairly quickly. Dr. Adams believed at that time this was the best decision for the University and it was time to get the matter resolved expeditiously.[100]

Mr. Nalley communicated this decision to Mr. Donnan and his agent, Mr.

Howell. Mr. Howell apparently asked if this guarantee could be put in writing, to which Mr. Nalley told him no.[101] Mr. Howell and Mr. Donnan finally concluded that while this was not optimal, they would accept this arrangement.[102] Mr. Nalley then called Dr. Adams the following Tuesday and again asked Dr. Adams for his confirmation to move ahead with this verbal side agreement, since Mr. Donnan had given his approval. Dr. Adams again gave his assent and subsequently the contract was signed.[103] It should be noted that the Athletic Director, Vince Dooley, and counsel to the Athletic Association, which was negotiating the remainder of the agreement, were completely unaware of this side agreement.[104] Mr. Dooley informed D&T he was shocked when, suddenly, Mr. Donnan and his agent seemed to fold on their demands and signed the contract as it then was negotiated.[105]

Two football seasons later, with a mediocre winning record and certain problem issues having arisen, it was decided that Mr. Donnan should no longer coach football at UGA. Not without some controversy between Dr. Adams and Mr. Dooley over the timing of his release, Mr. Donnan was terminated as UGA's football coach in December 2000.[106]

A few weeks after Mr. Donnan was terminated, Mr. Howell contacted Mr. Nalley and reminded him of the side agreement. Mr. Nalley, in turn, contacted Dr. Adams regarding same.[107] Dr. Adams acknowledged the fact this agreement had been made and stated the side agreement needed to be paid.[108] According to Mr. Nalley, he and Dr. Adams then had a discussion over how and from what source this payment could be made.[109]

Subsequent to this telephone call between Dr. Adams and Mr. Nalley, it became apparent that the only source of funds available for payment of the amount owed to Mr. Donnan was from the Athletic Association funds. Mr. Newton of King & Spalding recalls a conversation during which he advised the staff of the Athletic Association that it could not properly pay a sum in excess of $250,000 to an individual (Mr. Donnan) in the absence of a contract obligating such a payment unless the payment was authorized by the Board of Trustees of the Athletic Association, which, at the time, was unaware of this arrangement.

Later, a meeting was held involving the following individuals: Mr. Dooley, Mr. Ed Tolley, (the UGA Athletics Association NCAA compliance attorney), Mr. Shewmaker (UGA attorney that assisted Dr. Adams' office on legal matters), Mr. Floyd Newton (King & Spalding attorney that performed legal services for the Athletic Association and the Foundation) and another attorney friend of Mr. Dooley. At this meeting, Mr. Shewmaker stated the Athletic Association needed to absorb the cost of the approximately $250,000-plus side agreement and further suggested that this expenditure not be discussed with the Athletic Association board. Mr. Shewmaker did not indicate whether Dr. Adams had requested him to suggest this approach. Apparently, Mr. Newton challenged Mr. Shewmaker on this issue, stating that the full board needed to approve an expenditure of that size.[110]

Ultimately, in April 2001, the issue went before the full board of the Athletic Association. At that meeting, Dr. Adams explained what had happened relative to

Mr. Donnan.[111] The board decided that to avoid a lawsuit, they needed to approve the $250,000 expenditure for this side agreement. The expenditure was approved and the payment made.[112]

D&T Findings

D&T heard from several sources that Dr. Adams had asked Mr. Nalley to, in effect, take care of paying Mr. Donnan's side agreement.[113]

When D&T spoke with Mr. Nalley, while Mr. Nalley did not initially volunteer details of this conversation with Dr. Adams concerning the manner in which the side agreement would be paid, Mr. Nalley did upon subsequent questioning admit that he and Dr. Adams discussed whether athletic boosters could pay for the side agreement. Mr. Nalley stated that he volunteered to Dr. Adams he would try to raise money for this side agreement if it was legal to do so. Mr. Nalley was clear that it was he and not Dr. Adams that suggested this idea. Mr. Nalley further stated he thought he remembered Ed Tolley researched the legality of this and it was concluded that this was not a legal course of action to take. Finally, it should be noted that Mr. Nalley also denied to D&T the allegation that Dr. Adams asked him in some fashion to personally pay for the side agreement.

D&T also spoke with Mr. Tolley to obtain his recollection of any of these events. Mr. Tolley indicated that Mr. Nalley called him "out of the blue," sounding very nervous. According to Mr. Tolley, Mr. Nalley explained to him that a side agreement had been made with Mr. Donnan to pay him $250,000. Mr. Nalley then proceeded to explain to Mr. Tolley that Mr. Donnan had been terminated and now the $250,000 side agreement was being demanded by Mr. Howell. Of particular concern to Mr. Nalley was the fact that he personally had agreed to pay for this side agreement with Mr. Donnan. According to Mr. Tolley, Mr. Nalley indicated that he had agreed to pay for this arrangement at the time he and Dr. Adams had been golfing and Dr. Adams gave the order to get the deal done. According to Mr. Tolley, Mr. Nalley did not indicate whether Dr. Adams had asked him to take care of the side agreement. (D&T will note that some of the details provided through Mr. Tolley matched those relayed to us by Dr. Adams and Mr. Nalley.)

Mr. Tolley relayed the fact that he called Dr. Adams' office and received no response from Dr. Adams. However, Mr. Landrum did converse with Mr. Tolley about this issue and Mr. Tolley apparently informed him that having a coach paid outside of his contract terms by Mr. Nalley would be an NCAA violation. Mr. Tolley said that he told Mr. Landrum to inform the President that he should notify Mr. Dooley about this side agreement. Apparently, this did not occur before Mr. Tolley personally advised Mr. Dooley about this issue. Mr. Tolley further told D&T that he believed he relayed this information to Mr. Nalley as well. (D&T will also note that Mr. Tolley's account matched that relayed to D&T by Mr. Newton, King & Spalding partner whom Mr. Tolley had also called at that time in his role as the Athletic Association lawyer.)

In our discussions with Dr. Adams, Dr. Adams had no recall or failed to make any mention of such a discussion with Mr. Nalley about the possibility of having a booster pay for the side agreement. Dr. Adams stated it was decided long ago between he and Mr. Dooley not to "pass the hat" or do business in this fashion. Yet, Dr. Adams engaged in a discussion with Mr. Nalley where Mr. Nalley agreed to pay for this side agreement should it ever become necessary to do so. The side agreement that was reached by Dr. Adams and Mr. Nalley occurred in July/August 1998, less than one year into Dr. Adams' term as UGA President. Additionally, it appears that Dr. Adams made at least two subsequent attempts to have the Athletic Association pay for this side agreement before obtaining the approval of the full board of trustees of the Athletic Association. The first attempt appears to have been pursued by having certain individuals at the Athletic Association simply pay the expense without prior approval and the second attempt was by Mr. Shewmaker. It appears that Dr. Adams' intent in both attempts was to have this side agreement paid secretly, such that the Athletic Association board would not be aware of what had happened.

In D&T's interview with Dr. Adams, he expressed the opinion that while others may not agree with all of his decisions, he believes that he has always acted properly and within his discretion to act. Dr. Adams was emphatic about the fact that even with the Donnan side agreement, he had acted completely within his given authority in doing the deal and in how he did the deal. However, Dr. Adams did acknowledge that he "wished I could have this one back." It was the only time Dr. Adams admitted such an opinion to D&T.[114]

COSTA RICA ECOLODGE PURCHASE

Summary

1. Were Foundation funds used?

   • Yes. The initial purchase of $895,000 was accomplished with Foundation funds. Additional Foundation funds have been expended since then to renovate and maintain the Ecolodge.

2. Were proper procedures and policies followed by all parties connected to this transaction or were there improprieties?

   • Kathryn Costello, Senior VP External Affairs for UGA and Exective Director of the UGA Foundation, made a "mistake in judgment" by her own admission when she authorized what proved to be the authorization for the final closing on the Ecolodge on December 17, 2001. This authorization overstepped her authority, based on the December 7, 2001, directive issued by the Foundation.
   • The FEC made a good faith effort throughout this process to handle this transaction with all due diligence.

- Dr. Adams did not direct Ms. Costello to purchase the Ecolodge against the wishes of the Foundation's board of trustees. However, it appears Dr. Adams did not manage Ms. Costello effectively. Dr. Adams appears to have been aware of the risks Ms. Costello posed to UGA and the Foundation in the period preceding the purchase, and yet took no action to prevent or discourage this type of decision from being made.

3. What approval was obtained?

- Ms. Costello used her own approval based on her presumption that Dr. Adams wanted her to purchase the Ecolodge. In doing so, Ms. Costello exceeded the directive of the FEC.

Background and Timeline

The Costa Rica Ecolodge ("Ecolodge") is the site for a UGA program that allows students the opportunity to study abroad. In this instance the program focuses on environmental issues. The Ecolodge is one of several such UGA initiatives. The Ecolodge program started in the late 1990s, with some UGA faculty taking students to San Luis, Costa Rica for study and class credit. After a few years of activity, there was talk about the property being sold. Concerned faculty then began investigating various options, including the outright purchase of the Ecolodge land and buildings, in order to secure this site permanently for use in the study abroad program at UGA.[115]

D&T's review of the Ecolodge does not deal with the merits of having this program or whether this purchase has been financially accretive to the Foundation's bottom line. Rather, D&T's review focused on the manner in which the Ecolodge was purchased and why proper policy and procedures were not followed. Further, questions have persisted as to what role Dr. Adams played in the purchase of this property. Ultimately, the Ecolodge was purchased by the Foundation. Further, this particular program has been viewed as an academic success by everyone interviewed by D&T.

It should be noted that King & Spalding was tasked by the Foundation in March 2002 with reviewing the Ecolodge transaction in order to advise the Foundation on its legal obligations.[116] King & Spalding was not asked to determine the role Dr. Adams had in effecting the Foundation's purchase of the Ecolodge.

It is also important to know a few background facts about Ms. Costello, since much of what occurred with the Ecolodge purchase revolves around her role in the matter. Ms. Costello was a highly regarded university administrator and fundraiser prior to coming to UGA. Previously, Ms. Costello had held positions at several other universities, including the position of vice president for university advancement at Rice University. She had similar roles at the University of Maryland, the University of Texas Southwestern Medical Center in Dallas, Southern Methodist University and Vanderbilt University. In these roles, Ms. Costello planned or led campaigns that raised more than $900 million.[117] Prior to coming to UGA, Ms. Costello served on at least two boards with Dr. Adams and had also performed consulting work for Dr. Adams prior to his Presidency at UGA. Dr. Adams hired Ms. Costello to become Senior Vice President for External Affairs at UGA.[118] In this capacity she reported directly to Dr. Adams. In September 1998, Ms. Costello also became the Foundation Executive Director (also referred to as President) and was tasked with the primary responsibility of directing a fundraising campaign on behalf of the Foundation.[119]

As noted heretofore, the Ecolodge program enjoyed widespread support among Dr. Adams, UGA faculty and UGA students. When it became apparent that the Ecolodge might be sold, UGA faculty sought the help of UGA and Foundation officers and administrators to explore options whereby the Ecolodge might remain available permanently for use by UGA faculty and students.[120] Since it was clear that Dr. Adams supported the international study abroad programs, including the Ecolodge, and since the Foundation had the primary role in providing funding for these types of UGA initiatives, the task of establishing a more permanent arrangement for the Ecolodge fell to the Foundation Executive Director, Ms. Costello.

Sequence of Events

In March 2001, Ms. Costello traveled to Costa Rica to visit the Ecolodge and make her own assessment of its merits and report back to UGA and the Foundation. Subsequently, negotiations for the Ecolodge commenced in the summer of 2001 and an ultimate purchase price of $895,000 was agreed upon between the sellers and Ms. Costello.[121] On August 4, 2001, Ms. Costello met with King & Spalding attorney, Floyd Newton, and asked for help in executing the purchase of the Ecolodge.[122] King & Spalding began the process of assisting the Foundation in clarifying the business and legal issues associated with the Ecolodge. King & Spalding's initial assessment resulted in a warning to Ms. Costello from King & Spalding about getting involved with the Ecolodge deal because of concerns about how the proposed transaction had been presented and the role of the Liebermans, UGA part-time faculty members who managed the Ecolodge.[123] Nevertheless, negotiations continued between Ms. Costello and the sellers.[124]

On September 24, 2001, Ms. Costello issued a memorandum to the FEC trustees requesting a resolution to use Foundation funds to purchase the Ecolodge. The memorandum states that the purchase price was $895,000 and that a gift for same was anticipated to cover the cost. The memorandum further states that $40,000 in earnest money was needed to hold the land. Once executed, the Foundation would have 30 days to complete examination of the property and the business operations, and then close the purchase. Ms. Costello stated in her memorandum that Jack Rooker (Vice Chairman, Foundation board of trustees) concurred with the decision to purchase the Ecolodge. She further stated that, "Mike [Dr. Adams] and Karen [Holbrook—former Senior Vice President for Academic Affairs and Provost] are very supportive of the faculty request that we take advantage of this opportunity. I therefore request permission to use $40,000 of Foundation funds as earnest money as well as authority to pay the remainder of the acquisition price which will all be returned when gift monies are secured." A written consent document was attached for signature approval of the FEC trustees. This request was signed and approved by the FEC.[125]

On October 1, 2001, Ms. Costello informed the FEC via another memorandum that the $40,000 earnest money had been paid to the sellers and that the balance of the purchase price for $855,000 would be required in thirty days. A financial forecast was also made of additional expenditures required to renovate the site and cover various fees. Ms. Costello further stated that the Ecolodge had a positive cash flow with enough capacity to retire debt on a $1.3 million loan.[126]

On October 4, 2001 the FEC had a meeting and further discussed the Ecolodge. Minutes from this FEC meeting indicate that Dr. Adams "indicated his support of the purchase." A few of the trustees questioned whether or not the financing plan as outlined by Ms. Costello had been thoroughly reviewed. Mr. Rooker made a motion, seconded by Mr. William Espy and unanimously approved by voice vote, "to refer the financing plan to the Investment Committee for review and approval."[127]

On October 18, 2001, the Investment Committee deferred to the UGA Real Estate Foundation ("REF") for review and complete due diligence on the Ecolodge.[128]

By the end of October 2001, Ms. Jo Ann Chitty, REF President, had reviewed the Ecolodge budget numbers and concluded that "the project did not cash flow without debt and will definitely not cash flow with debt."[129] Sometime in November 2001, an extension was negotiated with the sellers on the closing date so that further due diligence could be performed. In exchange for this extension, the Foundation agreed to forfeit the $40,000 deposit. [130]

During the fall of 2001, efforts were being made by various UGA faculty and Ms. Costello to raise funds via donation for the Ecolodge. This fundraising effort fell well short of the $895,000 required to purchase the Ecolodge.[131]

At the end of November 2001, Ms. Chitty again concluded that the Ecolodge would not cash flow without paying a portion of the purchase price with donated funds. This message was relayed to the REF board at a meeting held during the same time period. Apparently, it was at this time that Dr. Adams made the first challenge, stating that if $500,000 was raised specifically for this project, he would endorse a "match" be given to fund the project from the Foundation's general endowment fund.[132] There is no evidence in the Foundation's minutes that such a commitment had been considered by, or approved by, the board of trustees, the FEC or the Finance Committee.

In a memorandum addressed to the Foundation Investment Committee and the Executive Committee, dated December 3, 2001, Mr. Pat Pittard, then Chairman of the Foundation notes the following:

"At the last Board meeting it was decided that further due diligence would be required before a commitment was made to this project. The process was put in the hands of the Real Estate Foundation.

First, it was necessary to decide if this property met strategic and programmatic goals. Dr. Adams and Ron Carroll, Director Academic of the Institute of Ecology, are emphatic that it does.

. . . So at present, the project is in the hands of the Real Estate Foundation; approval, or not, will come from its Board. I am confident that all appropriate oversight has been exercised, and if approved will satisfy University and Foundation requirements."[133]

On December 7, 2001, the FEC met to discuss a variety of issues including the Ecolodge. Mr. Rooker stated that because the Costa Rican government essentially shuts down from December 14 until the New Year, the Ecolodge project was on hold. At this point it was believed by the FEC that $300,000 in private pledges had been committed to fund the Ecolodge purchase, if in fact the property was acquired. Regardless of the funding, most FEC trustees recall that it again was reiterated at this meeting that the project was on hold until the REF gave approval to proceed with the purchase. It should be noted that the minutes to this FEC meeting do not reflect the fact that the trustees had reaffirmed their previous decision that the REF would have the final say on the project. In response to a question about directing gifts in the fundraising campaign, the minutes reflect that Dr. Adams stated that the Costa Rica project, along with another foreign study project, was a campaign objective. The minutes to this meeting indicate that all the FEC trustees but one were present, as was Dr. Adams, Ms. Costello and others.[134]

At the close of the meeting the FEC went into executive session, and all administrative staff, including Ms. Costello, and Dr. Adams left the room. It was then discussed and resolved that Mr. Pittard should relay to Dr. Adams the fact that the FEC had concluded they had lost their confidence in Ms. Costello for a variety of job performance reasons, particularly relative to the lack of progress in the fundraising campaign.[135] Subsequently, Mr. Pittard relayed such message to Dr. Adams within a couple days of this meeting.

Ms. Costello stated that sometime before December 17, 2001, when she authorized the purchase of the Ecolodge, she had a discussion with Dr. Adams about her work at UGA and the Foundation. At that meeting, Dr. Adams informed Ms. Costello that the FEC had lost confidence in her leadership and offered to give her a severance package if she resigned. Subsequently, in January 2002, Ms. Costello claims that Dr. Adams offered her a severance package from UGA that included 18 months worth of full salary and benefits. Additionally, Ms. Costello claims that Mr. Pittard offered her $70,000 to continue working on the campaign. Ultimately, it was agreed that Ms. Costello would relinquish her duties on March 1, 2002, but would continue to provide consulting services for another three months. Ms. Costello accepted both offers from Dr. Adams and Mr. Pittard. This decision to resign was formally announced to the Foundation board of trustees at their February 8, 2002 meeting in Atlanta, Georgia.[136]

Meanwhile, during all this time, Ms. Costello continued her efforts in raising funds for and closing the Ecolodge deal. On December 10, 2001, Ms. Holbrook sent a note to Ms. Costello stating Dr. Adams had called her from New Orleans and told her to tell Ms. Costello that he had spoken with Pierre Howard (Lt. Governor of Georgia and adjunct professor at UGA) and Mr. Howard believed he could raise $500,000 for the Costa Rica purchase. Dr. Adams again indicated to Ms. Costello, via Ms. Holbrook, that if this amount were on the table, UGA would find the remaining $500,000. Finally, Dr. Adams asked Ms. Costello to relay this decision on to Mr. Pittard.[137]

In an email dated December 11, 2001, from Ms. Costello to Milton and Diana Lieberman (a couple that were UGA faculty and working at the Ecolodge, but had taken an active role in facilitating the purchase/sale of the Ecolodge to UGA), Ms. Costello informed them that the fundraising effort was continuing and that Dr. Adams intended to use some of the Foundation funds as a challenge. In discussing how to proceed, Ms. Costello made it clear that; "I want to touch base with Karen [Holbrook] and Hank [Huckaby] and call Mike [Adams] before finalizing anything."[138]

On December 17, 2001, Ms. Costello gave the authorization via an email message from one of her assistants to Milton Lieberman to go forward with the closing. The closing apparently occurred on December 18, 2001.[139] At that time, no one at the Foundation (other than Ms. Costello) was aware the purchase had been made. Ms. Costello told D&T that she likewise did not realize at the time this action had triggered the purchase and obligated the Foundation to buy the property. Ms. Costello stated that this is what accounted for her own shock later in time when default notices came to UGA's offices at the end of February, 2002. Regardless of what she knew at that time, Ms. Costello had, in effect, countermanded the directive of the FEC not to proceed.

Ms. Costello also continued to pursue fundraising efforts on behalf of the Ecolodge through the month of January and February 2002.[140] These efforts included her acceptance of a loan from a personal friend, Mr. Barry Neumann, for $100,000 at a 15% interest rate at some point between December 11–18, 2001, which she obligated the Foundation to repay without authorization from the board of trustees.[141] It was this $100,000 loan that gave Ms. Costello sufficient cash to go forward with the December 18, 2001 closing. The balance of the purchase price came from the sellers, secured by a mortgage onthe Ecolodge. Later, Ms. Costello's desire to ensure that this $100,000 loan be repaid to her friend appeared to be a consideration on her part for finding sufficient donor funds in order to move the Ecolodge deal forward. It should also be noted that Ms. Costello contributed $6,000 of her own money to cover attorney's fees so that the closing could occur.[142] In a February 8, 2002 letter to Rachel Conway (FEC trustee and Secretary for the Foundation, who had been asked to donate funds to the Ecolodge), Ms. Costello stated:

"I have a letter that affirms the above. If you are prepared to sign it, it would be my best farewell gift as we have held the property largely because Barry loaned $100,000 to do so and I would love to complete this and get his money returned before I am gone."[143]

Sometime in February, perhaps as early as February 4, 2002, but no later than February 21, 2002, the Liebermans sent an email to Ms. Costello indicating that the payments to the sellers on the mortgage were late and additional penalties and attorney fees were owed.[144] Ms. Costello apparently did not inform anyone at the Foundation of this email, much less that the purchase had already occurred.

On February 21, 2002, Ms. Costello issued a memorandum to Dr. Adams stating that his challenge had been met and that $500,000 in donor gifts had been raised and the Foundation could proceed with contributing matching funds from the endowment. She then acknowledged and expressed her appreciation to Dr. Adams for the severance package offered to her to stay on as a consultant, saying, "Thanks for keeping me connected in such a nice way."[145]

On February 25, 2002, Dr. Adams responded to Ms. Costello's February 21, 2002 letter and in effect stated that the Ecolodge transaction was still subject to REF approval. He further instructed Ms. Costello that Ms. Chitty would be the point person for all future contacts and negotiations with all the parties involved in the Ecolodge purchase. Ms. Costello was also instructed to resign in her capacity as the Treasurer of the Board of Directors for the two Costa Rican corporations, which held title to the Ecolodge assets, with Tom Landrum replacing her in that capacity. In the letter, Dr. Adams reiterated that everyone be comfortable with the purchase price before proceeding and that the proposal be made subject to careful legal review. In closing, he states:

"Certainly, your counsel will be welcome in the coming weeks, and it would be good if you would share with Jo Ann as soon as possible all the details of the current status of the initiative. As always, I appreciate your advice. I am grateful for your efforts thus far in the Costa Rica initiative."[146]

Ms. Chitty states that she was not aware that the transaction had been consummated until she received a fax from the Liebermans to this effect on February 27, 2002. At this point, everyone with any interest in the Ecolodge was made aware of the fact that the Ecolodge had already been purchased and now a decision had to be made about how to proceed. Ultimately, after legal review from King & Spalding and further negotiation and business analysis, the Foundation completed the purchase of the Ecolodge and retired the seller financing. Regardless of how the Ecolodge transaction was conceived, financed and purchased, everyone D&T spoke with believes this program is a positive for UGA academically.

Ms. Costello's management role with UGA and the Foundation ended on March 1, 2002.[147] Ms. Costello stated that as soon as the Costa Rica purchase came to light, she was quickly removed from her responsibilities. As a result of this, the severance package she had been offered by UGA and the Foundation were both withdrawn. Instead, Ms. Costello was offered a 12 month (plus the additional three months agreed to in the original arrangement) consulting arrangement to continue to provide advice on the campaign. She was replaced in her capacity of Foundation Executive Director by Tom Landrum, Executive Assistant to Dr. Adams.[148] Mr. Landrum was initially the interim President and later in March 2003, became the permanent Executive Director.[149] Ms. Costello was replaced in her role as Executive VP of External Affairs by Mr. Steve Wrigley, who was until that time the VP for Government Relations of UGA.[150]

Costello Resignation

After being told by Mr. Pittard of the FEC's lack of confidence in Ms. Costello, Dr. Adams apparently confided in Mr. W. Charles Witzleben, a fundraising consultant to the Foundation, about the need to make a change regarding Ms. Costello. This discussion would likely have taken place in December 2001. Mr. Witzleben, who was also a friend to Ms. Costello, told Dr. Adams that he would attempt to encourage her to resign. Mr. Witzleben did speak with Ms. Costello after meeting with Dr. Adams.[151] Mr. Witzleben stated that Ms. Costello had talked about leaving her position with UGA and the Foundation for some time. [152] She again voiced her feelings that she should resign her post. Mr. Witzleben encouraged her to visit with Dr. Adams directly about her employment, stating that he thought Dr. Adams would help her out in some fashion. As discussed, Ms. Costello then visited with Dr. Adams who did offer Ms. Costello a severance package.[153] Ms. Costello apparently considered this offer over the holidays and accepted the package early in January 2002.[154]

In March 2002, Mr. Witzleben was in Raleigh, NC and received a call from Mr. Wrigley to discuss Ms. Costello's work situation. Mr. Witzleben recalled in vivid detail to D&T how that conversation transpired. Essentially, Mr. Witzleben recalls that Mr. Wrigley asked him if Mr. Witzleben would consider putting Ms. Costello on Mr. Witzleben's company's payroll with the Foundation directing Ms. Costello's payments through Mr. Witzleben's firm. This would occur by having Mr. Witzleben bill the Foundation back for the increased expense of having Ms. Costello on his payroll. Mr. Witzleben replied with an emphatic, "No." Mr. Wrigley then asked Mr. Witzleben if he would reconsider this matter for a few hours. Mr. Witzleben then responded that if he thought about it for a few hours, the answer would not be just "no, but hell no!" He then informed Mr. Wrigley that he considered this request totally insulting to his reputation and to his firm. He told Mr. Wrigley that he would never do this type of arrangement. Mr. Witzleben did note to D&T that Dr. Adams name did not come up in any of this conversation with Mr. Wrigley.

D&T also interviewed Mr. Wrigley regarding this issue. When pressed by

D&T, Mr. Wrigley admitted that he personally called Mr. Witzleben to ask if Ms. Costello could work for him, but Mr. Wrigley did not recall Dr. Adams asking Mr. Witzleben to put her on his payroll and charge UGA additional fees to pay for her compensation.

Dr. Adams' recollection about these events differs from Mr. Witzleben. When asked about Ms. Costello's post-employment work, Dr. Adams stated that Mr. Witzleben had made the initial contact and informed Dr. Adams that Ms. Costello had contacted Mr. Witzleben to ask if she could work for the Witzleben firm. Mr. Witzleben allegedly told Dr. Adams that he refused this request. Further, Dr. Adams stated Mr. Witzleben told him that having Ms. Costello work for Mr. Witzleben was just not possible in light of all that had transpired. In our interview with Dr. Adams, he was adamant that Mr. Witzleben called him. He further responded to our question about whether he directed anyone to approach Mr. Witzleben about hiring Ms. Costello and charging the increased fees back to UGA or the Foundation with an emphatic "no." When asked about this conversation with Dr. Adams, Mr. Witzleben repeated that he never, ever called or talked to Dr. Adams about any such thing. Ms. Costello also stated to D&T that she never called Mr. Witzleben and asked to work for him.

D&T Assessment

In general, it appears the Foundation board of trustees and the FEC made a good faith effort to handle the Ecolodge transaction with diligence and prudence. Ms. Costello overstepped the authority granted by the Foundation when she purchased the property. It appears Dr. Adams could have managed Ms. Costello in a better fashion than he did, knowing the facts made available to him. D&T will now expand on this assessment of how the Ecolodge was purchased. Again, as stated in the beginning of this report, D&T's assessment of how the Ecolodge purchase was managed and Dr. Adams' role in the matter are based to an extent on our assessment of all the issues that we reviewed and Dr. Adams' role in those issues.

It should be noted that Dr. Adams was a strong proponent of international study abroad programs, including the Ecolodge. While the Ecolodge as an environmental project was not, in and of itself, a significant issue with Dr. Adams, there is every indication Dr. Adams repeatedly stated his desire to purchase the Ecolodge and communicated the same to UGA administrators, including Ms. Costello, outside donors and the Foundation. Much of this has been already discussed above. Again, Dr. Adams' support for this project is not at issue.

Kathryn Costello's Responsibilities

Ms. Costello has admitted to making an error in judgment when she committed the Foundation to the purchase of the Ecolodge. She has further stated that this was her fault alone and no one else, including Dr. Adams. She has expressed this view repeatedly to various parties. Yet questions persist as to whether this admission tells the complete story.

Ms. Costello's working style and working relationship with Dr. Adams have helped to perpetuate questions regarding her admission. Almost no one interviewed considered Ms. Costello an individual capable or willing to defy the express orders of the Foundation or Dr. Adams up until that point in time. While Ms. Costello was acknowledged by many to be an executive who took initiative and had her own ideas, she had a track record at UGA and the Foundation of doing so within the confines of her expressed authority. Ms. Costello was said to be a team player and certainly not someone that would defy Dr. Adams or the Foundation's board of trustees. D&T has noted that this assessment by various people interviewed appears to be borne out by the memos, emails and letters authored by Ms. Costello. Ms. Costello repeatedly either asks for FEC member approvals, informs them of project status, references Dr. Adams, calls and reaches out to Ms. Chitty or the REF, contacts King & Spalding, etc. As noted previously, in the December 11, 2001 email from Ms. Costello to Milton and Diana Lieberman, Ms. Costello informed them that the fundraising effort was continuing and that Dr. Adams intended to use some of the Foundation funds as a challenge. In discussing how to proceed, Ms. Costello made it clear that, "I want to touch base with Karen [Holbrook] and Hank [Huckaby] and call Mike before finalizing anything."[155] All of this information indicates that making a decision of this magnitude without authorization would have been very much out of character for Ms. Costello.

In light of this work style profile, one can surmise that Ms. Costello was caught in a "moment of weakness" and, acting totally on her own, had an error in judgment. This has been suggested more than once. Conversely, one can conclude that Ms. Costello believed she was following orders and executed a transaction that she had been tasked with all along.

Ms. Costello has personally taken the blame for executing the Ecolodge purchase with numerous individuals. She has characterized it as an "error in judgment" made during a period when her personal life was in crisis due to a variety of reasons. This would appear to amount to a full confession with nothing further to be said. Yet, Ms. Costello has also stated to D&T and others that she would never have executed this purchase if Dr. Adams had told her not to do so. She believed that she was acting in the interests of and on behalf of Dr. Adams when she purchased the Ecolodge in December 2001, just as she was throughout the fundraising period for the Ecolodge.

Dr. Michael Adams' Responsibilities

The FEC clearly mandated on December 7, 2001 and before that the purchase of the Ecolodge would only be decided after the REF made its recommendations. It appears that Dr. Adams never explicitly told Ms. Costello to ignore this Foundation directive and purchase the Ecolodge. On the other hand, Dr. Adams admitted that it was likely he did not instruct Ms. Costello to stop her efforts to acquire and fund the Ecolodge. Dr. Adams stated to D&T that he just thought it was obvious from the FEC meeting in December that the Ecolodge was not to be purchased, so he assumed Ms. Costello would abide by that decision. Dr. Adams stated that he was shocked when he heard Ms. Costello had purchased the Ecolodge. Others on Dr. Adams' staff have likewise affirmed to D&T the surprise this action was to Dr. Adams. Dr. Adams also told D&T that it was Ms. Costello's purchase of the Ecolodge transaction that ultimately forced him to ask for her resignation. He indicated that he told Ms. Costello this action was so egregious that she had lost the Foundation boards' confidence and, therefore, needed to resign.

Dr. Adams' recount of this situation does not entirely match documented evidence. The FEC's indication of a lack of confidence occurred on December 7, 2001 which was prior to Ms. Costello's go-ahead order to purchase the Ecolodge on December 17, 2001. No one, including Dr. Adams, appears to have known about the Ecolodge purchase until the end of February 2002.

The other factor that must be considered in order to determine Dr. Adams' role in the Ecolodge matter is the incident with Mr. Witzleben. Mr. Wrigley and Mr. Witzleben both have a recollection of Mr. Wrigley initiating a call that included the question of whether Mr. Witzleben would consider hiring Ms. Costello to work for him. Dr. Adams was also aware in some fashion that this question had been posed. However, at this point the similarity of recollection ends. There are two questions. First, did Mr. Wrigley in fact ask Mr. Witzleben to hire Ms. Costello and charge her compensation back to the Foundation under his company's billing? Second, if in fact Mr. Witzleben's account is accurate, why try to handle Ms. Costello's compensation in this manner at all? Naturally, one must address the credibility of Mr. Witzleben's account.

D&T's review indicates that Mr. Witlzeben's account appears to be the most accurate and credible version of what happened. This appears true for several reasons. As to his discussion with D&T, Mr. Witzleben should be considered the most disinterested party to this incident. Mr. Witzleben did not volunteer this account to D&T nor was he even interested in talking to D&T about this incident. In fact, Mr. Witzleben expressed a strong desire to be left out of D&T's review process. Mr. Witzleben told D&T that he considered, and still considers, Dr. Adams a friend from over 10 years ago after working as a campaign consultant to Dr. Adams. On the basis of this personal friendship and business relationship, Mr. Witzleben preferred to be left out of D&T's review of this matter. At the time the conversation with Mr. Wrigley occurred, Mr. Witzleben was receiving substantial fees for his campaign fundraising work at UGA. Clearly, he wanted this work to continue, so the likelihood of fabricating this version of events would seem remote. Also, it is quite understandable that Mr. Witzleben stands to lose potential future business, since a good many of the current Foundation trustees sit on the boards of other charitable institutions. His comments, which do not reflect favorably on Dr. Adams administration, could be viewed very negatively by some of these trustees and thus impact Mr. Witzleben's business elsewhere in Georgia. Finally, D&T found Mr. Witzleben's recollection of this conversation and several other events as being much more precise and detailed than that of Mr. Wrigley or Dr. Adams, both of whom confessed to a poor recall of any topic dating back to 2001 and 2002 when the Ecolodge transaction occurred. D&T will note that Mr. Wrigley only admitted as much as he did when D&T continued to push him for the details of his conversations with Mr. Witzleben. All of these factors combined provide support that Mr. Wrigley did ask for this favor from Mr. Witzleben regarding Ms. Costello's compensation.

Regardless of how the severance package was funded, it does not appear reasonable to offer someone who has received a great deal of criticism for her job performance a 15-month consulting package that pays $10,000 per month to do the very thing that has been criticized. Ultimately, Dr. Adams and the Foundation reduced Ms. Costello's severance package significantly. Previously she was to receive 18 months worth of full salary and benefits. At the end of February 2002, she had a 12- to 15-month consulting agreement and was subsequently called a "rogue employee" by Dr. Adams.

Ms. Costello is the first to admit that Dr. Adams did not force her to actually execute the purchase, however, Dr. Adams was in favor of buying the Ecolodge and encouraged every effort to make the Ecolodge a reality. Again, this in and of itself was not wrong on Dr. Adams' part. Ms. Costello also stated to D&T that Dr. Adams indicated to her that he was "getting a lot of heat" from what happened and he would not take the blame for this, but that she would. As such, there does not appear to be a justifiable reason for why the President's office proposed the type of work arrangement with Mr. Witzleben, as appears to have been done.

In reviewing Ms. Costello's actions, D&T also determined it was common knowledge among FEC trustees and UGA administrators, including Dr. Adams, that Ms. Costello had a variety of crises that seemingly besieged her personal life during 2001. These issues appear to have negatively impacted her job performance even prior to the Ecolodge purchase. This fact alone, coupled with several warnings to Dr. Adams by FEC trustees and other influential individuals' privy to Foundation business, should have alerted Dr. Adams to the fact that Ms. Costello needed clear instruction.

Ms. Chitty stated that sometime in November 2001, she spoke with Ms. Costello and encouraged her to let the Ecolodge project die with the purpose of trying to come back in January 2002 to renegotiate a new deal on better financial terms. Ms. Chitty further spoke with Mr. Rooker and Dr. Adams in November 2001, to express her concerns that Ms. Costello was becoming too emotionally involved and fixated on purchasing the Ecolodge without regard to whether it made good business sense for UGA or the Foundation. Ms. Chitty states that Dr. Adams told her not to worry about it.[156]

Even prior to Ms. Chitty's warning to Dr. Adams, other influential individuals privy to Foundation and UGA business told D&T they also expressed deep concerns to Dr. Adams about Ms. Costello's job performance and the potential impact this could have on the fundraising campaign and her other areas of responsibility.[157] Some of these concerns were voiced as early as the summer of 2001. There is no indication

Dr. Adams heeded any of these warnings by intervening more directly with Ms. Costello's efforts to purchase the Ecolodge. It was only after the FEC decided that they were losing confidence in her leadership abilities and recommended removing Ms. Costello from her duties on December 7, 2001 that Dr. Adams took action.

Finally, Ms. Costello indicated to D&T that her working relationship with Dr. Adams was faltering as early as the spring of 2001. Apparently, Dr. Adams met with Ms. Costello at that time and indicated to her that she had lost the confidence of certain members of the FEC. After speaking with these members, Ms. Costello said she realized that it was likely that Dr. Adams had lost confidence in her.

Dr. Michael Adams' Authority Regarding "Matching" Funds

An additional question that has been raised is whether Dr. Adams had proper authority to make a $500,000 match to come from the Foundation if $500,000 in donations were received from donors to fund the Ecolodge purchase. D&T understands, based on our conversation with counsel, that Dr. Adams did not have the authority to issue this challenge which promised matching Foundation funds. Neither Dr. Adams nor any other trustee of the Foundation has the ability to authorize a challenge that would obligate the Foundation for $500,000 without proper approval by the board of trustees. For an expenditure of that magnitude, the authorization would have to come by vote from the full board of trustees.

ALUMNI CENTER PROJECT

Summary

1. Were Foundation funds used?

- Yes. $919,768 in Foundation funds have been expended on the Alumni Center, largely for architect fees. This expenditure is out of a total of approximately $1,406,722 in fees incurred, of which the Real Estate Foundation ("REF") paid the rest. We note, however, that the Foundation has guaranteed a substantial portion of the REF's indebtedness.

2. Were proper procedures and policies followed by all parties connected to this transaction or were there improprieties?

- Proper procedures and polices were not followed by Dr. Adams, particularly with regard to the involvement of his longtime friend, Mr. Filoni. Mr. Filoni's hiring was not in compliance with the self-imposed regulations that the REF followed from the Board of Regents. These regulations stipulate how projects should be bid and how companies should be retained prior to performing work of this nature. Further, the decision to utilize Mr. Filoni without due process showed questionable judgment on the part of Dr. Adams. Additionally, it appears Dr. Adams did not manage the Alumni Center properly such that unnecessary expenditures did not have to be incurred. As a result, it appears that the Foundation and the REF have little tangible benefit for these expenditures should Mr. Filoni's design be utilized, other than usable programming work approximating $250,000 to $400,000 of value.

3. What approval was obtained?

- Generally the proper approval processes were utilized as architects were hired. However, with regard to Mr. Filoni, Dr. Adams bypassed the normal bidding process and simply directed Mr. Filoni to create his own designs.

Background and Timeline

The idea of building an Alumni Center began in earnest under the administration of Dr. Knapp. Initially, the Alumni Center was conceived to be a three building complex that was budgeted to cost $8.6 million. At that time, Danny Sniff, UGA Director of Facilities Planning (campus architect) was charged with oversight for the Alumni Center. The original building was conceived without having made a site determination.[158] As will be seen, site location has been one of the ongoing issues with the Alumni Center. Another important note is that Dr. Adams became UGA's President on September 1, 1997.[159] This is noteworthy because the original Alumni Center was designed before the UGA Campus Master Plan was completed.[160] The Master Plan was a comprehensive and long-range plan for building facilities on the UGA campus that had been mandated by the Board of Regents. The Master Plan began to be developed prior to Dr. Adams' Administration.[161]

During 1999, a search and selection process was conducted for an architect. Mr. Michael Dennis of Michael Dennis & Associates was selected from a group of six architects to be the design architect for the Alumni Center. Mr. Dennis was not a resident of the state of Georgia. Therefore, in order to comply with regulations stipulated by Georgia's Board of Regents, the firm Jova, Daniels and Busby was selected as the project architect through whom Mr. Dennis worked.

The first site selected for the Alumni Center was Lake Herrick.[162] Apparently, Dr. Adams did not care for the Lake Herrick site in spite of the enthusiasm of others on the selection committee. Despite his misgivings, Dr. Adams reluctantly went along with the Lake Herrick site.[163]

It was understood by Mr. Sniff and UGA officials from the beginning that the Lake Herrick site had environmental issues due to having served as a landfill in the past. Approximately $1 million was originally budgeted by UGA to address the environmental issues. Mr. Dennis' plan ultimately changed from the original concept of having a three building complex to having only one building. Ms. Costello also became involved in the project and told Mr. Sniff that Dr. Adams wanted the Alumni Center to include space for Foundation offices, Communication offices, a TV studio, Career Planning and Placement and space for other functions. According to Mr. Sniff, as a result of these changes, the budget for the Alumni Center increased from $8.6 million to approximately $32 million. Additionally, the Alumni Center site now encompassed seven to eight acres.[164] Based upon various discussions, most people familiar with Mr. Dennis' designs favored his plans. However, Dr. Adams was uncomfortable with the design and ultimately opposed it. Apparently, Dr. Adams did not feel this design fit in well with the campus Master Plan.[165]

Sometime in late 1999, Dr. Adams instructed Mr. Sniff to terminate Mr. Dennis' work on the Alumni Center. After terminating Mr. Dennis, the firm Jova, Daniels and Busby took over as sole architect and attempted to create a design that complied with the Master Plan. None of the Busby firm designs were well received by anyone on the Alumni Center building committee, thus Dr. Adams was not shown any of their designs.[166]

During 2001, an architectural firm out of Boston, Massachusetts named Ayers, Saint, Gross, was brought in by Mr. Sniff as the design architect for the Alumni Center, since they were the architects that created the UGA Master Plan. The Busby firm continued its role as project architect. At this point it became clear that site size, location, topography, and shape were creating severe design challenges. It was also determined that the REF should assume responsibility for the contractual processes due to future bond financing requirements.[167] At this point, Mr. Sniff essentially was replaced by Ms. Chitty as effective project manager due to the involvement of the REF.

The Gross firm completed a set of designs that incorporated some features not heretofore seen by Mr. Sniff. For reasons that D&T was unable to determine, the Gross firm designs never made it past the review stage of Mr. Sniff and Ms. Chitty. Ultimately, the Gross firm designs were never submitted for review to Dr. Adams or the Alumni Center committee.

The REF decided to hold a design competition, providing an allowance to each of the competitors to help defray the expenses. Four architect firms competed and provided building designs. The architect selection committee consisted of Mr. Jack Rooker, Mr. Carl Swearingen, Mr. Carlton Curtis, Ms. Mary Adams, Ms. Kathryn Costello, Mr. Dave Muia and Ms. Jo Ann Chitty. The committee agreed to recommend the design proposed by Collins, Cooper and Carusi to Dr. Adams. The designs were presented to Dr. Adams and he concurred with the committee's selection. The Carusi firm was retained and the REF contracted with Carter & Associates to be the program manager.[168]

During this whole time period, it became clear to everyone involved in the Alumni Center project that the Lake Herrick site was too small for the size of building now being discussed. Perhaps more importantly, further environmental problems were uncovered at both the Lake Herrick site and the East Campus commuter parking lot which was also being considered as a potential site. The costs and potential liability of building on these sites were deemed to be prohibitive and entailed unacceptable levels of risk. Thus, further studies were conducted and eventually it was determined, with Dr. Adams' concurrence, that the Alumni Center should be built in the Central Precinct of the UGA campus.

Given the proposed Alumni Center's new Central Precinct location and the value of this particular property, it made sense to add other components of UGA life into the Alumni Center building. Dr. Adams believed the building should have a size and outline that conformed proportionally with its surroundings, particularly with the student center building that would sit opposite the Alumni Center. As a result, Dr. Adams principally added a parking deck underneath the complex and a UGA bookstore. Subsequently, debate occurred between all interested parties as to the purpose of the building, the UGA functions that should be included and the appearance of the Alumni Center.[169]

The Carusi firm set about designing the Alumni Center. Upon completion, the plan was presented to the Alumni Board's oversight committee. The oversight committee approved of the Carusi designs.[170] However, Dr. Adams was once again unimpressed and thought the design was mediocre at best.[171] Dr. Adams' thinking about the design of the Alumni Center was already being influenced by the opinions of an architect Dr. Adams regarded very highly and had utilized prior to his appointment as UGA President. This architect, Mr. Al Filoni, from Pittsburg, Pennsylvania, would apparently visit Mr. Sniff's office on a quarterly basis and make critical comments about the Carusi firm design.[172] Finally, Dr. Adams instructed his assistant, Ms. Kathy Pharr, to call Ms. Chitty and have her send the Carusi design for the Alumni Center to Mr. Filoni so he could attempt to create a design Dr. Adams liked. Ms. Chitty sent the Carusi designs to Mr. Filoni.[173] Ms. Chitty also instructed the Carusi firm to halt their work and likewise called Carter & Associates and terminated their work as program manager.

Mr. Filoni set to work, spending a lot of time with Dr. Adams, often one on one and without Ms. Chitty or Mr. Sniff involved. This is noteworthy because up until then, Dr. Adams never met directly with the previous architects to discuss his vision for the Alumni Center. Dr. Adams was the key decision maker, but until Mr. Filoni's design work, Dr. Adams involvement with the process of building the Alumni Center was minimal.[174] Dr. Adams and several other individuals visited Mr. Filoni's offices in Pittsburg. The consensus of the group was they liked the design. Most importantly, Dr. Adams liked the design. Dr. Adams directed Mr. Filoni to continue design work with the intention of visiting Athens, Georgia, and presenting his plan to an expanded group of people that included Mr. Sniff, Mr. Rooker and Ms. Chitty. This meeting occurred and further feedback was provided to Mr. Filoni. Finally, in February 2003, Dr. Adams presented Mr. Filoni's design to the full board of trustees for the REF, with Mr. Filoni in attendance. [175]

At the February 2003 REF board meeting, most questions revolved around costs for the project.[176] With the latest design iteration presented by Mr. Filoni, the programming for the building had changed again. The Alumni Center now included suites for the UGA President to facilitate meetings with Alumni, a senate like executive boardroom, additional stairwells, elevators and other features. Additionally, the buildings exterior facade now had a much more costly design.[177] Mr. Filoni quoted the REF a price tag of $50 million to complete the project.[178] Ms. Chitty and Mr. Rooker (Mr. Rooker is in the real estate business) had conducted their own independent analysis and also had a real estate specialist separately analyze Mr. Filoni's plans. This analysis determined Mr. Filoni's design would actually cost approximately $75 million.[179] During this meeting a discussion ensued over the project costs. Mr. Filoni argued with Mr. Rooker and Ms. Chitty about whether the $50 million that the REF had budgeted, represented the construction costs only, or whether $50 million represented total project costs. Mr. Filoni, apparently admitted that his design cost was $50 million for construction costs alone and, therefore, could not come close to being accomplished for a total project cost of $50 million. Apparently, Mr. Filoni was also defensive of his work and stated that he did not believe in designing a building to a square foot price. Subsequently, Ms. Chitty directed Mr. Filoni to cease his work, since it was deemed that this price tag could not be sustained by any anticipated funding through donations.[180]

D&T Findings

As of the writing of this report, work on the Alumni Center has ceased. Apparently, a proposal was made at a recent REF board meeting for representatives of the REF to visit other Alumni Centers around the country for design ideas. Nevertheless, approximately $1.4 million in fees have been incurred to date with $919,768 of that paid by the Foundation and the remainder paid by the REF. D&T has been told by Ms. Chitty and others that Mr. Filoni's designs can be better termed as sketches at this stage. Mr. Filoni estimated that his fee for designing the Alumni Center would be approximately $3.5 million. This is about twice the cost of the designs submitted by the Carusi firm.[181] As a result, UGA, the Foundation and the REF have received minimal value for their money since Mr. Filoni's plan appears to be the only acceptable plan to Dr. Adams and this design plan is too costly to build. The only portion of the $1.4 million that is still usable is the money spent on determining programming, site location and the like. Mr. Sniff and Ms. Chitty estimated that approximately $250,000 to $400,000 of value still resided in the expenditures made to date.

Al Filoni's Involvement

Ms. Chitty stated to D&T that soon after learning of Mr. Filoni's involvement in the Alumni Center, she informed Mr. Hank Huckaby, Senior Vice President for Finance and Administration, that the REF had not hired Mr. Filoni and, therefore, would not be paying any bills submitted by Mr. Filoni. Ms. Chitty believed that Mr. Filoni should have been properly retained from the outset, as the previous architects had been. As an out of state architect and with no project management firm or design firm currently being retained by UGA or the REF, it was necessary for Mr. Filoni to go through the Board of Regents bid process. Clearly, Mr. Filoni's fees would eventually exceed $100,000, which would mandate the Board of Regents approval process.

Apparently, Mr. Huckaby told Ms. Chitty that UGA would pay for Mr. Filoni's fees. However, when Mr. Filoni's bills were submitted to Mr. Huckaby's office for payment by the University, Mr. Huckaby held the bills. Mr. Huckaby apparently stated to Ms. Chitty that he would pay for Mr. Filoni under the current consultant contract. Ultimately, UGA did not pay Mr. Filoni's fees since Mr. Filoni had not been properly contracted through the normal bidding process. As a result, Mr. Huckaby asked the REF to pay Mr. Filoni's fees. The REF paid $74,762 of Mr. Filoni's fees. At this point Ms. Chitty indicated to Mr. Huckaby that if Mr. Filoni would be the architect of record, then he should be properly retained. After receiving an indication of what Mr. Filoni's fees were anticipated to be ($3.5 million), Ms. Chitty told Mr. Filoni that the REF only had $400,000 left.[182] This amount being entirely inadequate to fund further work and the proposed designs being too expensive, Mr. Filoni halted all further work. D&T notes that Dr. Adams accepted full responsibility for involving Mr. Filoni on the Alumni Center.[183]

D&T understands that the REF is a private entity, wholly owned by the Foundation. As such, it is not subject to the state regulations as promulgated by the Board of Regents. However, the REF self-imposed the state regulatory process that the Board of Regents put in place for the University System. This was done because the REF recognized that any building project that might be proposed would be on land owned by the Board of Regents. Therefore, it made good sense to follow this process and avoid any second-guessing and questioning about the practices being followed by the REF. Further, the REF has an informal agreement, if you will, to keep the Board of Regents informed of any project contemplated or in progress.[184] In light of this practice by the REF, it appears that proper policy and procedures were not followed by Dr. Adams.

Management of the Alumni Center Project

Based upon our review and analysis, the record indicates that the Alumni Center project was not properly managed. The Alumni Center project was a project that developed over the course of many years. Several site changes occurred. Numerous programming changes were made. Debate still rages over the merits of including the bookstore with this building and other features of the building. Due to all of the above, it was inevitable for a project this size to incur significant fees. However, our review of the records and discussions with numerous people involved in the development of the Alumni Center project indicate the process should have been managed in a better fashion than what has transpired to date.

There is no question that certain costs incurred on the Alumni Center project were unavoidable. No project of this type will ever be completed with 100% accuracy and efficiency by anyone. The question is one of reasonableness. To answer the question of reasonableness, a few additional facts may be helpful.

One factor that stands out with regard the Alumni Center project is the lack of leadership for driving the project forward. We asked numerous individuals with knowledge of the Alumni Center project as to who was in charge of the project or who should be held responsible for what has happened to date. The answers varied. Even Dr. Adams seemed unsure as to who should be held accountable for the Alumni Center project, although he finally offered up that perhaps the Senior VP of Finance and Administration, Mr. Hank Huckaby, could be held responsible. With no one clearly in charge from start to finish and with no real accountability, the Alumni Center project was destined to flounder.

It appears Dr. Adams had the final say over every plan that was proposed. The only plan acceptable to Dr. Adams was the plan from Mr. Filoni. If Dr. Adams had the final say over any proposed design and yet by the same token was unsure over who should be responsible for what has occurred to date, D&T would suggest that Dr. Adams was in charge and, therefore, should be the one held accountable for the Alumni Center project. Other facts point to the same conclusion.

It is clear from our various interviews that Dr. Adams has strong ideas about the overall design of the campus. Mr. Sniff noted that Dr. Adams will often get involved in making decisions over what trees should be cut down or left standing on different projects. By way of example, D&T has even heard accounts of Dr. Adams having the walls of a building under construction moved two to three times. As a direct result of Dr. Adams actions and at his orders, Dr. Adams caused the dismissal of some of the architects that worked on the Alumni Center project. All of these facts indicate that Dr. Adams was the one individual in charge of the Alumni Center project since his arrival at UGA in September 1997 throughout the entire project to date.

The question remains as to how Dr. Adams managed the Alumni Center project. First, both Mr. Sniff and Ms. Chitty made it very clear that Dr. Adams was very involved in the decision making of each design. However, both individuals indicated that to the best of their knowledge, Dr. Adams never met with Mr. Dennis, the Busby firm or the Carusi firm to give them his input of how he wanted the Alumni Center project design to look. In contrast to this, Dr. Adams met numerous times with Mr. Filoni as he worked on sketching the Alumni Center. It is no wonder that Dr. Adams liked Mr. Filoni's design and did not like the previous designs.[185]

Other management questions arise due to the manner in which Dr. Adams brought Mr. Filoni into the process without going through the normal state bidding requirements. The response from Dr. Adams and others to this occurrence has been twofold. First, Mr. Filoni is not the named design architect and a decision has not been made to utilize him. Secondly, Mr. Filoni is only acting in his ongoing role as a consultant to UGA.

While technically these arguments may be true, it cannot be denied that Mr.

Filoni's sketches still cost approximately $75,000, which D&T understands is substantially more than the cost allowed to any of the four firms that participated in the previous design competition of which Mr. Filoni was not involved. It is also unclear why UGA refused to pay Mr. Filoni's fees. However, a possible explanation is the fact Mr. Filoni was not properly retained. He was not selected through the normal Board of Regents bidding process. Further, Mr. Filoni was an out of state architect and the Board of Regents requires that in such situations he would have had to work as a subcontractor of a Georgia architectural ftrm. This also was not done.

We note, as have others, that bringing in an old friend, no matter how talented and accomplished, raises eyebrows even to the most casual observer. At a minimum Mr. Filoni should have been required to pursue the normal bidding process. For Dr. Adams to single-handedly put Mr. Filoni to work on the design and terminate the Carusi firm simply does not appear proper. In short, it creates an appearance of impropriety on the part of Dr. Adams to have proceeded in this manner.

D&T's final comment regarding the Alumni Center project is with regard to certain comments made by Dr. Adams in our interview with him.

When discussing the Alumni Center issues with D&T, Dr. Adams presented a different recollection of the facts from others we interviewed. An example of this was with regard to the design plans of Mr. Dennis and those by the Carusi firm. In both instances, Dr. Adams stated to D&T that no one liked their designs. Our interviews indicate that with both of these plans, there was widespread, if not unanimous support for the designs offered, with Dr. Adams being the sole holdout. It appears that this again is an attempt to deflect criticism away from his role in the matter. Certainly this desire is apparent when he holds Mr. Huckaby responsible for the overall Alumni Center project, when Mr. Huckaby never appeared to have more than a casual and, at best, ancillary role with the Alumni Center project.

Conclusion

Deloitte & Touche has performed the special review as described throughout this report at the request of the University of Georgia Foundation through its counsel, King & Spalding. Such services do not constitute an engagement to provide audit, compilation, review or attestations services prescribed in pronouncements on Professional Standards issued by the American Institute of Certified Public Accountants. This document has been prepared for and is intended solely for the use of the University of Georgia Foundations and its legal counsel.

Our analyses and findings are based upon the various interviews conducted and information and documents reviewed to date. Should additional information be made available to Deloitte & Touche and we are requested by King & Spalding or the Foundation to perform additional reviews or analyses, we will provide a subsequent report of our findings as appropriate.

Exhibit A—Interviews

Exhibit B—Endnote Documentation

1. Policies and Procedure - The University of Georgia Foundation, 1. Introduction, A. Mission

2. Minutes of The Georgia Foundation Board of Trustees Winter Board Meeting, February 4, 2000, page 4 - remarks by Mr. Jim Nalley, Foundation Trustee

3. Interview with Mr. Tom Landrum

4. Minutes of The Georgia Foundation Board of Trustees Winter Board Meeting, February 4, 2000, page 4 - remarks by Mr. Jim Nalley, Foundation Trustee

5. Minutes of The University of Georgia Foundation Board of Trustees Winter Board Meeting, February 14, 2003

6. Interview with Mr. Allen Barber and Foundation trustees; Document from Mr. Tom Landrum to Mr. Jack Rooker "Draft" version "Fiscal Controls for UGA Foundation Funds which Support the President's Office, p. 06/09

7. Interview with Mr. Allen Barber

8. Interview with Mr. Allen Barber, Mr. Claude Williams, Jr., Mr. C. Richard Yarbrough, Mr. Robert Woodson

9. Interview with Mr. Tom Landrum

10. Interview with Mr. Jim Nalley and various other FEC trustees

11. Interview with Ms. Cindy Coyle, Foundation CFO

12. Interview with Mr. Tom Landrum and Ms. Cindy Coyle

13. Interview with Mr. Tom Landrum

14. Interview with Ms. Cindy Coyle

15. General Guidelines for President's Office Expenditures, p. 6; and Specific Policy Guidelines for the President of the University and the President/Executive Director of the Foundation

16. Interview with Mr. Wyck Knox and Mr. Jack Rooker

17. Interview with Ms. Cindy Coyle

18. Interview with Mr. Gerald McCarley; Document from Mr. Tom Landrum to Mr. Jack Rooker "Draft" version "Fiscal Controls for UGA Foundation Funds which Support the President's Office, p. 05109

19. Interview with Ms. Cindy Coyle

20. Document from Mr. Tom Landrum to Mr. Jack Rooker "Draft" version "Fiscal Controls for UGA Foundation Funds which Support the President's Office, p. 09109

21. September 7, 2003, *Athens Banner-Herald*, titled "Foundation supports Adams by footing the bills,"

22. Letter dated October 3, 2003 from Dr. Adams to Mr. Jack Rooker

23. Interview with Mr. David Shipley, UGA Law School Professor and former law school Dean

24. *Athens Banner-Herald*, Friday, October 3, 2003 - "Some in law school cry objection over Adams party"

25. *Athens Banner-Herald*, Saturday, October 4, 2003 - "Adams reimburses foundation for luncheon costs"

26. Check #2126 from Dr. Michael F. Adams or Mary L. Adams, for $10,000

27. Interview with Ms. Cindy Coyle and The University of Georgia Foundation Reimbursement of University Related Entertainment Form

28. UGA Foundation Disbursement Request #0139402 and #0139800

29. The University of Georgia Foundation Disbursement Request No. 0133750

30. Check #2080, dated August 12, 2003 from Dr. Adams to the UGA Foundation

31. Handwritten memo dated June 5, 2002 from Ms. Cindy Coyle to Doris and interview with Ms. Cindy Coyle

32. Letter dated August 14, 2003 from Mr. Tom Landrum to Ms. Cindy Coyle

33. Exhibit C - Dr. Michael Adams' Compensation Analysis

34. Letter dated June 5, 1997 from Mr. Stephen R. Portch to President Michael Adams

35. Interviews with Dr. Adams and various FEC trustees

36. Exhibit C - Dr. Michael Adams' Compensation Analysis

37. Deferred Compensation Agreement entered into on February 9, 2001 between the Foundation and Dr. Adams

38. Exhibit C - Dr. Michael Adams' Compensation Analysis and Foundation records

39. Interview with Peter Amann and Jack Rooker

40. Interviews with Dr. Adams and various FEC trustees

41. Interview with Mr. Peter Amann

42. Resolution of the Trustees of The University of Georgia Foundation, Inc., adopted on

February 14, 2003

43. Interview with Mr. Floyd Newton, Partner with King & Spalding

44. Minutes of The University of Georgia Foundation Board of Trustees Winter Board Meeting, February 14, 2003

45. Resolution of the Trustees of The University of Georgia Foundation, Inc. - dated February 14, 2003

46. Resolution of the Trustees of The University of Georgia Foundation, Inc. - dated February 14, 2003; Interview with Mr. Peter Amann

47. Interview with Mr. Peter Amann and Mr. Carl Swearingen

48. Interview with Mr. Peter Amann and Mr. Carl Swearingen

49. The $12 million number referenced was actually $12,699,323 in funds received from Ticket Priority

50. Interview with Mr. Peter Amann and Mr. Carl Swearingen

51. FY2002 New Funds Raised

52. Interviews with Dr. Adams, Mr. Peter Amann, Mr. Swearingen, Mr. Rooker, Mr. Floyd Newton

53. Interview with Mr. Peter Amann, Ms. Cindy Coyle

54. Action of the Executive Committee of the Board of Trustees of the University of Georgia Foundation, Inc. on December 13, 2002

55. Interview with Dr. Adams

56. Interview with Ms. Coyle

58. Memorandum dated August 29, 1997 from Dan Amos, Chairman of the Foundation to the Executive Committee University of Georgia Foundation

59. Letter dated October 4, 2000 from Mr. Patrick S. Pittard to Dr. Stephen Portch

60. Letter dated October 4, 2000 from Mr. Patrick S. Pittard to Dr. Stephen Portch

61. Exhibit C - Dr. Michael Adams' Compensation Analysis

62. Interview with Mr. Floyd Newton

63. Memorandum dated October 30, 2001 from Mr. Tom Landrum to Melissa Stokes and "Attachment 2"

64. University of Georgia Foundation - Complimentary Ticket Usage forms

65. University of Georgia Foundation - Complimentary Ticket Usage form for UGA vs. Vanderbilt football game on October 17, 1998, October 14, 2000 and October 19, 2002

66. University of Georgia Foundation - Complimentary Ticket Usage forms

67. Interview with Mr. Allen Barber

68. Interview with Ms. Cindy Coyle

69. Exhibit C - Dr. Michael Adams' Compensation Analysis

70. Memo from Ms. Cindy Coyle to Doris, dated June 5, 2002

71. Note dated August 14, 2003 from Mr. Tom Landrum to Ms. Cindy Coyle

72. Interview with Mr. Jim Nalley and Mr. Rooker

73. Interview with Dr. Adams

74. Interview with Mr. Nalley and Mr. Rooker

75. Interview with Mr. Pittard

76. Interview with various FEC members

77. Interview with Mr. Pittard

78. Document titled "Mary Adams Compensation" MS:excel/myfiles/maryadams1, dated 12/21/00

79. Minutes of The University of Georgia Foundation Board of Trustees Fall Board Meeting, October 12-14, 2000, Athens, Georgia, p.5

80. Letter dated December 5, 2000 from Ms. Costello to Mr. Pittard, Chairman of the Foundation board of trustees

81. Interviews with Ms. Cindy Coyle and Ms. Costello

82. Letter dated December 5, 2000 from Ms. Costello to Mr. Pittard, Chairman of the Foundation board of trustees

83. The University of Georgia Foundation Board of Trustees Directory 2002 - 2003

84. Interview with Mr. Rooker

85. Interview with Mr. Swearingen

86. Minutes from the Meeting of the Executive Committee, University of Georgia Foundation, The Cloister, Sea Island, May 22, 2003 - Part III

87. Interview with Mr. Rooker, Mr. Swearingen and Mr. Pittard

88. Interview with Mr. Rooker

89. Interview with Dr. Adams

90. Interview with Mr. Wyck Knox and others

91. Minutes from the Meeting of the Executive Committee, University of Georgia Foundation, The Cloister, Sea Island, May 22, 2003 - Part III

92. Interview with Mr. Wyck Knox

93. Interview with Mr. Wyck Knox

94. Interview with Mr. Rooker

95. Interview with Mr. Jim Donnan, Mr. Richard Howell

96. Interview with Dr. Adams, Coach Vince Dooley, Mr. Richard Howell, Mr. Donnan

97. Interview with Mr. Donnan and Mr. Richard Howell

98. Interview with Dr. Adams

99. Interview with Dr. Adams

100. Interview with Dr. Adams

101. Interview with Mr. Nalley

102. Interview with Mr. Howell

103. Interview with Dr. Adams

104. Richard Howell letter to Mike Adams dated January 16, 2001, p. 1

105. Interview with Mr. Dooley

106. Interviews with Dr. Adams and Mr. Dooley

107. Interview with Mr. Nalley

108. Interviews with Dr. Adams and Mr. Nalley
109. Interview with Mr. Nalley
110. Interview with Mr. Dooley and Mr. Newton
111. Interviews with Mr. Newton, Mr. Dooley, Dr. Adams, Mr. Damon Evans
112. Interview with Mr. Newton
113. Various FEC members
114. Interview with Dr. Adams
115. Interviews with Ms. Costello and Mr. Ron Carroll
116. March 6, 2002 Letter from Jack Rooker, Vice-Chairman of the Foundation Board of Trustees to King & Spalding confirming the desire for an internal review of the Ecolodge.
117. The University of Georgia, Public Affairs Bulletin dated February 8, 2002 - writer Tom Jackson
118. Per interview with Ms. Costello and others
119. Resolution Empowering Kathym R. Costello as Executive Director to Execute Contracts of The University of Georgia Foundation
120. Interview with Mr. Ron Carroll
121. Jo Ann Chitty timeline - Interoffice Memorandum dated March 5, 2002
122. Jo Ann Chitty timeline - Interoffice Memorandum dated March 5, 2002
123. Interview with Floyd Newton
124. Memorandum by Ms. Costello to the UGA Foundation Executive Committee dated September 24, 2001
125. Memorandum by Ms. Costello to the UGA Foundation Executive Committee dated September 24, 2001
126. Memorandum by Ms. Costello to the UGA Foundation Executive Committee dated October 1, 2001
127. Minutes from the Meeting of the Executive Committee University of Georgia Foundation held at the Atlanta Financial Center, Thursday, October 4, 2001
128. Notes from FEC trustee, Mr. Billy Espy
129. Jo Ann Chitty timeline - Interoffice Memorandum dated March 5, 2002
130. Jo Ann Chitty timeline - Interoffice Memorandum dated March 5, 2002
131. Interview with Ron Carroll, Ms. Chitty and others
132. Jo Ann Chitty timeline - Interoffice Memorandum dated March 5, 2002
133. Pat Pittard Memorandum to Investment Committee and Executive Committee regarding the Ecolodge, dated December 3, 2001
134. Minutes from the Meeting of the Executive Committee, University of Georgia Foundation held at the Atlanta Financial Center, December 7, 2001
135. Interviews with several FEC members present at the meeting December 7, 2001 FEC meeting
136. The University of Georgia, Public Affairs Bulletin dated February 8, 2002 - writer Tom Jackson

137. Note dated December 10, 2001 from Karen [Holbrook] to Kathryn Costello

138. Email from Kathryn Costello to Milton and Diana Lieberman, dated Tue, 11 Dec 2001

139. Jo Ann Chitty timeline - Interoffice Memorandum dated March 5, 2002

140. Jo Ann Chitty timeline - Interoffice Memorandum dated March 5, 2002

141. Letter dated January 15, 2002 from Ms. Costello to Mr. Barry G. Neumann, the December 11, 2001 email from Ms. Costello to Milton and Diana Lieberman and the handwritten letter from Diana and Milton Lieberman to Ron Carroll dated December 4, 2001.

142. Jo Ann Chitty timeline - Interoffice Memorandum dated March 5, 2002

143. Letter dated February 8, 2002 from Ms. Costello to Ms. Rachel Conway

144. Jo Ann Chitty timeline - Interoffice Memorandum dated March 5, 2002

145. Memorandum from Ms. Costello to Dr. Adams, dated February 21, 2002

146. Letter from Dr. Adams to Ms. Costello, dated February 25, 2002

147. The University of Georgia, Public Affairs Bulletin dated February 8, 2002 - writer Tom Jackson

148. The University of Georgia, Public Affairs Bulletin dated February 8, 2002 - writer Tom Jackson

149. Letter dated August 12, 2003 from Mr. Tom Landrum to Mr. Jack Rooker

150. The University of Georgia, Public Affairs Bulletin dated February 8, 2002 - writer Tom Jackson

151. Interview with Mr. W. Charles Witzleben

152. Interviews with Ms. Costello, Mr. Witzleben and Ms. Chitty

153. Interview with Ms. Costello and Mr. Witzleben

154. Interview with Ms. Costello

155. Email from Kathy Costello to Milton and Diana Lieberman, dated Tue, 11 Dec 2001

156. Interview with Ms. Jo Ann Chitty, REF President

157. Interview with Dr. Alan Barber and Mr. Billy Espy

158. Interview with Mr. Danny Sniff, UGA Campus Architect

159. Letter dated June 5, 1997 from Mr. Stephen R. Portch, Chancellor, to Dr. Adams

160. Interview with Mr. Danny Sniff and Interoffice Memorandum dated July 8, 2003 from Ms. Chitty to Mr. Rooker

161. Interview with Mr. Tom Landrum, Executive Assistant to Dr. Adams

162. Interoffice Memorandum dated July 8, 2003 from Ms. Chitty to Mr. Rooker

163. Interview with Mr. Danny Sniff

164. Interview with Mr. Danny Sniff

165. Interview with Mr. Danny Sniff and Ms. Chitty

166. Interviews with Mr. Danny Sniff and with Ms. Chitty

167. Interoffice Memorandum dated July 8, 2003 from Ms. Chitty to Mr. Rooker

168. Interoffice Memorandum dated July 8, 2003 from Ms. Chitty to Mr. Rooker

169. Interviews with Mr. Sniff, Ms. Chitty, Dr. Adams and others

170. Interviews with Mr. Sniff and Ms. Chitty

171. Interview with Dr. Adams

172. Interviews with Mr. Sniff and Ms. Chitty

173. Interview with Ms. Chitty

174. Interviews with Ms. Chitty and Mr. Sniff

175. Interoffice Memorandum dated July 8, 2003 from Ms. Chitty to Mr. Rooker

176. Interoffice Memorandum dated July 8, 2003 from Ms. Chitty to Mr. Rooker

177. Interview with Mr. Sniff

178. Letter dated February 18, 2003 from Mr. Albert L. Filoni to Ms. Jo Ann Chitty, Re: Fee Proposal for the UGA Alumni Center

179. Interviews with Mr. Sniff and Ms. Chitty

180. Interview with Ms. Chitty

181. University of Georgia Alumni Development Center - Architectural Fee Comparison

182. Letter dated February 18, 2003 from Mr. Albert L. Filoni to Ms. Jo Ann Chitty, Re: Fee Proposal for the UGA Alumni Center

183. Interview with Dr. Adams

184. Interviews with Ms. Chitty and Mr. Danny Sniff

185. Interviews with Ms. Chitty and Mr. Sniff

Appendix B: Regents' Response

Following is the text of the October 29, 2003, statement of the Board of Regents in response to the Deloitte & Touche audit:

The University of Georgia (UGA) Foundation submitted a report to the Board of Regents and the Chancellor on Friday, October 27, 2003. This report by Deloitte and Touche (D&T) was ordered by the UGA Foundation. The report dealt with six primary areas and other areas involving President Michael Adams, President of UGA, that were identified by the Foundation Executive Committee.

The Regents were told through the Chancellor that the Foundation would publicly release the report on Wednesday, October 29, 2003, giving the Regents only three working days to solicit a response from UGA although the report took over three months to generate.

Since neither the Chancellor, the Regents nor President Adams was given the opportunity to see the report prior to its distribution last Friday, there has been no opportunity to prepare a response until this late date. No reasonable explanation was provided for this unusual approach.

At the Chancellor's request, President Adams has now personally responded to the report and, again at the Chancellor's request, the senior management team at UGA has also responded in great factual detail to the report from Deloitte and Touche. Both responses are attached with the D&T report which is being released in concert with the Foundation as agreed.

After carefully considering all three submissions, the Board of Regents expresses extreme disappointment in the report from Deloitte and Touche and is deeply distressed it has received such attention from the Foundation.

The Regents find the report offensive in a large number of ways, for example:

- numerous significant factual errors;
- assumptions not based on facts;
- selective use of information;
- lack of understanding of a complex research institution's operations;
- innuendos;
- hearsay;
- statements attributed to sources unidentified; and
- inappropriate conclusions drawn.

For such a report to be submitted by Deloitte and Touche and for the report to be accepted by the Foundation and forwarded to the Regents without giving the President of the University an opportunity to respond or even to see the report is neither reasonable nor fair and has no place in the world of academia.

Given the way this report was initiated and the timing, the Regents find it impossible to divorce this action from the personnel decision made by President Adams regarding Athletics Director Vince Dooley. Although some contend this is not the case, the facts speak for themselves.

The Regents find the report submitted by President Adams and the report submitted by the UGA senior management team to be far more credible than the report submitted by Deloitte and Touche.

Has President Adams been perfect for the six years he has served as president at UGA? Of course not! Have there been times when he might have used better judgement? Absolutely, but those times are relatively few and he has admitted those. Do any of the accusations against President Adams reflect any criminal intent? Not at all! Has he always acted in what he considered to be in the best interests of the University of Georgia? Absolutely! Has he led the flagship institution of the state of Georgia into a position of greater academic prominence in American higher education? Without question!

The UGA Foundation has the potential to be an extraordinary resource for the University. However, its responsibility goes beyond managing assets. It not only must actively raise private resources, but its members must also give of their own time and assets in a way so as to serve as a positive model and a catalyst for others to give. It must also serve in a support role for the President. If and when Foundation members have questions regarding the President's activities with Foundation funds, it should meet with the President or the Chancellor privately and specifically address those concerns in a professional way and not in the manner demonstrated with the D&T report.

From the D&T report, it is obvious that the Foundation's own internal procedures and past practices contributed to some of the concerns and confusion. The Foundation's policies are not clear enough to accomplish what some would wish. The University has moved to a level of complexity which may require a different Foundation structure than now exists. The Regents are hopeful the Foundation will not look internally for advice on restructuring but will look to the best experts in the country for counsel to improve their procedures and governance.

As stated previously, the Regents have received these reports and have evaluated their contents. As a result, the Regents reiterate their total and complete support for President Adams and ask the Foundation to close this chapter and now move forward and be about the business of raising private funds for the University. Individual Foundation members will have to decide whether or not they desire to continue as a Trustee.

It must not be forgotten that the health and well-being of the University of Georgia must be the ultimate concern of the Board of Regents and the UGA Foundation in this matter. This great university must have a close working partnership between these two bodies. Therefore, the Regents will enhance their communication link with the UGA Foundation.

The Regents now consider this matter closed.

APPENDIX C: ADAMS'S RESPONSE

Following is the text of the October 27, 2003 statement by UGA President Michael Adams to Chancellor Thomas Meredith in response to the Deloitte & Touche audit:

Dear Tom:

Last Friday, you and Regents Vice Chair Joel Wooten were given a copy of the report commissioned by Mr. Floyd Newton of King & Spalding on behalf of the Executive Committee of the University of Georgia Foundation. I received a copy of that report at approximately 5 P.M. on October 24. You requested a response from me to that report, and I'm pleased to do so.

When I completed a reading of the report, I must say l hardly knew the "Dr. Adams" the report seems to describe. Per our conversation last Friday, I have had no choice but to spend virtually every waking hour for the last three days trying to respond to issues that a team of professional forensic auditors have prepared full time for nearly four months. The total cost in dollars of the report and the negative impact on the University, unfortunately, may be significant as well. The right of due process is another issue.

What is most significant to me, however, is the need to do whatever can be done not only to respond to this report, but to respond to whatever alterations in substance or style that might be needed. I am certainly not perfect and I am greatly bothered by this entire situation. I am willing to do within human reason whatever can be done to work with the Regents, the Foundation Trustees, or any other group to move this great institution for which we all care so deeply to the next level of success and unity.

As you know, on June 23, a special meeting of the Foundation Trustees was called by Mr. Wyck Knox and Ms. Rachel Conway "to have an open discussion about recent events." This notice went out less than three weeks after the announcement that I would abide by the employment contract that Athletic Director Vince Dooley and I reached in February 2001. Since the date of the meeting notice and the subsequent Trustees meeting on July 1, which I was not asked to attend, I have been patient and trusting with "hang in there" advice from the Regents' leadership, the Trustees' leadership and others. After reading the report and seeing how truly biased it is, I am proud to have "stayed above the fray."

I have talked to anyone who asked me about anything at every turn, including you, Mr. Rooker, the press, and Deloitte & Touche without notes, calendar, or professional representation, because I believed that there was a level of trust and mutual respect by all of those parties on which I could depend.

Never once was I told by anyone that I was the object of a study by individuals of a fraud and forensic investigations unit, but rather that the Foundation Trustees wanted Deloitte & Touche auditors to question me and examine material relating to the six issues that had been raised about University spending, some of which involved funds from the UGA Foundation. Undoubtedly, the Foundation has a right and responsibility to manage fiduciary matters under its care. Those issues were: Costa Rica, the Alumni Development Center, the Jim Donnan agreement, Mary's stipend, the honorarium for Hank Huckaby, and certain expenses I might have incurred in the line of work.

The audit report says on page one that no single issue should be a basis for judgment, but rather that the report "must be read in its entirety" for making any ultimate judgment. I would submit that the entire actions of the President and his administrative team over the past six and one-half years need to be looked at in their entirety and the end results of such measured against any shortcomings that may have occurred. Also, it seems to me that the D&T report gives greater emphasis to the opinions of my most vocal detractors.

I recently submitted to the Board of Regents a summary of recent achievements by the University of Georgia and I am attaching it to my memo to you. The faculty and administrative leadership of the University have worked hard in recent years to enhance the University's national reputation and level of academic excellence. By all indications, we have achieved a special level of success and I am proud to have served as president over this time of growth and progress.

The University of Georgia spends approximately four million dollars a day from numerous sources, and we have dealt at one stage or another with approximately one billion dollars in physical plant issues during my time here. We have also interacted with thousands of employees, dealt with thousands of issues, and participated in hundreds, if not thousands, of calendar commitments.

What one does not know, in this role, about the thousands of activities, comments, and actions taken by almost ten thousand employees everyday is always of concern at a place of this size. I didn't know until last year, for instance, that the Foundation paid for the Skybox on the south side of the stadium. I was just told when I got here that it was available to me to be used and that the previous president had used it rather than the "Big Box." As you know, during football season, I have chosen to spend the greater part of my time in the traditional large President's box on the north side of the stadium. That was simply because I thought such furthered the ultimate causes of the University. We have used the box periodically on the south side of the stadium for Mary to entertain donors as well as personal guests and friends that always accumulate in any center of responsibility.

I was also surprised to see in the auditor's opening statement at the bottom of page one that they were apparently willing to accept information as fact given by unidentified individuals with the promise of confidentiality and leaving no way for anyone to question the individuals, to test their observations, or to know what data or motives might be driving them.

I would be the first to admit that the procedures of the Foundation have been "looser" than many such groups might be, but from my understanding, that is a pattern of longstanding with this group. The D&T report at one point characterizes the Foundation as a "social club." I believe that goes too far, but there have been benefits as well as downsides to a more informal operating mode. Until the last six months, there was a high level of trust and comradeship which I still think can be redeveloped with and among most members.

While you know my view that the genesis of this report emanates from certain trustees with strong disagreements with my personnel decision of last June, frankly there was evidence of some concern and discontent before then. For example, two years ago at a Fall Foundation meeting, I was presented with new operating guidelines for expenses by a trustee substituting for Finance Chair Wyck Knox who was absent from the meeting. I had been given no opportunity for comment or discussion before the meeting and did express some concern to him about that at that time. But realizing the level of concern that he had raised and that the Trustees had raised, I readily accepted the provisions of the new guidelines and took additional personal measures of my own. I signed for a personal credit card on which I now only put University expenses. I also created a checking account with both my name and the name of my personal assistant on it and now deposit any state or Foundation checks only into that account. I have staff pay any appropriate bills from that account when they come in. For over two years, when I became aware of these issues, I have not put a single nickel back in my own pocket from that holding account despite whatever level of outgo from my pocket has occurred.

I would also point out that there is no indication in this report that anything illegal or, I believe, unethical, has occurred. Twenty-twenty hindsight can always question the wisdom of some actions. Clearly, mistakes in a large organization like UGA are always made and that includes me. I apologize for any that may have occurred during my time here, but I believe they were few and relatively inconsequential in the whole scheme of things. Where mistakes have occurred, Tom, we have corrected them soon after they came to our attention. Any decision we have made in that regard has always been done with what I believe to be in the University's best interest.

On the other hand, I believe this report is laden with pejorative and accusatory language and value judgments and I'm led to wonder exactly what instructions were given to Deloitte & Touche. Page two of the report at the bottom indicates that D&T has relied on the advice of counsel throughout this report in making a determination of the propriety of any action or inaction by all involved parties. I would submit that that level of direction, in and of itself, is a conflict of interest. Furthermore, the trustees were given this report without my knowledge of its contents or any opportunity for me to discuss with the Foundation as is usually the case. This placed me in an inherently unfair and difficult position.

Expenses of the President of the University of Georgia

Pages 5–9 of the report deal with the processes and the perception of expense uses by the President of the University of Georgia. The report correctly states that according to the bylaws the President is a managing trustee of the Foundation. They furthermore state that the President serves as an Ex Officio member of the Executive Committee. I believe that those arrangements are proper and that as President, this process would have been well served had that process continued and the President been invited to discuss any of the matters now under D&T review. Quite to the contrary, for the past six months, I have been excluded from the various meetings where I could have addressed whatever questions needed to be addressed. I must also point out that the new Foundation Trustee book, contrary to last year's, now lists the President erroneously as advisory rather than as a managing trustee of the Foundation. It is my belief that I should have been in any and all meetings, full board or executive committee, and especially the ones that occurred on July 1, October 24, and at several executive committee meetings in the interim.

As President, I deal with a multiplicity of affiliate groups and an alphabet of other entities that range from the University Council on campus to the American Council on Education in Washington. In every case, one principle is important. I have operated on assumed trust between myself and the principal of these other groups. On Real Estate Foundation matters, I have dealt with the Chair of the Real Estate Foundation and the President of the Real Estate Foundation, Ms. Joann Chitty. On alumni matters, I have dealt with the current chair of the Alumni Association and sometimes the executive director. I chair the Athletic Association and deal directly with the AD. I also chair the University of Georgia Research Foundation and deal directly on most issues with the University's Vice President for Research. I have also chosen to attend about half of the Regents meetings when my schedule allows. Additionally, I have some direct interaction with the various regents because of the nature of a flagship institution. My direct reporting line and most conversations have been with the two Chancellors under whom I have served, Dr. Portch and yourself. In every case, a principal to principal relationship was employed.

Page three of the D&T report indicates that of all the organizations with whom I work, the UGA Foundation has most "operated like an alumni club." In some ways, those relationships have been more familial and less legal or professional than the other entities. While this is sometimes difficult, it has been balanced by the very strong personal relationships I have developed with now the fourth and soon to be fifth chair, Dan Amos, Jim Nalley, Pat Pittard, Jack Rooker, and soon, Lynda Courts.

Furthermore, I must point out that among the literally hundreds, if not thousands, of expense transactions that have taken place, even the D&T report on page seven says that "the majority of expenses have complied with all policies and procedures." The auditors further say that "when this has not been the case, it has often been due to human error."

In regard to the issue about auditing the President's personal accounts, I have had no objection philosophically or practically to such audits. I have simply believed that internal controls and external controls with other existing audit programs were sufficient to guard against any misuse. On page seven, where D&T concludes that both I and the Foundation erred in the initial decision not to continue mandatory audit, they speculate without any possible basis what the President apparently believes. Furthermore, on page eight, they point out that the majority (I would say overwhelming majority) of Dr. Adams' expenses have complied with all policies and procedures of UGA and the Foundation. They also correctly point out that a substantial portion of my private life is intertwined with, and in many instances indistinguishable, from my duties as President. There have clearly been times when personal friends have attended a dinner or a ball game, but such in the whole scheme of things has been very, very minor. As a matter of fact, both my wife and I have given ourselves to the University of Georgia almost seven days a week for going on seven years. As the report indicates, there is "a good deal of subjective judgment" (page eight) in these kinds of arrangements. Additionally, D&T indicates on page nine that since "new procedures were implemented in 2001," (effectively almost the first procedures) no expenses submitted have been rejected by the Foundation Chairpersons (either the Chair or the Foundation Committee Chair). The report further correctly states, given the fact that most of this paper processing (a huge amount) is done by staff who are human beings, that to some degree, some level of mistake is almost "inevitable."

Furthermore, the Chief Financial Officer of the Foundation points out on page nine that since new policies and procedures were implemented in 2001, there has been "an improvement in both the quality of documentation provided and the nature of expenditures incurred by Dr. Adams." Clearly, such shows cooperative intent at the very least on the part of both myself and the staff.

Specific Expense Findings

The Deloitte & Touche report reviews the reception for some law school students and their family members held in the Spring of 2002. I have hosted many events for student groups in my home, and these events vary greatly in size and purpose. When this particular event came to my attention as one questioned, I asked for the back-up documentation and came to the conclusion that while a level of benefit inured to the University, the appearance of impropriety existed because my son, David, was among the graduates at the event. The next day, I wrote a check for $10,000 payable to the Foundation to cover the expenses related to this reception. This expense was a mistake on my part and I apologize.

There is one other incident in which I have written a reimbursement check to the University. I believe that also occurred earlier this year and relates to a 1997 charge to the Foundation when one of my sons stayed at the University Georgia Center. When I learned of this $58.50 charge that had been paid with Foundation funds, I immediately wrote a reimbursement check.

When it comes to the matter of Presidential discretionary funds, I have never viewed them as funds with which I can "do as I please." As D&T states on page 11, rather, I have made some discretionary use of funds when donors told me to cover things that either might not be covered by the state or were in some "grey area." I know of no single incident in which a donor has had problems with any use of these funds. Still, I have and remain committed to comply with whatever appropriate rules and regulations both the Foundation and donor might wish.

Michael Adams' compensation

Since I have appropriately always been excluded when matters of compensation were discussed by The Executive Committee (to my knowledge, always in executive session), I cannot speak to the issue of the actual processes that were followed by the Executive Committee. I do know that I've been told in every instance that there is a paper trail to justify whatever compensation matters were resolved. I will leave to the Regents and the Trustees the debate about which portion of what compensation should be paid by each and what conflicts of direction and "ownership" might occur. I do know a considerable amount about direct dealings on compensation because those discussions were always principal to principal between me and either the Chancellor or the Board Chair. I take great exception to the notion that I have ever misled anyone about levels of compensation or specific offers. I don't believe any mistakes have occurred, but if they have, they have certainly not been purposeful nor intentional. I repeat that in whatever questions or interviews I've been requested to have on these matters, I have not only cooperated fully, but responded immediately from memory without the basis of notes or specific times.

I have never before seen a breakdown of compensation like the one that occurs on page 13 of the report, including, for example, allowances and club memberships, but I will assume the amounts have been accurately stated.

I accepted the UGA position in 1997 for slightly more than I was making at Centre, hardly an indication of someone taking on a much more complex and challenging position simply for the money. I did believe that if I performed that additional compensation would come, and such was so indicated by the then Chancellor. The report is correct in noting that a deferred compensation plan was created for me in 2001 with a $200,000 deposit and that a board member added another $78,673 in stock the following year.

What is also correct about the report is that the motivating force in the 2002 time frame was to make my compensation at least comparable to similar positions (and there has been a substantial rise in public presidential compensation over the past seven years) and to also get my total compensation at a level of around $600,000, similar to that to be received by the President at Georgia Tech, and close to that received by the System Chancellor. Presidents in Georgia, including me, are not paid beyond national norms. I am not privy to all of the conversations that would have taken place in that regard, but I believe you and Jack Rooker knew I was forthright with you about any visits I made or offers I considered. Such decisions were not made as page 14 pejoratively indicates in an environment where faculty and staff had received little or no pay increases. Nor, as is insinuated on page 15, was there ever any desire on my part or expectation that any financial agreement I might have would not become public. I have voluntarily released any such material when questioned including the agreement reached with the appointed ad hoc compensation committee last year under which I thought we were operating. Two open records requests relating to my compensation package were made last spring and the information was provided in full. Copies of that entire record were sent to every member of the Executive Committee. As to why such an agreement was never "signed," I would simply point out that the board chair, as did I, thought that the compensation agreement drafted by King & Spalding was so technical and overbearing that it did not address the kind of relationship that existed here and that all of us had a high level of trust and belief in one another. Furthermore, there were communications and letters (now available) between the board chair and the Chancellor representing both the Regents and the Foundation that gave validity to these new arrangements. I still believe that to be the case. I am attaching a copy of the correspondence relating to compensation.

On the matter of fringe benefits and football tickets, to the best of my knowledge, I have never signed or given any indication about any person who might have received a football ticket through my office. Every detail of such has been handled by staff who manage the distribution of tickets and invitations to the games. Although have never been involved in this documentation, I would pay taxes on any that might be personal (i.e., my mother and father and other immediate relatives), I hasten to point out that even if the numbers in the report are correct, there have been very few such tickets in seven years during a time when we have entertained thousands of individuals at game events. Surely, some reasonable crossover of people who might be friends with some personal history is allowable.

On the matter of administrative fees for deferred compensation, no one ever discussed that matter with me. When I learned that my deferred compensation accounts are treated like donor fund accounts, I agreed that such should be applicable. I might point out that today's value of the funds deposited to my deferred compensation account, because of market conditions, is significantly less than the numbers (again, front end numbers were used to present the worst possible pejorative case) rather than current dollar value.

OSU offer

The part of the report that troubles me the most and the one that I most regret becoming public is the situation regarding a potential 2002 opportunity to return to one of my Alma Maters, Ohio State University, as its President. I regret such becoming public because first of all I have never talked about any specific offer publicly. There have been opportunities both at institutions and educationally related entities that have sought me out, but the only one where I have really "walked up to the line" on accepting was the Ohio State offer. Second, I deeply regret this matter becoming public because of any potential embarrassment or chagrin it might cause my dear friend, Karen Holbrook, whom I am so proud to count as the current President at Ohio State. Karen, of course, was formerly Provost at UGA.

I did meet in early 2002 with a search committee at Ohio State University at a meeting in Washington, DC and was very favorably received and encouraged by members of the search committee. Although I was drawn to that opportunity, I still felt a major commitment to the University of Georgia and to my family who live in Georgia, and so on July 1, 2002 (copy attached), I wrote Dr. Jan Greenwood of the A. T. Kearney Search Firm indicating that I did not feel now was the right time or personal circumstances for me to pursue this opportunity. I believe there was an additional communication or two by phone with representatives of A. T. Kearney including Dr. Greenwood in the ensuing days. As that search drew to a close, I was called again, I believe by Dr. Greenwood and then subsequently by the Chair of the Board at OSU and was urged to come back and have a discussion with the full board one more time.

Given the fact that such was a particularly busy time for me, I indicated a very narrow time range in which my wife and I could visit Columbus and meet with all the trustees. On July 16, Ohio State sent a Net Jet to the Athens Airport, flew us to Columbus, Ohio where I met for approximately two hours with the full board of Ohio State in the conference room of the Nationwide Insurance hangar. When the discussion was completed and I stood to leave, thanking them, I walked into the lobby to wait for my wife who had been given a tour of the university by a Mrs. Basinger, who was an employee of Ohio State. She and Mary had not returned from the tour.

About ten minutes into my wait in the lobby, the Board Chair came out and approached me and asked me if I would give them about 30 minutes before we flew on to Washington. I was doing so at their expense to attend the well-reported congressional reception that included an appearance by UGA mascot, UGA VI. About 20 minutes later, the Chair reappeared with a sheet of paper in his hand.

I tore off a sheet of paper from a packet of information on the various trustees that had been given me as a part of the meeting, and he sat down and talked me through, issue by issue, an offer that added up to in excess of $600,000 in direct compensation, an agreement to live in the University residence in Bexley, notation that the garage apartment was being redone and would be turned into a very nice office for my wife, that a stipend would be paid her just as it had been paid the previous President's wife, that she would be offered a part-time secretary, and that we would have two cars made available to us. I made only two additional inquiries, the first whether or not the University would pay for spouse accompaniment on travel (he said that they would) and whether or not I would be eligible to participate in any corporate boards and he said yes to this also. Several OSU presidents had done so, and he was sure that there would be acceptance of membership on a couple of boards. By any estimation such gets into the range that D&T reported with a degree of skepticism.

Furthermore, one should remember at the time I was not seeking compensation or that nature, but was interested in the opportunity, as most of us are, to return to one of our Alma Maters. Furthermore, the real issue for me was not the difference between what Ohio State offered and what Georgia offered, but whether or not my compensation would be similar to that at Georgia Tech and other comparable institutions. I believe UGA to be of much greater size, challenge, and complexity than any other in the USG system. In other words, I was not playing off an Ohio State offer against what I was making at UGA or would make at UGA, but had simply talked to Mr. Rooker and the Chancellor about what might be equitable. I never spoke in any terms of either/or.

To further legitimize the fact that I could have gone to Ohio State, two very prominent Ohio officials called me the next day urging my acceptance. I also, over the next two days, had discussions with the outgoing President and the President of the National Association of State Universities and Land Grant Colleges.

The notion that I misled you, the Chairman, or the compensation committee here in that regard is frankly preposterous and an insult.

Again, I deeply regret that this entire episode has become public. On July 18, after deep thought and prayer, my wife and I decided no matter what happened here, and nothing more than a general range of compensation had been mentioned by the Chancellor or the Board Chairman at that time, we wanted to be here. My deep regret springs from the fact that this encounter could serve to embarrass either Ohio State or its current president, both of which I dearly love.

The Mary Adams stipend

Since our arrival here in mid-1997, Mary Adams has given an almost full time commitment to the University of Georgia. Frankly, as the first year of an empty nest homeplace, she was glad to do so and happy for a year or two to have no commitments beyond those which she chose.

This matter was discussed with both chairs Jim Nalley and Pat Pittard. The more Mary gave, the more in demand she was by others, and there were opportunities where I feel she would have likely been hired by certain units at the University if she had chosen to do so and if such was allowed. Rather than question the Regents' nepotism rule, it was clear to me that increasingly some sort of simple spousal stipend was being paid to spouses of a number of university presidents. That seemed to me then and still seems to be appropriate under certain circumstances, given the Georgia nepotism rule. Certainly, any such arrangement should be fully vetted and proper procedures followed. Since I was not in the room when any of these discussions were held by the Foundation's Executive Committee, my assumption was that all had been handled properly.

Frankly, I'm too biased toward someone who has been a soul mate for 34 years to be very objective. I believe the original agreement called for annual reviews of this arrangement between Mary and the Board Chair with the assumption being that if it was not advisable and advantageous, the arrangement could be stopped on an annual review basis. Funds which came from a restricted discretionary account were used to pay the stipend. Our main interest was not the income, but the validation that came from some simple arrangement that indicated value to what was being done. We were grateful, however, that a portion was directed toward her retirement because that was frankly a bigger concern than regular income. (I am attaching memorandum of summary of some of her activities last year.)

The Hank Huckaby Honorarium

I do not remember the exact date or time, but I was approached initially by either Jack Rooker or Carl Swearingen regarding some proposed bonus for Hank Huckaby. I do not remember which one approached me first (I believe it was Mr. Swearingen), but I discussed it with both. Both acknowledged that since Hank reported to me that my approval and support would be essential to any such honorarium. I was pleased to give it and believe that such a payment was well deserved given the "double duty" Mr. Huckaby had carried on for some six months. Furthermore, I had discussed previously with the Chair the request by the Governor-elect to make Mr. Huckaby available for several months to the new administration. That, too, was done with the full knowledge of all participants. No one at the University of Georgia deserves every dollar he makes more than Hank Huckaby.

The Jim Donnan incident

This story has been told multiple times and I have some wonder why it is in this report since there is no Foundation money or activity involved. Clearly, Mr. Nalley and I had several discussions about the matter at the time, but in no way did he ever present this as a Foundation issue. It was something in which he, like many other football fans, was very interested early on in my time here. Everyone involved in the matter has acknowledged that the Foundation Executive Committee has no authority and no dollars in this matter.

Frankly, this is one where the truth has been told over and over. Coach Donnan and his lawyers were right on this one. The D&T record does not show the numerous inquiries by many people to the President's Office on Donnan's behalf. There was clearly an estrangement between Coach Dooley and Coach Donnan at this time and the recounting of what I did is accurate. The 1998 season was approaching and I wanted the issue resolved.

I would clearly do this one differently today, as I have said on numerous times. I was surprised at the end pejorative statement in this section that it was "the only time Dr. Adams admitted such an opinion to D&T."

Costa Rica

The Costa Rican situation is also clear. I've attached a memo that has been released before from Joanne Chitty explaining the situation.

Kathryn Costello, a very good human being, because of personal challenges and emotional distress she was suffering at the time, made a mistake in judgment out of concern for what she believed to be a good academic program in the best interest of the University of Georgia. Effectively, that judgment has been borne out.

However, the way this was done, without authorization, was a serious mistake in judgment and the loan of personal money from a friend involved in any University transaction was an even more egregious mistake, especially since Kathy had been instructed by me not to do so.

The University has dealt with this matter at some considerable personal cost to Kathryn Costello, and effectively we have made lemonade out of what was a "lemon deal." I believe this full story has been told and while mistakes were made, I firmly believe that this program and the entire international affairs program as expanded will accrue to the ultimate benefit of the University. I was supportive of exploring for possible purchase the Costa Rican ecolodge because I believed in its potential as a successful academic program. I thought it had great promise as both an environmental and a Spanish-speaking site.

I indicated at the Executive Committee meeting on December 7, 2001, that the University might be able to commit $500,000 if $500,000 in gifts could be given for both the Costa Rica and Cortona projects ($500K to each). This statement is confirmed in the minutes of the Executive Committee of December 7, 2001. I never committed $500,000 from the Foundation's General Endowment fund for I knew that such would require Foundation Board approval if that was the source.

Alumni Center Project

Every now and then in an organization, there is a challenge that seemingly "just can't get solved" and one of the few in that category recently at the University of Georgia has been the alumni development center project.

My first involvement with this project came on the day of final interviews for UGA President when then Alumni Chair Sonny Seiler asked me if I would commit a plot of ground to the Alumni Association on which they might build an alumni center. I indicated that I would certainly consider it and thought such a project to be generally advantageous on the campuses where I had seen them. I also told him I would want to make a full analysis of the individual sites and tradeoffs before I made such a commitment. He seemed satisfied by that response.

After becoming President of UGA, the issue of where to place the alumni center was put before me. Although I had some instinctive misgivings about an alumni facility that did not incorporate development, communications, career counseling, and other alumni services, I certainly did not want any major argument early on with the Alumni Association so I acquiesced to both the plan and to the site. Certainly, I had some concern about the proposed Lake Herrick site because I wondered about its isolation from the main flow of the campus. Indeed, one of my perceptions when I came to the University of Georgia was that development and alumni affairs had been treated more as a stepchild or afterthought than as an integral part of the whole that served to move the entire University forward. In other words, from the beginning, I had some doubts about the program and the location, but I decided after some soul searching that it was probably better to go along with the proposal. As the D&T study indicates, Mr. Michael Dennis, I believe of Boston, Massachusetts, was hired to be the design architect and paired with a Georgia firm, Jova, Daniels & Busbee.

The report indicates that I instructed campus architect, Danny Sniff, to terminate Mr. Dennis's work on the alumni center. I do not remember such a conversation, but do remember some concern by several members of the administration about Mr. Dennis's design and I will confess to having my own misgivings about where we were headed. I don't deny responsibility for whatever was done. However, I have been assured by Mr. Sniff that it was he who ended the Dennis arrangement, not me.

There were subsequent efforts directed by Mr. Sniff and his staff with the Ayers St. Gross team out of Baltimore and later the Collins Cooper Carusi group, chosen by an appropriate selection committee. When the Carusi firm was recommended to me, I accepted their recommendation and moved forward. The report is correct that as the center developed, additional concerns arose about the Lake Herrick site. I remember Hank Huckaby, the Senior Vice President for Finance and Administration, saying to me one day, "I want you to listen to Joann Chitty and me about another potential site for the alumni center." I was somewhat frustrated with the entire process by the year 2001 because the project had bounced around planning wise for almost four years with little progress made, few dollars raised, and still considerable discussion about actually what such a center was to be. When Mr. Huckaby and Ms. Chitty met with me and made their suggestion about a site opposite the then under construction Student Learning Center, I thought their idea made a lot of sense and inquired as to what the Alumni Association's opinion was. I was told that they believed there was a good chance that the Alumni leadership, at least, would go along.

Again, we changed direction and I concurred because I thought the approach brought by Ms. Chitty was reasonable and because I believed that the newly preferred site was near what would become the center of campus when the Student Learning Center was completed. Also given the history of football at the University of Georgia, I thought the alumni center's proximity to the stadium made a lot of sense. At this point, the project had been under University consideration for almost five years. I decided I wanted someone I trusted to give me an independent opinion on a project that had grown to the 35–50 million dollar range in most people's minds. Admittedly, there were still then, and I believe are today, programming decisions to be made about what actually should go into an alumni development center.

I did determine to call an architect with whom I had worked before for another opinion. I believed this was one of those signature facilities for a campus that you only had an opportunity to get right one time. I did contact Mr. Al Filoni of Pittsburgh and asked him to give me that independent opinion. I will say more about him in just a moment.

The context in which I want to place this decision, though, is one of dramatic changes in the campus of the University of Georgia. Because our facilities were rather outmoded when I got here and represented in many ways both poor planning and poor design, I have been very involved in the management of the campus plan. Also, the Regents requested this. While presidents always have their detractors, one of the things for which I am generally applauded is the dramatic improvement of the campus. I believe at some level of completion, development, construction, or planning, we have literally talked about and/or executed 40 or 50 major projects with potential expenditures of over a billion dollars. There have been significant improvements such as the Herty Field, the renovation of Moore College, the renovation of Meigs Hall, the renovation of the Law Library, the renovation of Candler Hall for the School of Public and International Affairs, the renovation of the old art museum into an administration building, the construction of the magnificent Student Learning Center, the East Campus Housing Development, the East Campus Commons, the Complex Carbohydrate Research Center, the development of the Paul Coverdell Research Center, and getting Regents' approval for state funds for a new school of art, an expansion of the Pharmacy School, and approval for a new research library. I would contend that such is a pretty good record for a seven-year President.

But to be fair about it, the Alumni Center has been somewhat troublesome. I turned to a longtime acquaintance, though not a close personal friend as the report indicates, Mr. Al Filoni of Pittsburgh.

Mr. Filoni and I had come to know one another through a professional relationship. I believe we have spent two social occasions together over a fifteen year period outside lunches or dinners that might be compatible with work. On one occasion, my wife and I visited him for a night of dinner and opera in Pittsburgh and on one occasion he visited me at my lake house in Kentucky. I believe he is a friend, but not one at the level described in the report. Furthermore, Mr. Filoni is a distinguished art graduate of Bethany College and possesses an architecture degree from Harvard University. He is one of the best known campus planners in the country and has done significant projects at Case Western, Carnegie Mellon, Pittsburgh, Centre, Davidson, and numerous other top flight campuses. My belief was that I was hiring him at UGA as a consultant to give us another opinion on a very important building. I thought the University had paid and was paying him until I read this report. I am certain that we never got to the point of nominating him to be the architect of record. I knew he would have to be paired with some Georgia firm if we wished to make him the architect of record.

I did make some mistakes with the planning of the newest Alumni Development Center proposal because we tried to put too much in the building and thus escalated the cost beyond anything that was reasonable. There was also considerable opposition by prominent alumni to the bookstore being in the building and I have since agreed that they were right. My concern was not just to build a new bookstore, but to hopefully have the space that the bookstore currently occupies connected to an expanded Tate Center that could provide badly needed student affairs space. In the past year, we have tabled that notion and yet need to get back to the issue of what ultimately goes in the Alumni Development Center.

My own view is that Mr. Filoni did provide more than adequate assistance to us in the project. We spent $74,000 for Mr. Filoni's participation in this matter. On a building that is to cost roughly $50 million and additionally be built on top of a parking deck at the center of campus, I believe the expenditure was a sound one. I do believe that the University should reimburse the Foundation for the $74,000. We yet need to sit down, both senior administrative officials and interested alumni parties and see if we can come to ultimate programming decisions that both work and we can afford. Such is yet to be done.

Summary

As the attached record of the past years of achievements indicates, these have been seven years of progress at the University of Georgia. The accomplishments are not mine, but belong to the entire University community, although I believe I have been a catalyst for some of them.

At the same time, I have made some mistakes and have moved to correct them when possible. I remain committed to working with all University parties, including those who may have disagreed with me on the Dooley situation or any other matter. This University is too important to the future of the state for us to all not come together to continue enhancing our mutually established record of excellence.

Appendix D: Robert Miller Correspondence

Following are letters written by Atlanta attorney Robert Miller to and received by him from various University and Georgia officials concerning the issues raised in the Deloitte & Touche audit:

November 3, 2003, from Robert Miller to John W. Rooker, Chairman, Board of Trustees, The University of Georgia Foundation

Dear Mr. Rooker:

This letter is about the Deloitte & Touche Special Review, dated October 24, 2003 (the "D&T Report"), The University of Georgia Foundation (the "Foundation") and the President of The University of Georgia, Dr. Michael F. Adams. I apologize in advance for the length of this letter.

1. Background. Mary Helen (ABJ, 1963) and I (AB, 1964) have been and will continue to be supporters of The University of Georgia. For the past 20 years or so, our annual gift to the Foundation has ranged between $1,500 and $5,000 and in some years has exceeded $5,000. We are almost the sole funding source of the Charles M. Hicks Fund (balance at June 30 of $176,000) which provides summer study abroad support for Honors Program students. We hate to see Vince Dooley retire, but a clear agreement was reached on that issue several years ago.

We think Dr. Adams has done some very good things for the University, including particularly Herty Field, the superb Student Learning Center and the renovation of Moore College and its dedication to use by the Honors Program.

In the past five years, I have served on the audit committee of the boards of directors of four publicly-held companies. Presently, I serve on two such audit committees and am chairman of one audit committee. I have read and attended meetings about numerous reports similar to the D&T Report and the responses of management and others to those reports. Thus, I am used to reading and making judgments about the types of documents involved in the review relating to Dr. Adams.

I have read (i) the D&T Report; (ii) the October 27, 2003, Memorandum from

Dr. Adams to Chancellor Thomas Meredith that responds to the D&T Report (the "Adams Response"); (iii) the undated University of Georgia's Management Response to the D&T Report (the "Management Response"); (iv) the three-page Management Summary of Key Points; (v) the Board of Regents' Statement in Response to the D&T Report, dated October 29, 2003; (vi) the Memorandum, dated October 29, 2003, from Chancellor Meredith to the Board of Trustees of the Foundation; and (vii) related documents such as the Ohio State University correspondence released by Dr. Adams and the Dr. Adams compensation analysis.

In the remainder of this letter, I will give you my reactions, conclusions and observations about the D&T Report and the related documents. These are based on what I have read. I obviously did not conduct any interviews and accordingly cannot personally make credibility judgments when two or more statements about the same event differ. If I had conducted interviews, I might well have made credibility judgments that differ from those made in the D&T Report and that could change a small portion of what I write in this letter.

2. The Foundation and its Board of Trustees. The Trustees of the Foundation have not been good stewards of the money entrusted to you by alumni like Mary Helen and me. From such a distinguished group, we expected more. The sloppiness, the failure to follow sound practices, and the inherent conflict in having Foundation expenses approved by an Executive Director who was also the President's Chief of Staff are hardly the way you ought to have looked after the $400 million entrusted to you as fiduciaries for the benefit of The University of Georgia.

I gather from press reports that major reforms in governance, procedures and controls are in the works; but I am dismayed that these changes will apparently be delayed until February 2004 at the earliest. You need to do something prior to that time to let those of us who normally give in December know that we will be giving to a reformed Foundation. Otherwise, we may conclude we need to hold our 2003 contributions until we see that real changes have been made.

Personnel changes also seem necessary, in addition to new governance and controls policies. The Trustees are supposed both to aid in fund raising and to act as fiduciaries over $400 million. It seems we have many qualified to do the former but likely need more who will do a good job on the latter. And, based on my reading, the President or Executive Director of the Foundation should never again be an employee of the administration of the University.

In the Trustees' defense, I suspect many of you have never dealt with an administration that makes undocumented, unapproved $250,000 promises or engages in end-runs on established procedures like what seems to have happened in the architect Filoni matter. It is a sad commentary that in this day and time a foundation trustee—much like a corporate director—has to design controls and processes on the assumption people will try to abuse the system.

3. President Adams and UGA Management. In many instances the authors of the D&T Report, when faced with conflicting statements, have made credibility decisions that are not to the liking of President Adams, UGA Management and the Board of Regents. For the most part, my comments are not dependent on those D&T credibility decisions, although my experience is that qualified professionals like D&T tend to do a good job of making decisions about whose version of an event is credible and whose is not.

(a) **Al Filoni.** The hiring of Mr. Filoni by Dr. Adams seems to have been an end-run on or subterfuge of the architect engagement rules of the Real Estate Foundation (the "REF") and the Board of Regents, with the result that the Foundation paid $74,000 of fees (i) the University refused to pay and (ii) incurred without going through the applicable bidding process. The REF, a subsidiary of the Foundation, refused to pay Mr. Filoni because he had not been engaged through the REF-adopted bidding process for engaging the services of architects. (D&T Report, p. 42).

The response of Dr. Adams is that Mr. Filoni was hired as a consultant and, apparently, not as an architect (Adams Response, p. 13). Management also says that the architect was hired as a consultant and not as an architect—though he in fact is an architect and developed a preliminary or other design for the alumni center—and that "all appropriate procedures were followed" (Management Response, p. 19). Neither response undertakes to explain why—if Mr. Filoni were properly engaged—the University refused to pay his fees.

Based on any fair reading of the D&T Report and the two responses, the Foundation should have refused to pay Mr. Filoni's fees and should have reported the end-run on the architect engagement rules to the Board of Regents. It should now demand a refund from someone.

(b) **Coach Donnan.** In the matter of Dr. Adams' verbal, undocumented, undisclosed, non-Athletic Board approved side agreement for $250,000 of severance compensation to Coach Jim Donnan in addition to severance compensation provided for in his contract, there is little factual disagreement. Dr. Adams did it and two years' later disclosed the verbal side agreement when Coach Donnan was fired. With considerable reason, neither the Adams Response nor the Management Response has much to say about this episode except that it is old news.

Indeed, both responses go out of their way to point out that Foundation funds were not used to satisfy the side agreement or that it was not within the purview of the Foundation. (Adams Response, p. 10; Management Response, p. 14). These response comments are intended to question why the matter is even in the D&T Report. The answer is clear to this contributor: as soon as the Foundation found out in late 2000 that its money was being spent by someone who makes undisclosed, undocumented, unapproved quarter-million dollar commitments, it should have promptly tightened all its controls over expenditures of Foundation funds by Dr. Adams and his office.

There is one other aspect: the D&T Report cites (endnote 110) two interview statements to the effect that Legal Affairs Executive Director Steve Shewmaker took the position that payment by the Athletic Association of the $250,000 side agreement should be made without obtaining approval of the Athletic Board. Mr. Shewmaker "flatly denies" that he took such a position. (Management Response, p. 14). This conflict in statements needs to be resolved in a forum where statements are made under oath; Attorney General Baker should look into the matter. I highlight this because, if attorney Shewmaker did advocate bypassing the Athletic Board, then he should not be employed by the University any longer.

(c) **McLeod Funeral.** Dr. Adams in 1998 spent $2,255 of Foundation funds to charter a plane to attend the funeral of a former president of Centre College, and his Chief of Staff—apparently acting on behalf of the Foundation—approved this use of Foundation funds. (D&T Report, p. 11). The Management Response justifies charging the Foundation because "there is an expectation that collegiality and respect be shown by presidents whose presence at funerals . . . is representative of the respect an educational institution shows for the academic community." (Management Response, p. 7). This mushy language is not close to being an acceptable reason for spending donors' gifts that are supposed to be dedicated to supporting the University.

Even if there were a proper purpose for the expenditure, the amount is an outrage. The funeral was in Winter Park, Florida, which borders Orlando. I do not have 1998 schedules and fares, but on November 3, 2003, Delta has 12 flights to Orlando from Atlanta and AirTran has 10 flights; and walk-up roundtrip fares vary from $182 to $432.50. I think a refund to the Foundation of the excess over commercial airfare plus transportation to/from the Atlanta airport is in order.

(d) **Law School Party.** The Foundation was charged $10,000 for a graduation party for the 2002 class at the law school. Two Foundation officials approved the expense. No such party had been held before, and none has been held since; the distinction is that a son of the President was in the graduating class. Only after public disclosure did Dr. Adams reimburse the Foundation for this expenditure. (D&T Report, p. 10).

Management notes Dr. Adams reimbursed the Foundation "despite benefits that inured to UGA," and Dr. Adams claims "a level of benefit inured to the University" (Management Summary of Key Points; Adams Response, p. 5). No specific benefits are cited and almost surely cannot be cited. UGA Management calls charging the $10,000 party to the Foundation "an error in judgment" (Management Summary of Key Points). It was far more than an "error in judgment"; it raises real questions about the integrity of those involved.

(e) **Steve Wrigley-Charles Witzleben Telephone Conversation.** The D&T Report concludes that the more credible version of this conversation is Mr. Witzleben's. (D&T Report, pp. 34 and 36). If that version is the truth, then Mr. Wrigley, a Senior Vice President of the University, advanced a scheme for defrauding the Foundation or the University. Mr. Wrigley's version of the conversation differs. (D&T Report, pp. 34, 36; Management Response, p. 17). This conflict in statements should be referred to

Attorney General Baker for resolution because of the seriousness of the matter if the version found credible by D&T is in fact the truth.

(f) You Should Have Had Rules. Management in its response seems to send a signal about how it operates with regard to the Foundation. In denying intentional misappropriations of Foundation funds, Management blames misuses on "the absence of clear Foundations guidelines and procedures" (Management Response, p. 2). Later, and with regard to football tickets, Management blames problems on the lack of "written or clear guidelines" (Management Response, p. 9).

Do not misunderstand the message being sent by UGA Management. Paraphrased, it is "Your failure to have very specific rules gives us the opportunity to push every issue to the limit and perhaps beyond. If money is improperly spent, it is your fault for not having tight enough rules."

That is a fair characterization of the argument made by Management. Management makes no mention of things like integrity and propriety. The Foundation should take this attitude into account when adopting its new procedures and rules.

(g) Other. For the most part, the events I discussed above and my views about them are not dependent on D&T credibility judgments. I do not think one needs to delve into those items where the credibility judgment is crucial in order to conclude there have been some real problems with the stewardship of Foundation funds by Dr. Adams and UGA Management. Nothing in the D&T Report and the responses relating to Dr. Adams' compensation, the Hank Huckaby bonus, the Costa Rica imbroglio or Mary Adams' compensation would change that conclusion—even if D&T had made different credibility judgments on those matters.

The Adams Response and the Management Response repeatedly claim the D&T Report is biased. They offer no real examples of bias. Indeed, the example of "bias" in the first full paragraph on page 3 of the Adams Response is a misreading of what is stated at the bottom of page 1 of the D&T Report—D&T states it did not pursue things where individuals insisted on confidentiality.

It is not "bias" to listen to and to research differing versions of an event and then make a judgment about which is the more credible. One can be wrong without being biased.

4. The Chancellor and the Board of Regents. The Board of Regents Statement, the Chancellor's Memorandum to Foundation Trustees and the statement made by the Chairman of the Board of Regents would be laughable if they were not so pathetic. They seem unaware of Enron, Worldcom, Tyco and the current mutual fund investigations and their affects on stewardship of funds—whether those of shareholders or contributors.

In conclusion, I am not asking for resignations or confidence-no confidence votes. I leave those to others. But I would like for the Foundation (i) promptly to implement needed reforms that take into account preventing in the future the type of abuses described in this letter, (ii) request the refunds described in this letter, and (iii) refer two matters to the Attorney General of the State of Georgia.

Sincerely,
Robert W. Miller
cc: Michael F. Adams, PhD
Wyckliffe A. Knox, Jr.

FEBRUARY 27, 2004, FROM ROBERT MILLER TO GEORGIA ATTORNEY GENERAL THURBERT E. BAKER

Dear Attorney General Baker:

The purpose of this letter is to request and urge you and your Department of Law to investigate and, if warranted, take appropriate action with respect to three matters described in the Deloitte & Touche Special Review, dated October 24, 2003, (the "D&T Report") prepared at the request of The University of Georgia Foundation (the "Foundation").

The three matters are (1) the payment by the Foundation of $74,000 to Architect Al Filoni; (2) the payment by the University of Georgia Athletic Association (the "Athletic Association") of $250,000 to Coach Jim Donnan under an undocumented, non-Athletic Board approved side agreement and the alleged act of Legal Affairs Executive Director Steve Shewmaker in urging payment of the $250,000 without obtaining Athletic Board approval; and (3) the alleged conduct of Steve Wrigley, a Senior Vice President of The University of Georgia (the "University" or "UGA"), with respect to severance compensation for Kathryn Costello. (The D&T Report addresses a number of other disturbing uses of funds that may also merit investigation by you and the Department of Law.)

In an effort to hold down the length of this letter, I will not describe these three matters in detail. They are described in (i) the D&T Report, (ii) the October 27, 2003, Memorandum from Dr. Michael F. Adams to the University System Chancellor that responds to the D&T Report (the "Adams Response"), and (iii) the undated University of Georgia's Management Response to the D&T Report (the "Management Response"). I assume you and your Department of Law have copies of these documents. If not, they can be obtained from the UGA Office of Public Affairs; or I will loan you my copies.

First, the Al Filoni Payment. The hiring of Mr. Al Filoni, an architect, by University President Adams seems to have been an end-run on or subterfuge of the architect engagement rules of the Real Estate Foundation (the "REF") and the Board of Regents, with the result that the Foundation paid $74,000 of fees (i) the

University refused to pay and (ii) incurred without going through the applicable bidding process. The REF, a subsidiary of the Foundation, refused to pay Mr. Filoni because he had not been engaged through the REF-adopted bidding process for engaging the services of architects. (D&T Report, p. 42; and see generally the D&T Report, pp. 39-44).

The response of Dr. Adams is that Mr. Filoni was hired as a consultant and, apparently, not as an architect (Adams Response, p. 13). Management also says that the architect was hired as a consultant and not as an architect—though he in fact is an architect and developed various designs for an alumni center—and that "all appropriate procedures were followed" (Management Response, p. 19). If it walks like a duck and talks like a duck, it is probably a duck; and Mr. Filoni was an architect who provided what clearly seem to be architectural services. Neither response undertakes to explain why—if Mr. Filoni were properly engaged—the University refused to pay his fees.

Based on any fair reading of the D&T Report and the two responses, the Foundation should have refused to pay Mr. Filoni's fees and should have reported the end-run on the architect engagement rules to the Board of Regents. Restitution seems to be the proper remedy. The Attorney General, after an investigation and in addition to any other appropriate remedies, should take action for restitution against some or all of Mr. Filoni, Dr. Adams, and Foundation Trustees who approved the payment of the $74,000. Such action, if warranted after your investigation, would be consistent with the supervisory and enforcement powers of the Attorney General over non-profit corporations (O.C.G. §14-3-170, among other provisions of law) such as the Foundation and its real estate subsidiary.

Second, the Coach Donnan Payment. In the matter of Dr. Adams' verbal, undocumented, undisclosed, non-Athletic Board approved side agreement for $250,000 of severance compensation to Coach Jim Donnan in addition to severance compensation provided for in his contract, there is little factual disagreement. Dr. Adams made such an oral agreement with Coach Donnan and neither disclosed that agreement to the Athletic Association or the Athletic Board nor asked for and obtained approval by the Athletic Board of the verbal side agreement. Dr. Adams was and continues to be the Chairman of the Athletic Board. Two years after the side agreement was made, it was disclosed when Coach Donnan was fired.

As part of your supervisory and enforcement powers over non-profit corporations, such as the Athletic Association, you have the authority to seek "appropriate relief" (O.C.G. §14-3-170) for improper actions. Assuming that your investigation determines the facts in the matter are substantially as stated in the D&T Report—and not contested in the Adams Response or the Management Response—then appropriate relief perhaps should include barring Dr. Adams from serving on the Athletic Board or, at the least, serving as Chairman. I do not know whether restitution from some source would be indicated as a result of your investigation, but it might be.

There is one other aspect: the D&T Report cites (p. 27 and endnote 110) interview statements from Athletic Director Vince Dooley and Athletic Association counsel Floyd Newton to the effect that UGA Legal Affairs Executive Director Steve Shewmaker took the position that payment by the Athletic Association of the $250,000 side agreement should be made without discussing the matter with the Athletic Board. Mr. Shewmaker "flatly denies" that he took such a position. (Management Response, p. 14).

This conflict in statements needs to be resolved in a forum where statements are made under oath; and your authority to investigate acts of state employees, in addition to your powers with respect to non-profit corporations, satisfy this need.

I highlight this because, if attorney Shewmaker did advocate not discussing with the Athletic Board a $250,000 undocumented, unapproved payment, then he should not be employed by the University any longer. And, if Mr. Dooley and Mr. Newton's recollections are determined to be the more credible, then attorney Shewmaker should also not be allowed to provide advice with respect to the Athletic Association, including advice to an individual member of the Athletic Board.

Third, the Steve Wrigley matter. According to the version of events found credible by Deloitte & Touche in their special review, Mr. Steve Wrigley, a Senior Vice President of the University, asked a UGA fund raising consultant, Mr. Charles Witzleben, to put Kathryn Costello on his company's payroll and then bill the increased expense back to the Foundation (or the University). The apparent purpose was to provide severance to Ms. Costello without the cost being clearly labeled as such on the Foundation's or the University's records. (It is not entirely clear from the D&T Report and the Management Response whether the Foundation or the University was involved.) (D&T Report, pp.34 and 36).

If the version found credible by Deloitte & Touche is the truth, then a Senior Vice President of the University advanced a scheme for defrauding the Foundation or the University. Mr. Wrigley's version of the conversation with Mr. Witzleben differs from that of Mr. Witzleben. (D&T Report, pp.34, 36; Management Response, p. 17). I believe this serious allegation should be investigated by you so that the conflict in statements can be resolved by use of your subpoena and other investigative powers and appropriate action, if warranted, can be taken.

For your information, I graduated from the University (AB, 1964) and have been a regular contributor ($3,100 in 2003) to the Foundation. I have not written this letter because of actions taken or not taken with regard to Vince Dooley. Indeed, I am weary of the Board of Regents, the University System Chancellor and *The Atlanta Journal-Constitution* claiming mindlessly that expressions of concern over misuse of Foundation and other funds by the University's administration come solely from angry Vince Dooley supporters. What I am is a citizen and UGA alumnus who thinks the Attorney General should exercise his authority, investigate some serious

allegations and take appropriate actions.
    Sincerely,
    Robert W. Miller

FEBRUARY 27, 2004, FROM ROBERT MILLER TO GEORGIA ATTORNEY GENERAL THURBERT E. BAKER

RE: Supplement to Prior Letter

Dear Attorney General Baker:
    This is a supplement to my letter of earlier today to you. This morning's *The Atlanta Journal-Constitution* reports that last week the newspaper complained to your office about closed or partly closed meetings of The University of Georgia Foundation trustees when discussing compensation to Dr. Michael F. Adams, President of The University of Georgia. Today's edition further reports that on Thursday, February 26, you made a determination in the matter and directed the Foundation not to hold such closed meetings with respect to Dr. Adams' compensation from the Foundation.
    I trust and assume that you and the Department of Law will act with comparable promptness to investigate the matters described in my letter to you of earlier today. Those matters go to the substance of funds uses by Dr. Adams and the University administration and deserve at least equally prompt action.
    Sincerely,
    Robert W. Miller

MARCH 11, 2004, FROM ASSISTANT ATTORNEY GENERAL SAMANTHA M. REIN TO ROBERT MILLER

Dear Mr. Miller:
    Thank you for your letter concerning the above-referenced matter. Please be aware that according to the provisions of the Georgia State Constitution, the Attorney General serves as legal counsel to the executive branch of state government. Therefore, the Attorney General and those lawyers employed by him are prohibited from providing representation or advice directly to private individuals. As a result, our office is unfortunately unable to assist you in this matter.
    However, your information will be forwarded to the Board of Regents of the University System of Georgia. The Board has the authority to manage and govern public higher education in Georgia. Therefore, I have taken the liberty of forwarding your letter to the Board for their review at the address below:

Board of Regents of the University System
270 Washington Street S.W.
Atlanta, GA 30334
www.usg.edu

I regret we are unable to provide you with further assistance, but trust you will find this responsive to your request.
Sincerely,
Samantha M. Rein
Assistant Attorney General

MARCH 13, 2004, FROM ROBERT MILLER TO ASSISTANT ATTORNEY GENERAL SAMANTHA M. REIN

Dear Ms. Rein:

I have received your letter of March 11 in which you interpret my February 27 letters to the Attorney General to be requests for representation of or advice to me as a private individual. I find it difficult to believe the Attorney General and the Department of Law could so interpret my letters. My letters in no way requested representation of me or advice to me as a private individual.

To the contrary, my letters urged the Attorney General and the Department of Law to do their duties under Georgia law. The Attorney General's website lists his duties. These include, "prosecuting public corruption cases" and "conducting special investigations in questionable activity concerning any state agency or department." Those are precisely what I urged the Attorney General and the Department of Law to do with regard to The University of Georgia and three university officials.

In addition, my letters urged the Attorney General and the Department of Law to investigate and take actions under Official Code of Georgia provisions that give the Attorney General various powers over non-profit corporations, in this case The University of Georgia Foundation and the University of Georgia Athletic Association. As I mentioned in my letter, one code section in particular, §14-3-170, entitled in part, "Powers of the Attorney General," gives the Attorney General the power to investigate, to issue subpoenas, and to petition the superior court to compel, among other things, restitution or other appropriate relief. In light of serious, and apparently documented by the D&T Report, allegations involving non-profit corporation funds misuse, the Attorney General should investigate and take action under that code sections and other appropriate code sections.

I trust that the Attorney General and the Department of Law will now move to carry out the duties listed on the Attorney General's website and to exercise the powers provided by Georgia law to the Attorney General with respect to non-profit corporations.

Sincerely,

Robert W. Miller,

cc: The Hon. Thurbert E. Baker

Board of Regents of the University System

MARCH 22, 2004, FROM ROBERT MILLER TO SENIOR ASSISTANT ATTORNEY GENERAL KATHRYN L. ALLEN

Dear Ms. Allen:

I have received your letter of March 18 in which you state that the Attorney General and the Department of Law received my second letter of February 27 but not my first letter of February 27. I am enclosing with this letter (1) a copy of my first February 27 letter; and (2) a copy of my March 13 letter to Samantha M. Rein, which letter I wrote in response to her letter to me of March 11. I think, but do not know, that Ms. Rein had a copy of my first February 27 letter when she wrote me her March 11 letter—a letter that misinterpreted my first February 27 letter.

I believe you will now have a full record of my correspondence on this matter. I assume that the Attorney General and the Department of Law will now promptly investigate the matters covered in my letters and take appropriate action.

Sincerely,

Robert W. Miller,

cc w/o encl: Samantha M. Rein

APRIL 2, 2004, FROM ROBERT MILLER TO BOARD OF TRUSTEES, THE UNIVERSITY OF GEORGIA FOUNDATION

c/o Mr. Allan W. Barber, Executive Director

Athens, Georgia

Dear Ladies and Gentlemen:

The purpose of this letter is to urge you to take appropriate action with respect to matters described in the Deloitte & Touche Special Review, dated October 24, 2003 (the "D&T Report"), prepared at the request of The University of Georgia Foundation (the "Foundation").

In my view, Foundation Trustees who receive information of the type contained in the D&T Report have two equally important duties. The first duty is to adopt new or revised practices and controls to prevent future occurrences of similar events. The second duty is to determine, with respect to each item in such a report, whether or not further action is necessary or appropriate. If a determination is made that no further action is necessary or appropriate, then the reasons for that determination should be documented and approved by the Trustees.

From newspaper articles since the release of the D&T Report, I understand that the Board of Trustees of the Foundation is considering or has adopted new or revised practices and controls intended to avoid *in the future* the types of events and problems described in the D&T Report. But I have not read about any Board of Trustees action to redress or remedy those *past* events and problems in the D&T Report that merit remedial action, including (as appropriate) an accounting, restitution or referral to other agencies for investigation. I also have not read about any Board of Trustees determination that no further action is necessary or appropriate.

To make it clear what the second duty of trustees encompasses, below this paragraph are two examples of how the Board of Trustees (or a special committee of independent Trustees) might respond to items in the D&T Report. In order to hold down the length of this letter, only two items in the D&T Report are reviewed; and the more complex items—such as Dr. Adams' compensation and the Costa Rica Ecolodge purchase—are omitted for the same reason.

The $74,000 Al Filoni Payment. Based on the D&T Report and the undated University of Georgia Management's Response to the D&T Report (the "Management Response"), the hiring of architect Filoni seems to have been an end-run on the architect engagement rules of the Board of Regents, the University and the Real Estate Foundation (the "REF"). I understand REF is owned and controlled by the Foundation. Mr. Filoni billed the University, but it did not pay because ". . . Mr. Filoni had not been properly contracted through the normal bidding process." D&T Report, p. 42. Mr. Hank Huckaby, the University's Senior Vice President for Finance and Administration, asked REF to pay the $74,000 of fees. Although REF had previously informed Mr. Huckaby that REF would not pay Mr. Filoni's fees and that Mr. Filoni had not been retained by REF under its engagement process that is based on Board of Regents' policy, REF ended up paying the $74,000 to an architect that neither it nor the Foundation had retained.

An action for restitution seems the appropriate remedy in order for the Foundation's subsidiary to recover improperly spent assets. The primary issue is from whom should restitution be sought: from the Foundation Trustee (Dr. Adams), who retained Mr. Filoni apparently without following applicable procedures; Mr. Huckaby, who urged REF to pay the bill; any Foundation or REF Trustees, who approved the payment when they knew or should have known REF did not retain Mr. Filoni and certainly not as the result of its process for engaging architects; Mr. Filoni, who knew or should have known that there were required engagement procedures and they were not followed in his case; or all of the above?

The **Steve Wrigley-Charles Witzleben Telephone Conversation.** The conversation is described on pages 34 and 36 of the D&T Report and discussed on page 17 of Management's Response. If Mr. Witzleben's recollection of that conversation is the truth, then Mr. Wrigley, a Senior Vice President of the University, advanced a scheme for defrauding, by creation of misleading or false records, the Foundation or the University. The D&T Report states the conversation related to Foundation records and funds. Management's Response states it does not believe the Witzleben version of the conversation is correct; and, in any event, the records and funds that would have been involved in a scheme were University funds and records.

This allegation has potential criminal implications. It should be referred by the Foundation to the appropriate District Attorney or Attorney General Baker for investigation. The Foundation itself lacks subpoena and other investigative powers and should limit its activities to making the referral to the proper law enforcement official and requesting an investigation.

The Board of Trustees owes it to Foundation contributors to make a determination about action to take or the reasons for not taking action with respect to each item in the D&T Report. I suspect (but I leave that advice to others) that the Trustees also have a legal obligation as fiduciaries to make determinations about the D&T Report items. Last, in my view a Trustee for his or her own protection should want a documented record of determinations made about the items in the D&T Report.

For your information, I am an alumnus (AB, 1964) and have been a regular contributor ($3,100 in 2003) to the Foundation. My wife and I are almost the sole funding source of the Charles Hicks Fund (balance of about $180,000) that provides summer study support for Honors Program students.

Sincerely,
Robert W. Miller

APRIL 30, 2004, FROM DEPUTY ATTORNEY GENERAL MICHAEL E. HOBBS TO ROBERT MILLER

RE: Deloitte & Touche Special Review for the University of Georgia Foundation dated October 24, 2003.

Dear Mr. Miller:

I am in receipt of copies of your letters dated February 27, 2004 to Attorney General Baker, the March 11, 2004 letter to you from Ms. Samantha Rein of this office, your March 13, 2004 reply to Ms. Rein, and your letter dated March 22, 2004 to Senior Assistant Attorney General Kathryn Allen.

Your correspondence raised important issues concerning the operation of the Univrsity of Georgia Foundation and its relationship with the University and the Board of Regents. Please be advised that I am now in the process of reviewing the Deloitte & Touche report, the response to the report provided by the Board of Regents by management at the University of Georgia, as well as the Board's October, 29, 2003 statement made in response to the report.

Thank you for bringing your concerns to the attention of this office. If you have any questions or comments, please do not hesitate to contact me.

Sincerely,

Michael E. Hobbs

Deputy Attorney General

MEH/mh

cc: Jeff Milsteen, Chief Deputy Attorney General

MAY 5, 2004, FROM ROBERT MILLER TO ATTORNEY GENERAL THURBERT E. BAKER

Dear Attorney General Baker:

This letter is a supplement to my February 27, 2004, letter to you in which I requested you and the Department of Law to investigate and, if warranted, to take action with respect to three matters described in the Deloitte & Touche Special Review, dated October 24, 2003, (the "D&T Report") prepared at the request of The University of Georgia Foundation (the "Foundation"). My February 27 letter also stated the D&T Report addressed a number of other items that may merit investigation by the Department of Law.

The purpose of this letter is to bring to your attention one additional matter that merits investigation. I apologize for not mentioning this matter in my February 27 letter to you. However, it involves an attachment to the D&T Report; the attachments to that report were not available on the website I used to obtain a copy of the D&T Report; and I learned of the attachment only last week.

I enclose with this letter a three-page document entitled "Resolution of the Trustees of The University of Georgia Foundation, Inc." (the "Certified Resolution"), and I believe this is the document described in footnote 42 of the D&T Report and discussed on page 14 of the D&T Report.[1]

The Certified Resolution begins in the first paragraph by stating the Trustees of the Foundation "hereby adopt" on February 14, 2003, "the following resolution" and "hereby direct that such action be filed with the minutes of the proceedings of the Foundation." There then follows the text of a two-page resolution that authorizes

---

[1]   The handwritten marks on the enclosed copy of the Certified Resolution were apparently made by the person who provided me with a copy.

entering into agreements with Dr. Michael F. Adams relating to supplemental and deferred compensation for Dr. Adams, the terms of which are described in some detail in the resolution. The last page of the document states that "to reflect the approval of the Trustees to [sic] this Resolution at the meeting of the Trustees on February 14, 2003" the Chairman of the Board of Trustees and the Secretary of the Foundation "do hereunto set their hands and seals as of this 14th day of February, 2003."

The Certified Resolution is then signed by those two persons. I cannot tell from my copy whether or not the corporate seal, which is called for by a bracketed notation, was affixed to the original version.[2]

The text of the D&T Report makes it clear that, although there was a meeting of the Foundation Trustees on February 14, 2003, the resolution set out in the Certified Resolution was not adopted at that meeting or, to my knowledge, at any prior or subsequent Trustees' meeting. (D&T Report, p. 14). The D&T Report also makes it clear that the resolution was not adopted by the Executive Committee of the Foundation. (D&T Report, pp. 14,15).

The existence of a signed and sealed document that falsely certifies the adoption of a resolution by the Foundation Trustees approving supplemental and deferred compensation for Dr. Adams (a Trustee and an employee of the State of Georgia) is a concern. The Certified Resolution raises questions: Who drafted the document? With whom, if anyone, did the signers confer, negotiate or agree to sign the Certified Resolution prior to their signing of the document? What was the intended use and the actual use of the Certified Resolution? To whom were copies delivered and for what purpose? Were any funds expended pursuant to the authorization contained in the Certified Resolution?

I respectfully request and urge you and the Department of Law to use your authority under O.C.G.A. §14-3-170 and your other powers to investigate the circumstances surrounding the Certified Resolution and, if warranted, to take appropriate action.

Sincerely,

Robert W. Miller,

State Bar # 508200

cc: Kathryn L. Allen, Senior Assistant Attorney General

Samantha M. Rein, Assistant Attorney General

---

[2]   I do not know why the last page is marked, at the bottom, "Page 3 of 4." I have not located a fourth page, but it might be the "Exhibit A" referred to in the resolution. I also do not know why the first two pages are marked "Page 1 of 1" and "Page 2 of 2" when they seem clearly to be part of a three (or four) page document. All pages have the same word processing document number at the bottom: 169967.1.

JUNE 7, 2004, FROM ROBERT MILLER TO ATTORNEY GENERAL THURBERT E. BAKER

Dear Attorney General Baker:

This letter is a supplement to my May 5, 2004, letter to you in which I requested you and the Department of Law to investigate and, if warranted, to take action with respect to a falsely certified resolution (the "Certified Resolution") of the Trustees of The University of Georgia Foundation (the "Foundation"). A copy of that letter is enclosed for your reference.

The need and the reason for an investigation of the circumstances surrounding the Certified Resolution have become more necessary in light of the recent action by the Board of Regents with respect to The University of Georgia Foundation. It appears that the Certified Resolution is related to and involved in the action by the Board of Regents to end the relationship between The University of Georgia and the Foundation. For example, a June 2 article in the *Athens Banner-Herald*, written by Lee Shearer, reports that University System Chancellor Meredith approved a Foundation-funded compensation package for University of Georgia President Michael Adams, ". . . but the legal status of that package remains in question after auditors found the package had never been approved by the Foundation's board, as required in the non-profit corporation's bylaws." (article taken from www.onlineathens.com).

Assuming this article is correct, the falsely Certified Resolution was delivered to Chancellor Meredith; and he approved the compensation package for Dr. Adams described in that resolution. Who participated in drafting, using, delivering or setting the terms of the false Certified Resolution relating to the compensation of a state employee (Dr. Adams) who is also a trustee of the Foundation? What were the participants in the preparation and delivery of the false Certified Resolution attempting to achieve? Was the purpose to deceive the Chancellor, a state employee? Did the Chancellor know the resolution had in fact not been approved by the Foundation Trustees? Did the Chancellor expect the Foundation to pay to Dr. Adams the amounts provided for in the Certified Resolution, even though the resolution had not been approved by the Foundation Trustees?

I again respectfully request and urge you and the Department of Law to investigate the circumstances surrounding the Certified Resolution.

Sincerely,

Robert W. Miller,

cc: Kathryn L. Allen, Senior Assistant Attorney General
Samantha M. Rein, Assistant Attorney General

MAY 25, 2005, FROM ROBERT MILLER TO ATTORNEY GENERAL THURBERT E. BAKER

Dear Attorney General Baker:

The lead story in *The Atlanta Journal-Constitution* today (Wednesday) is about the termination of three employees of Georgia's Department of Technical and Adult Education ("DTAE"). DTAE took action after an investigation of, among other things, falsification of records—a falsified degree transcript and a falsified resume, both used to make an unqualified person appear qualified to hold his $72,000 per year position at DTAE. A spokesman for your department stated that the Law Department is investigating the matter to determine whether or not there was criminal wrongdoing.

I enclose with this letter a copy of my May 5, 2004, letter to you. My letter requested an investigation of a different falsified document relating to the compensation of a state employee, UGA President Michael Adams. Dr. Adams was also a trustee and thus a fiduciary of The University of Georgia Foundation at the time the false document certified the Foundation's Board had approved a compensation program for Dr. Adams when in fact it had not. (Georgia's Attorney General, of course, has supervisory powers over non-profit corporations, such as The University of Georgia Foundation, in addition to the authority to investigate state employees and to enforce criminal laws.)

To my knowledge, no action by a state agency or investigation by your Law Department has occurred in the case of the falsified document relating to the compensation of Dr. Adams, a state employee. The contrast between the DTAE actions and your department's investigation, as reported today in *The Atlanta Journal-Constitution*, and the apparent lack of action by a state agency or your Law Department in the case of the falsified document relating to Dr. Adams is striking and, to this citizen, puzzling.

I renew my May 5, 2004, request that the falsified document relating to Dr. Adams' compensation be investigated.

Sincerely,

Robert W. Miller

Appendix E: Attorney General Baker's Letter

Following is the complete text of Georgia Attorney General Thurbert E. Baker's December 5, 2006, letter to Allan Vigil and Erroll B. Davis Jr., chairman and chancellor, respectively, of the University System of Georgia Board of Regents:

Dear Chairman Vigil and Chancellor Davis:

While the Board of Regents, the University of Georgia and the former University of Georgia Foundation have experienced a difficult period over the last several years, it is my opinion that establishment of the Arch Foundation operating under new policies and procedures has alleviated much of the public concern relating to the relationships among these organizations. However, after due consideration, I have determined that a number of issues warrant further discussion. Therefore, I offer the following in my capacity as the chief legal officer of this state (O.C.G.A. § 45-10-3) as well as under my responsibilities relating to non-profit corporations (O.C.G.A. § 14-3-170).

In my opinion, many of the problems previously encountered by the Board of Regents, the University and the former foundation stem from a failure to fully recognize that the foundation is a separate entity from the University. Foundations have been established for the support and benefit of colleges and universities in virtually every state and for virtually every institution in our university system. In *Macon Telegraph Publishing Company v. Board of Regents*, 256 Ga. 443 (1986), the Supreme Court of Georgia recognized that such organizations may be used by institutional authorities as a means of managing legitimate collegiate programs, such as intercollegiate athletics. In 1995 Op. Atty. Gen. 95-36, this office described the relationship between the non-profit corporation and the institution it supports as "symbiotic," with what might be described as interlocking directorships and influence.

However, by their very nature, foundations maintain a separate corporate existence and governance from the institutions they support. Indeed, Board of Regents Policy No. 1905, Section II, Paragraph F requires that "cooperative organizations" such as foundations must enter into memoranda of understanding setting forth the respective responsibilities of the institution and the organization "so that it is clear to third parties dealing with the cooperative organization that the organization is acting as a legal entity separate from the System institution . . ."

Foundations have been created largely because they are not limited by the budgetary and operational restrictions placed on state government agencies. As has been painfully learned from past experiences, however, the interests of the foundations may not always be consistent with the interests of the Board of Regents and its institutions. I have observed that state officials and employees on the university level are often called upon to perform services for or on behalf of these foundations, creating an ambiguity as to which entity the official or employee owes a duty of loyalty. Frankly, the availability of money from the foundations engenders a loyalty by state officials or employees that might be described, at least in some instances, as incompatible with the duty of loyalty owed to the Board of Regents and the state.

I recognize that Georgia law has declared that it is permissible for full-time employees of the Board of Regents to serve as members of the governing boards of private non-profit foundations and associations organized for the support of our colleges and universities. O.C.G.A. § 45-10- 23(a).

I am certain that such relationships foster greater efficiencies in the process of setting and communicating institutional funding and operational priorities. I do not believe, however, that this code section permits full time employees of the Board of Regents to perform services for such foundations on a full-time or part-time basis, while being paid with state funds, unless such services have been provided pursuant to a contract with substantial consideration flowing from the foundation to the Regents.

The interlocking involvement of full-time employees of the Board of Regents requires that additional care must be taken by all who are involved to avoid actual conflicts of interest, and to effectively deal with those situations when they occur. Therefore, it is my hope that the following discussion will assist the Board in avoiding the highly disruptive disputes of the past.

As public officers we are all "trustees and servants of the people, and are at all times amenable to them." Ga. Const., Art. I, Sec. II, Para. I. This concept has been part of the constitutional framework of this state since 1877. Public office in Georgia carries with it the same fiduciary obligations of honesty, integrity, and fidelity that attaches to other trustees, including those who govern the operations of non-profit organizations such as the University of Georgia Foundation and the University of Georgia Athletic Association. *Georgia Department of Human Resources v. Sistrunk*, 249 Ga. 543 (1982); *Malcolm v. Webb*, 211 Ga. 449 (1955). These standards of conduct affirmatively require loyalty to the best interests of the people in the case of a government officer, or to the organization in the case of a director or trustee. Such loyalty cannot be tainted by undisclosed conflicts of interest, divided loyalties to multiple employers or inappropriate external influences. Dealing for the personal benefit of the officer or trustee is a violation of one's fiduciary duty. Pragmatism and business convenience do not diminish the obligation to act at all times with honesty and integrity, with all regard for the interests of the beneficiaries of the trust.

This office received correspondence from Mr. Robert W. Miller urging that an investigation be initiated into certain findings contained in the Deloitte & Touche

Special Review which was commissioned by the University of Georgia Foundation and its counsel, King & Spalding. I have reviewed the Deloitte & Touche report, the response of Dr. Adams to the report, and the response prepared by senior administrators at the University of Georgia.

The Deloitte & Touche report stated that both Dr. Adams and Senior Vice President of Finance and Administration, Mr. Hank Huckaby, received $40,000 and $30,000 bonuses, respectively, from the University Foundation in 2003. Apparently this action was taken by the Foundation's executive committee without the measures ever being submitted to the full board of trustees. Aside from a possible breach of the Foundation's corporate by-laws, the receipt of this additional compensation by two public employees from a private source of funding is troubling.

The bonus to Dr. Adams and the "honorarium" for Mr. Huckaby appear to violate the spirit of the Georgia Constitution. In each case it appears that the payments were made with the knowledge and consent of both the president and former chancellor. According to the University Management Response, both the former chancellor and the president "agreed for this action to be taken to the Foundation . . ." University Management Response, p. 13. In each case, the payments were justified as additional compensation for exemplary work already performed on behalf of the University. Deloitte & Touche concluded, however, that Mr. Huckaby's work on the governor's transition team provided no meaningful benefit to the University. In response, the University Management indicated that Mr. Huckaby was deserving of the additional compensation because "[u]nder [his] leadership, the governor and the General Assembly passed Senate Bill 73 which allows the university . . . to carry over unexpended funds into the next fiscal year." University Management Response, p. 13.

Article III, Section VI, Paragraph VI of the Georgia Constitution prohibits state government from granting gifts or gratuities or authorizing "extra compensation to any public officer . . . *after* the service has been rendered or the contract entered into." See, e.g. 1976 Op. Atty. Gen No. 76-62 (no agency may award retroactive pay increases). The constitutional provision speaks not only to the prohibition against the gift of public funds, but also to the evil that may arise from providing additional compensation to public officials, no matter what the source of the funds. The grant of additional private funds to a public official for performing his public duties in an exemplary manner raises serious conflict of interest issues that the constitutional provision was designed to preclude. In this case, it appears that even though the additional compensation originated with a non-governmental source, its receipt was "authorized" by the Board of Regents and President Adams. Thus, the imprimatur of the state was placed on this award of additional compensation to two state employees.

The bonus to Dr. Adams also appears to have been a means by which the Foundation circumvented the limitations the Board of Regents placed on the Foundation's level of participation in the president's overall compensation plan. It is my understanding that during this time the Board of Regents permitted the Foundation to supplement Dr. Adams's salary up to 49 percent of his state pay. It appears that the Foundation exceeded that limitation every year after it was established. In fact, during the period covered by the Deloitte & Touche report, much more than half of Dr. Adams's overall compensation was from Foundation funds, not state pay.

I have become aware that the Board of Regents has developed a standard memorandum of understanding for cooperating organizations as well as guiding principles for these organizations, last revised on August 4, 2004. The guiding principles provide in part that:

> No employee of the institution, or member of their [sic] immediate family, may receive remuneration (salary, stipend or gifts for service) from the Cooperative Organization without the approval of the institutional president or, in the case of the president or the president's immediate family, the chancellor, or in the case of the chancellor or the chancellor's immediate family, the Board.

Thus, the Board's own guidelines have institutionalized the "authorization" of additional compensation which, if applied to "gifts for service" or compensation for work already performed, is clearly prohibited by the Georgia Constitution.

While it is certainly important for the Board of Regents to control the level and sources of compensation for institutional presidents and employees, it must do so in accordance with the Constitution of this state which prohibits the grant of additional compensation for past efforts, no matter how exceptional. Indeed, the law of this state contemplates that every state official and employee will put forth his best efforts on behalf of the people. See O.C.G.A. § 45-10-3, III; *McIntosh v. Williams*, 160 Ga. 461, 4643 (1925) (Public office is a public trust. The holder may not use it directly or indirectly for personal profit.)

By receiving compensation from two separate and distinct sources, particularly at the levels of participation here, Dr. Adams was in fact serving two masters. This presents a common law conflict of interest which jeopardizes the undiluted allegiance Dr. Adams owes to the Board of Regents, and through it, the people of Georgia. The Board of Regents should make it clear that it, and not any other body, is responsible for establishing and regulating the compensation of board officials and employees. It has not done so in the standard memorandum of understanding or guidelines. While a non-profit corporation might designate donated funds for whatever legitimate purposes it deems appropriate, including salary enhancements, the specific decisions on the expenditure of those funds must be left to the Board. Therefore, no compensation should be made directly to any president or other official or employee of the Board of Regents by any cooperating organization. All compensation should be made through the Board of Regents.

The Deloitte & Touche report also addressed the $250,000 side agreement with former head football coach, Jim Donnan. It is most troubling that such an agreement would be verbal and made without the knowledge of the Athletic Director, the attorney for the Athletic Association who was negotiating the remainder of Mr. Donnan's contract, and the Board of Trustees for the Athletic Association. According to the Deloitte & Touche report, at a later meeting Mr. Stephen Shewmaker, Senior Vice President for Legal Affairs, suggested that the Athletic Association should absorb the cost of the side agreement, and further suggested that the payment be made without discussion with the Athletic Association Board. Ultimately, the matter was presented to the full board, which approved the payment to avoid a lawsuit. Although Dr. Adams is the chairman of the Athletic Association Board and has been delegated significant authority for the overall operation of the athletic program at the University of Georgia, it is the Association's board which has responsibility for oversight, policy, and major decisions. While I cannot say definitively that Dr. Adams was without authority to agree to the $250,000 severance for Coach Donnan, if the findings of the Deloitte & Touche report are accurate, the failure to notify the Association's governing body of a major decision concerning a large amount of money may constitute a violation of Dr. Adam's fiduciary obligation of forthrightness as president and as chairman of the Association. As Justice Cardozo once stated,

> [M]any forms of conduct permissible in a workaday world for those acting at arm's length are forbidden to those bound by fiduciary ties. A trustee is held to something stricter than the morals of the marketplace. Not honesty alone, but the punctilio of an honor most sensitive, is then the standard of behavior. Uncompromising rigidity has been the attitude of courts of equity when petitioned to undermine the rule of undivided loyalty by the 'disintegrating erosion of particular exceptions...' Only thus has the level of conduct for fiduciaries been kept at a level higher than that trodden by the crowd.
> *Meinhard v. Salmon*, 249 N.Y. 458, 464 (1928).

Moreover, any attempt to conceal this side agreement violates the principles of open government embodied in the Georgia Open Records Act, O.C.G.A. § 50-18-70 through O.C.G.A. § 50-18-77. See also *Macon Tel. Publishing Co. v. Board of Regents*, 256 Ga. 443 (1986). Frankly, I have never heard of any corporation, much less a nonprofit such as the Athletic Association, entering into an oral contract which creates an obligation of a quarter million dollars. Not only would such thwart the legitimate interest of the citizens of this state in the manner in which this quasi-public body operates, but such is an indescribably bad business practice. The Board of Regents should act to ensure that this kind of situation never occurs again.

Item 7 of the Guidelines for Cooperative Organizations attempts to address this kind of problem. It provides that: "[t]he Cooperative Organization shall develop policies to ensure that its business, governance and programming activities are conducted in an open and responsible manner, consistent with the laws of the State of Georgia." In my view, however, the Board would be well advised to specifically require, as a condition of its recognition of a cooperating organization, that all activities of such organizations be open to the public, and governed by the provisions of the Georgia Open Meetings Act, O.C.G.A. § 50-14-1 through § 50-14-6, as well as the Georgia Open Records Act, O.C.G.A. § 50-18-70 through § 50-18-77.

One more comment needs to be made about this issue. Apparently, Dr. Adams was approached about finalizing this aspect of Coach Donnan's contract by Mr. Jim Nalley, a member of the University of Georgia Foundation Executive Committee, and allegedly a friend to Coach Donnan. Coach Donnan believed that his negotiations with Athletic Director Dooley were not making progress, and he had asked Mr. Nalley to see if Dr. Adams would intervene on his behalf (Deloitte & Touche Report, pp. 25–26). Apparently, after this conversation, Dr. Adams was convinced that the negotiations had to be concluded. He allegedly instructed Mr. Nalley to "get the deal done," and if the termination pay had to be made, they would deal with it at that time. Mr. Dooley had previously been involved in the negotiations with Coach Donnan and his agent. The undisclosed decision by Dr. Adams may well be seen as the result of influence by a member of the Foundation's executive committee— an external influence by a member of an organization substantially supplementing Dr. Adams's salary, but having no direct responsibility for the contract with Coach Donnan. This situation raises the specter of a conflict of interest which might have been avoided had the matter been dealt with in the open.

I understand that the Board, the University of Georgia and the successor to the University of Georgia Foundation, The Arch Foundation, have now established new working relationships. This office stands ready to consult with you and the Board on any aspect of its relationships with cooperating organizations. I hope that in the future the Board of Regents and the chancellor will call on me and my staff for in-depth assistance and consultation on issues such as those discussed above. The resolution of such matters can have a profound effect on public confidence in their public institutions.

Sincerely,
Thurbert E. Baker
Attorney General